Illustrator
Victoria Ponikvar Frazier

Editor
Walter Kelly

Editorial Project Manager
Ina Massler Levin, M.A.

Editor-in-Chief
Sharon Coan, M.S. Ed.

Creative Director
Elayne Roberts

Associate Designer
Denise Bauer

Art Coordination Assistant
Cheri Macoubrie Wilson

Cover Artist
Larry Bauer

Product Manager
Phil Garcia

Imaging
James Edward Grace

Publishers
Rachelle Cracchiolo, M.S. Ed.
Mary Dupuy Smith, M.S. Ed.

Author

Rosalind Thomas, M.A.

Teacher Created Materials, Inc.
6421 Industry Way
Westminster, CA 92683
www.teachercreated.com

©1999 Teacher Created Materials, Inc.
Reprinted, 2003
Made in U.S.A.
ISBN-1-57690-209-9

Table of Contents

Introduction 4
File Folder Themes and Activities 8
Theme: Colors
   Activities:
- Teddy Bear, Teddy Bear 8
- Lily Pads 18
- Gingerbread Boys 24
- Color Bead Patterns 29

Theme: Shapes
   Activities:
- M & M® Shapes 33
- Shape Puzzles 35
- Shape Bus 38
- Hidden Shapes 41

Theme: Apples
   Activities:
- Wormy Apples 46
- Apple Sorting 57
- Apple Trees 61
- Apple Book 74
- The Worm and the Apple 80

Theme: Families
   Activities:
- Family Sizes 84
- Family Fun 86
- Families Do Things Together 89

Theme: Nursery Rhymes
   Activities:
- "One, Two, Buckle My Shoe" 94
- "Humpty Dumpty" 96
- "Jack and Jill" 98
- "Hey Diddle, Diddle" 100
- "Pease Porridge" 102
- "Jack Be Nimble" 104

Theme: Transportation
   Activities:
- How We Travel 106
- Our Travel Graph 111
- Number Convoy 114
- Going Places 116

Theme: Winter
   Activities:
- Snowman Buttons 120
- Snowman Book 133
- Crystal Painting 139
- Snowman Guess 141

Theme: Numbers
   Activities:
- Number Beans 143
- Wrapping Paper Count 145
- Frog Count 156
- Chocolate Chip Numbers 171
- Number Clay 173

Table of Contents *(cont.)*

Theme: Alphabet
Activities:
- Alphabet Hopscotch 177
- Flannelboard Alphabet 179
- ABC Feel and Guess 181
- ABC Follow Directions 182

Theme: Dinosaurs
Activities:
- Fossil Search 190
- Dinosaur Sorting 193
- Dinosaur Food 195
- Dinosaur Puzzles 200

Theme: Caterpillars and Butterflies
Activities:
- Caterpillar Number Puzzle 203
- Hungry Caterpillar Sock Book 206
- Butterfly Life Cycle 215
- Caterpillar Art 217
- Word Caterpillar 219

Theme: Halloween
Activities:
- Pumpkin Sequencing 224
- Pumpkin Faces 226
- Frozen Pumpkin Squares 228
- Pumpkin Float 230

Theme: Thanksgiving
Activities:
- Pilgrim or Indian? 232
- Where Is the Turkey? 236
- Indian or Pilgrim Graph 245
- Turkey Fingerprint 248

Theme: Winter Holidays
Activities:
- Christmas Surprise 250
- Martin Luther King, Jr., Award 253
- Groundhog Pop-Up 256
- Abraham Lincoln's Log Cabin 264
- President Washington Flag 266
- Valentine Heart Puzzle 271
- ✔ Missing Valentine Heart Numbers 285
- ✔ Valentine Heart Candy Patterns 290
- Valentine Candy Graph 292
- St. Patrick's Green Book 295

Theme: Easter
Activities:
- Bunny Finds His Egg 298
- Bunny Number Book 331
- My Easter Handful Book 338
- Easter Bunny, Easter Bunny 341

Activities Listed by Skills 351

Introduction

File Folder Activities

File folder activities can be filled with fun while serving as creative tools to enhance the early childhood curriculum. They may be used in a variety of ways throughout the day, such as in centers, during free choice time, with volunteers, in one-to-one teaching, with small groups, etc. Children enjoy the activities once they understand the rules and how they relate to the current theme being studied. Children also love to come back to activities they have already learned.

This book is designed to show you how to make file folder activities, the materials needed for each activitiy, ideas for storage of file folder activities, how to introduce the activities to the children, rules and standards to be used for each activity, when to use a file folder activity during the day, and how to incorporate volunteers in carrying out the file folder activities. There are both self-checking activities and hands-on activities. In addition, this book will identify your file folder activities by themes and by skill areas so that it will be easy to pull out an activity to reinforce the concept you are working on. Also included are activities that children can make copies of to take home to show parents what they are doing in the classroom.

File Folder Activities for Learning Centers will provide you with a rich source of creative file folder activities that may be used in interactive ways in your classroom.

What File Folder Activities Will Include

Each activitiy will include the following items:

- ❑ Instructions for making each activity
- ❑ Directions for the activity for both children and adults
  - Children's directions included for older children who may be reading
  - Verbal directions and demonstrations necessary for younger children
- ❑ Activity pieces (as applicable)
- ❑ Pages to reproduce (as applicable)
- ❑ Charts (as applicable)
- ❑ Graphs (as applicable)
- ❑ Answer keys (as applicable)
- ❑ Activity labels for file folder tabs (sample)
- ❑ Decorative activity titles for the fronts of the folders (sample)

Introduction (cont.)

Materials Needed for Each Activity

Some or all of the following materials will be needed to complete the file folder activities in this book.

- ❑ Scissors
- ❑ Glue or paste
- ❑ Markers, crayons, colored pencils
- ❑ Tagboard
- ❑ Large and small resealable plastic bags for storage of the activity and for loose pieces (Another option would be to use plastic pockets.)
- ❑ Letter-size file folders with tabs
  (Use various colors to denote skill areas. For example, all math skills would be in red folders, all science skills in blue folders, etc.)
- ❑ File boxes or accordion folders
  (Use separate boxes or folders for each theme. As you look at a theme component, you will know immediately what to pull out of it for math, science, etc.)
- ❑ Individual laminating sheets, contact paper, or laminating machine
- ❑ Check-off sheet for each activity
  (Use a class roll sheet or blank paper for children to print their names as they complete the activity.)
- ❑ Labels for file folders—two sizes
  - Tab size to mark the game titles and skills
  - Larger labels to mark the folders as to the names, themes, skills, etc.

Storage of File Folder Activities

File folder activities may be stored in filing cabinets, desk drawers, storage boxes, baskets, plastic containers, etc. A self-sealing storage bag (large or small depending on the sizes of the pieces) should be with each file folder activity. All loose pieces should be inside the bag. Color code each piece in case it gets separated from where it belongs.

When you have finished making the activity, place each folder in a large self-sealing bag so it all stays together.

When the activity is ready to be used, it may be hung on a chart holder or clothesline with rings, hooks, or clothespins.

File each activity by theme with the label on the tab showing the activity name and the skill, as in the following example.

Name: Gingerbread Boys

Skill: sequencing

Folders should be color coded so you will know what skill is covered—e.g., all math skills could be in red folders, etc.

Introduction *(cont.)*

Rules and Standards for File Folder Activities

For file folder activities to work successfully, the rules and standards need to be carefully taught and consistently reinforced. Children need to understand not only the activities but also how to take care of them. In this way, the activities become excellent teaching tools.

- ❏ Discuss the care of file folder activities and how to use them.
- ❏ Discuss the parts of the file folder activity:
  - Folder
  - Pieces
  - Name check-off and how to do it
  - Where to store the game
  - Self-checking features (if applicable)
  - What to do about lost pieces (Have a place in the classroom to put all lost pieces so there is a consistent place to check for missing pieces.)
- ❏ Discuss where to do the file folder activity—at a center, the floor, a table, desk, etc.
- ❏ Discuss and reinforce how to participate in the activity with a friend.
- ❏ Discuss how to clean up by yourself or in a group.

How to Introduce File Folder Activities to the Children

- ❏ Introduce the theme to the children before activities are introduced, or they will not understand how it all comes together.
- ❏ Demonstrate to the children how to play the file folder activity.
- ❏ Demonstrate how they are to make the activity to take home after they have completed the activity successfully. (You may wish to choose only some activities for the children to take home to share with parents. However, be sure they still understand how to complete the activity.)
- ❏ Teaching the activity step by step in the beginning will save time when the children actually do the activity.

  Example: *Sequencing activity*
  - Discuss the correct order of the pictures.
  - Have children come up to the front to put the pictures in order.
  - Demonstrate how to glue the pictures to the paper.
  - Show the children where to put their names and what to do with the picture when finished.
  - Show them how to check off or sign their names when they have completed the activity.
  - Show the children how to clean up and where to put folders and game pieces when they are finished.
- ❏ Cooperative learning with file folder activities is best in pairs or groups of three at this age.
  - Cross-age tutors or parent volunteers are especially helpful with small groups so they may observe and help as needed.
  - Show the children where to sit when they do the activities in cooperative groups.
  - Demonstrate how to take turns and how to help one another.
  - Demonstrate how to praise one another.
  - Demonstrate how to clean up after finishing the activity together.

Introduction *(cont.)*

When to Use File Folder Activities

File folder activities work well in a variety of settings. They may be used at table groupings, centers, during free-choice time, in small groups with volunteers, or in one-to-one teaching.

- ❑ *Table Groupings*—Set out four to six folder activities, depending on how many children are at the table grouping. Children may complete the activities and then trade with a friend.

- ❑ *Centers*—After a theme is introduced, all related file folder activities may be placed at the center for the children to use. Be sure the activities have been introduced and taught to the children first.

- ❑ *Choosing Time*—This may be a free-choice time or a time when the children have completed their work. The activities may be placed on shelves, at centers, in storage containers, on windowsills, etc. When the children have time, they love to do activities they already know and feel successful with.

- ❑ *Volunteers*—When cross-age tutors or parent volunteers come into the room, file folder activities are an easy, effective method for them to use with the children. Tutors and volunteers may use them in small groups or do one-to-one teaching with them. Be sure the volunteers know where the activities are, how to do them, and where to have the children do them. Then it will not be necessary to disturb the teacher when they come into the room.

- ❑ *One-to-One Teaching*—When a child is having difficulty with a concept, pull out file folder activities that deal with that concept. When a volunteer comes in, have all materials laid out with the child's name, and the volunteer may then work with that particular child to reinforce the concept.

Training Volunteers and Cross-age Tutors to Use File Folder Activities

One of the most important areas to focus on with volunteers is training. To use untrained volunteers is both frustrating and a waste of time for the volunteer, the teacher, and the children. Set aside a short time each month for training cross-age tutors and volunteers.

- ❑ Explain the upcoming themes to the volunteers.

- ❑ Show them how to do the file folder activities and where to do them.

- ❑ Explain the rules to the volunteers, making sure they are the same rules the children will be using.

- ❑ Show the volunteers where the activities will be stored.

- ❑ Volunteers may also be used to help make activities when they come into the room to help, or they may take them home to make.

Teddy Bear, Teddy Bear

Colors are an important component of the early childhood curriculum. Depending on the ability levels of the children, a variety of activities may be incorporated. Use the popular book, *Brown Bear, Brown Bear* by Bill Martin, Jr., (Henry Holt and Company, 1996) to introduce this theme. Add the song "Going on a Bear Hunt," and the children will love this theme. Later, the book and the song may be reviewed to do a unit on bears.

Activity: Teddy Bear, Teddy Bear
Skills: color word recognition, writing

Materials Needed
- duplicating masters of Teddy Bear Book
- color words printed in the folder
- contact paper
- markers
- pencils

How to Make This Activity
- Reproduce enough copies of the Teddy Bear Book for each child and staple each book together.
- Place the books in the folder.
- Print the color words in their colors on one side of the folder.
- Print the color words in black on the other side of the folder.

Teacher's Directions
- Demonstrate how to trace over the words.
- Show how to find the color words in the folder.
- For younger children, a volunteer would need to be at the center to read each page to the children as they complete the book.

Self-Checking Feature: The children may look in the folder to find the color words.

Children's Directions
1. Select one Teddy Bear Book.
2. Color the teddy bear.
3. Read the color word.
4. Trace over the color word with your pencil.
5. Color the next page that color.
6. Draw a picture of yourself on the last page.

Labels

> **Activity:** Teddy Bear, Teddy Bear
> **Skills:** color word recognition, writing

(Tab)

> **Theme:** Colors
> **Activity:** Teddy Bear, Teddy Bear
> **Skills:** color word recognition, writing

(Folder)

Teddy Bear Book

Teddy Bear, Teddy Bear, what do you see?

I see a __red__ apple looking at me.

Teddy Bear Book (cont.)

Red Apple, Red Apple, what do you see?

I see an _____orange_____ jack-o'-lantern

looking at me.

Teddy Bear Book (cont.)

Orange Jack-o'-Lantern, Orange Jack-o'-Lantern,

what do you see?

I see a ___yellow___ sun looking at me.

Teddy Bear Book (cont.)

Yellow Sun, Yellow Sun, what do you see?

I see a ___green___ tree looking at me.

Teddy Bear Book (cont.)

Green Tree, Green Tree, what do you see?

I see a ___blue___ star looking at me.

Teddy Bear Book (cont.)

Blue Star, Blue Star, what do you see?

I see a  heart looking at me.

Teddy Bear Book (cont.)

Purple Heart, Purple Heart, what do you see?

I see a _____black_____ cat looking at me.

Teddy Bear Book *(cont.)*

Black Cat, Black Cat, what do you see?

I see_____ looking at me.

Teddy Bear Book (cont.)

Draw a picture of you!

Lily Pads

Activity: Lily Pads
Skills: color recognition, color word recognition, large muscle control, cooperative learning

Materials Needed

- duplicating master of frogs
- duplicating master of lily pads
- 9" by 12" (23 cm by 30 cm) construction paper—in red, yellow, green, orange, blue, brown, purple, and black
- 9" by 12" (23 cm by 30 cm) construction paper—four green sheets for frogs
- laminate or contact paper

How to Make This Activity

- Duplicate the lily pad master onto the construction paper in the eight different colors.
- Laminate or contact the lily pads and cut them out.
- Duplicate the frogs onto the green paper.
- Laminate or contact the frog papers and cut them out.
- Print the color words in the folder in colors and in black.

Teacher's Directions

- Show the children where to place the lily pads for hopping.
- Demonstrate how to hop over the lily pads.
- After the older children hop over the lily pads, they may match the lily pad to the color word frog.

Self-Checking Feature: Look in the folder to match the color word frog to the color word.

Children's Directions

1. Find a partner.
2. Pretend you are a frog.
3. Take turns hopping over the lily pads.
4. Tell your partner the color as you hop.
5. Match the lily pad to the color word frog.

Labels

> **Activity:** Lily Pads
> **Skills:** color recognition, color word recognition, large muscle control, cooperative learning

(Tab)

> **Theme:** Colors
> **Activity:** Lily Pads
> **Skills:** color recognition, color word recognition, large muscle control, cooperative learning

(Folder)

Lily Pad Master

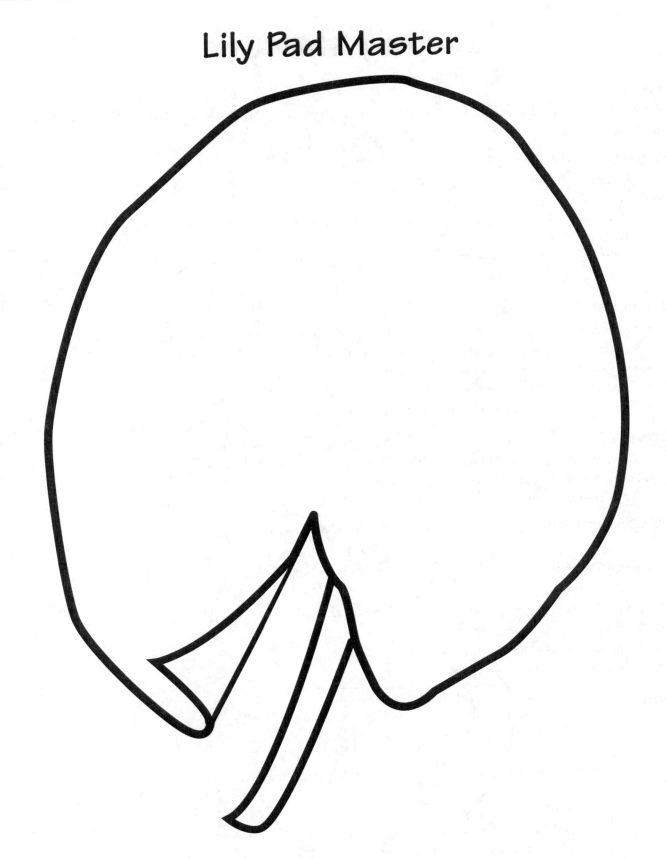

Frog Master

Frog Master *(cont.)*

Frog Master (cont.)

Frog Master (cont.)

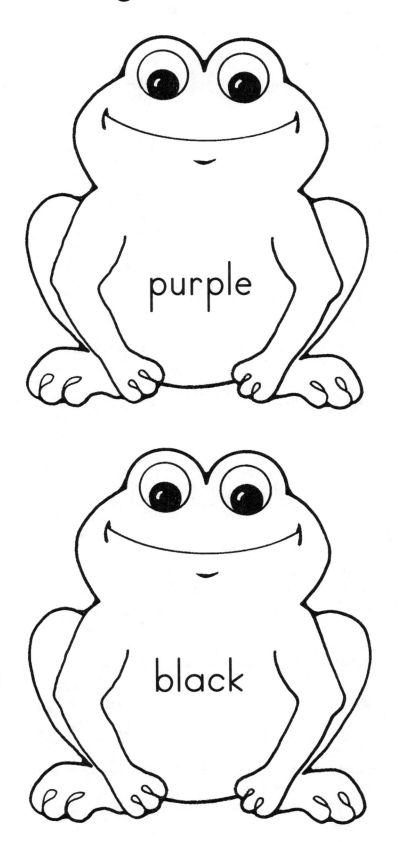

Gingerbread Boys

Activity: Gingerbread Boys
Skills: color matching, color discrimination

Materials Needed

- duplicating master of gingerbread boys
- 9" by 12" (23 cm by 30 cm) construction paper—16 to 24 pieces
- laminate or contact paper

How to Make This Activity

- Reproduce the gingerbread boys, making two or three of each color.
- Laminate or cover with contact paper and cut them out.

Teacher's Directions

- Demonstrate how to sort by colors.
- Demonstrate how to sort by the faces, pointing out the facial differences.

Children's Directions

1. Sort the gingerbread boys by colors.
2. Mix up the gingerbread boys.
3. Sort the gingerbread boys by their faces.
4. Tell how the gingerbread boys are feeling.

Labels

> **Activity:** Gingerbread Boys
> **Skills:** color matching, color discrimination   (Tab)

> **Theme:** Colors
> **Activity:** Gingerbread Boys
> **Skills:** color matching, color discrimination   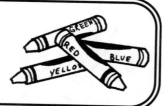   (Folder)

Surprised Gingerbread Boy

Shy Gingerbread Boy

Sad Gingerbread Boy

Happy Gingerbread Boy

Color Bead Patterns

Activity: Color Bead Patterns
Skills: patterns, color recognition

Materials Needed
- colored beads for stringing (These may be purchased at a teacher supply store.)
- heavy string or shoelaces to use for stringing
- sentence strips
- colored markers
- bead patterns
- laminate or contact paper

How to Make This Activity
- Cut the pattern strips in half horizontally.
- Following the bead pattern samples, make enough patterns for two or three children to work at the center together.
- Color in the bead patterns with markers.
- Create more difficult patterns, adjusting to the children's ability levels.
- Laminate the pattern strips.

Teacher's Directions
- Demonstrate how to string beads.
- Demonstrate how to follow a pattern.
- Demonstrate how to make a new pattern.

Children's Directions
1. Select a string and a box of beads.
2. Choose one pattern.
3. Begin by the star.
4. String your beads to look like the pattern.
5. Tell a friend or your teacher the colors in your pattern.
6. Make your own pattern.

Labels

> **Activity:** Colored Bead Patterns
> **Skills:** patterns, color recognition   (Tab)

> **Theme:** Colors
> **Activity:** Colored Bead Patterns      (Folder)
> **Skills:** patterns, color recognition

Pattern Strips

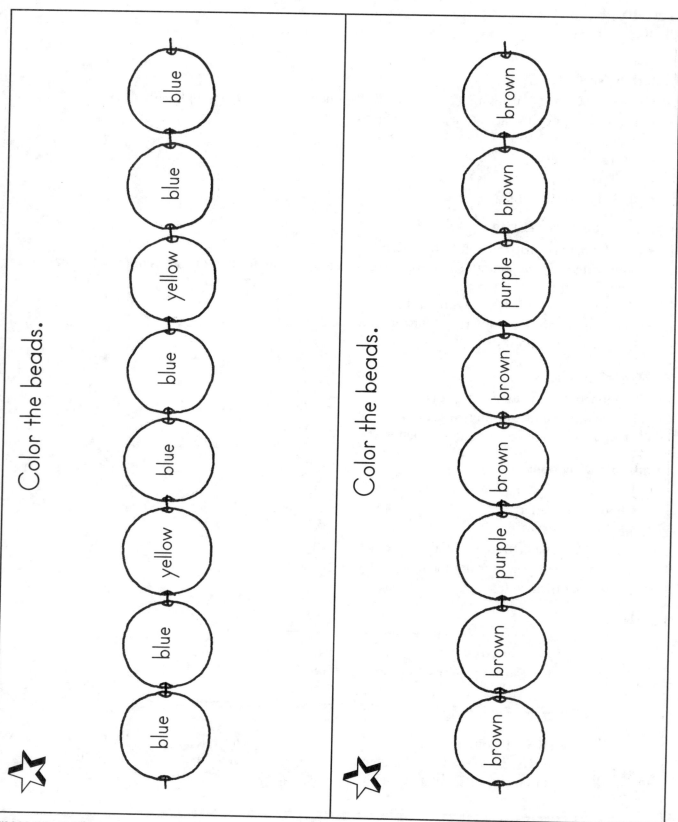

Color the beads.

blue · blue · yellow · blue · blue · yellow · blue · blue

Color the beads.

brown · brown · purple · brown · brown · purple · brown · brown

Pattern Strips *(cont.)*

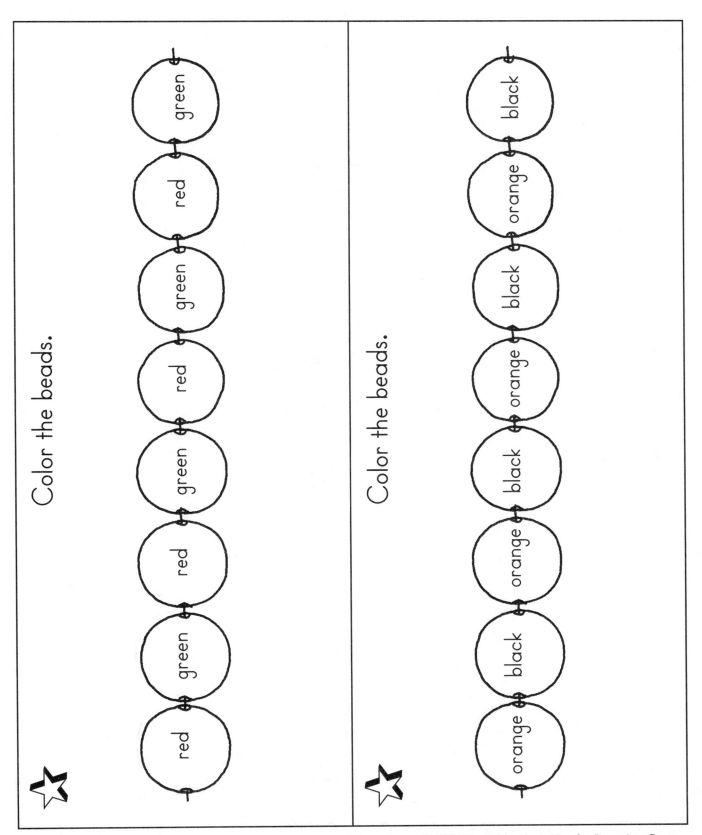

Pattern Strips *(cont.)*

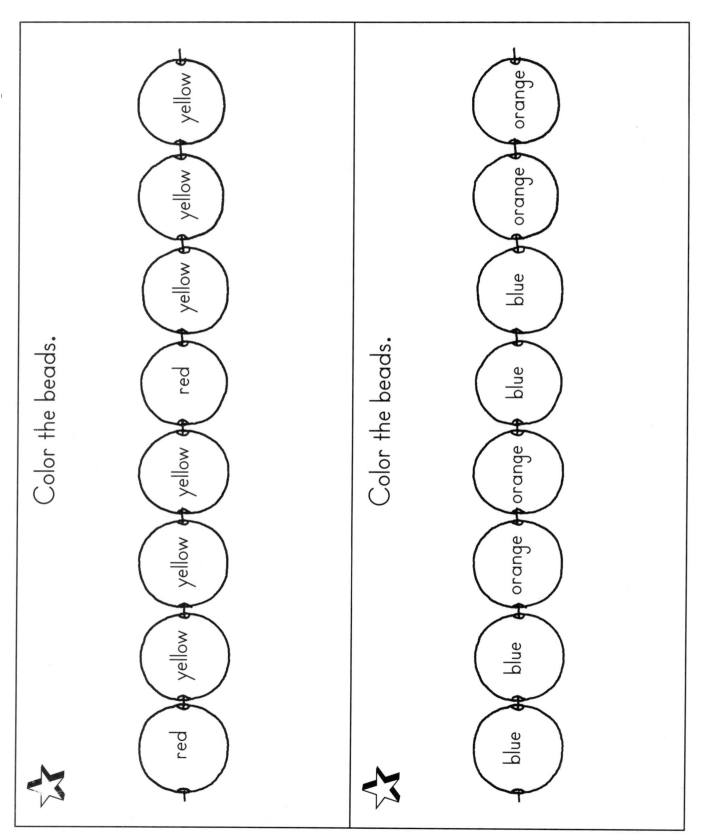

Color the beads.

yellow yellow yellow red yellow yellow yellow red

Color the beads.

orange orange blue blue orange orange blue blue

M & M® Shapes

Shapes are an integral part of the early childhood curriculum. A creative way to introduce this theme would be to use yarn and a flannelboard. Cut a piece of colored yarn 15" (38 cm) long. Place the yarn on the flannelboard and tell the children that "Willie the Worm" has come to visit. He will teach them about different shapes. Use the yarn to introduce the shapes to the children. Later, give each child a "Willie" and let each practice making shapes on the rug, tables, counters, etc.

Activity: M & M® Shapes
Skills: shape recognition, small muscle coordination

Materials Needed

- M & M® candies
- master sheet of tracing shapes
- resealable plastic bags—quart size
- one sheet of construction paper
- crayons

How to Make This Activity

- Reproduce the master of tracing shapes—one for each child and one for the folder.
- Fill one plastic bag full of M & Ms.
- Mark the plastic bag "For Table Use Only."
- Fill another bag with M & Ms to eat and mark the bag "To Eat."
- Glue the master to the construction paper and laminate.
- Cut it to fit the back of the folder and glue on. This will be for self-checking.
- Place the run-off papers and M & Ms in the folder.
- Place the folder and plastic bags at the shape center.

Teacher'sDirections

Demonstrate this activity for those children who cannot read the instructions. Show how many two are for those who cannot count.

Self-Checking Feature: *The children may look on the back of the folder if they forget how to make a shape.*

Children's Directions

1. Use your M & Ms to make these shapes: triangle, square, circle, rectangle, straight line, curved line, and oval.
2. Eat two M & Ms.
3. Take one paper and trace the shapes.

Labels

> **Activity:** M & M® Shapes
> **Skills:** shape recognition, small-muscle coordination

(Tab)

> **Theme:** Shapes
> **Activity:** M & M® Shapes
> **Skills:** shape recognition, small-muscle coordination

(Folder)

Shape Tracing Master

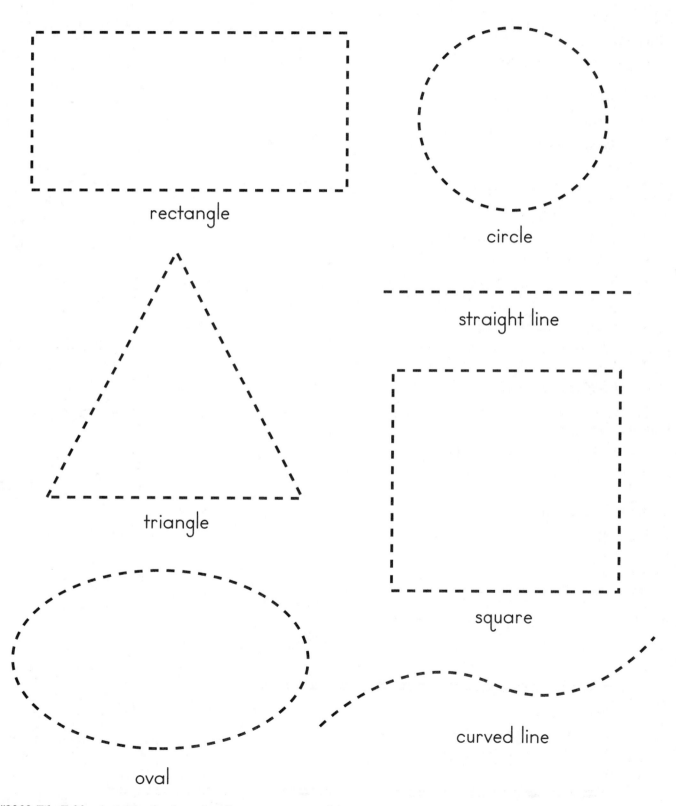

rectangle

circle

straight line

triangle

square

oval

curved line

Shape Puzzles

Activity: Shape Puzzles
Skills: matching, eye-hand coordination

Materials Needed

- tagboard or heavy paper
- shape master
- shape pieces
- shape picture
- resealable plastic bags
- glue

How to Make This Activity

- Reproduce shape masters.
- Reproduce three shape pieces.
- Reproduce one shape picture.
- Mount uncut shape pieces on tagboard or heavy paper. Then laminate and cut out the shapes. Store in a plastic bag. Place in folder. Glue shape picture on the back of the folder.

Teacher's Directions

Demonstrate forming a shape so children will know how to manipulate the pieces to form a picture.

Self-Checking Feature: The children may turn the folder over to see the pictures.

Children's Directions

Use the puzzle pieces to make a picture.

- Square
- Triangle
- Boat
- Fish
- Bunny

Labels

> **Activity:** Shape Puzzles
> **Skills:** matching, eye-hand coordination

(Tab)

> **Theme:** Shapes
> **Activity:** Shape Puzzles
> **Skills:** matching, eye-hand coordination
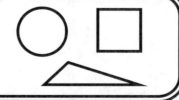

(Folder)

Shape Master

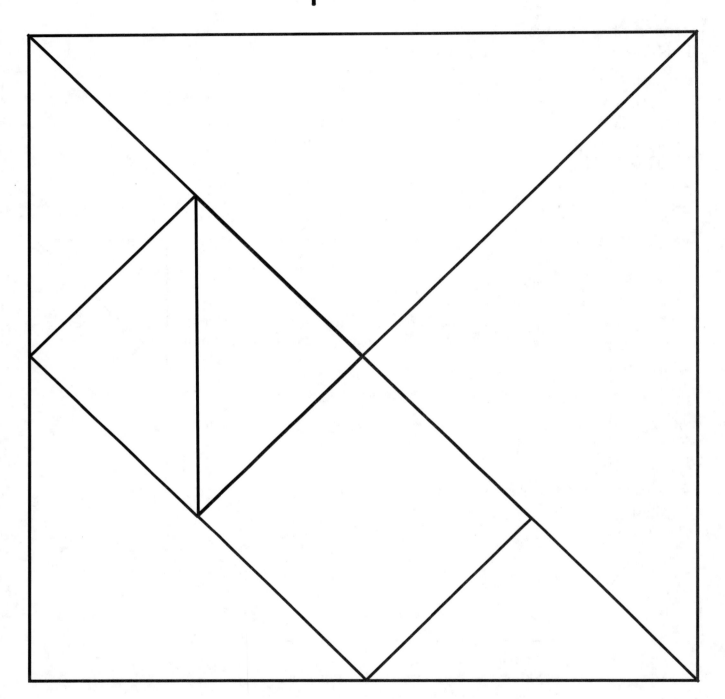

Shape Pictures

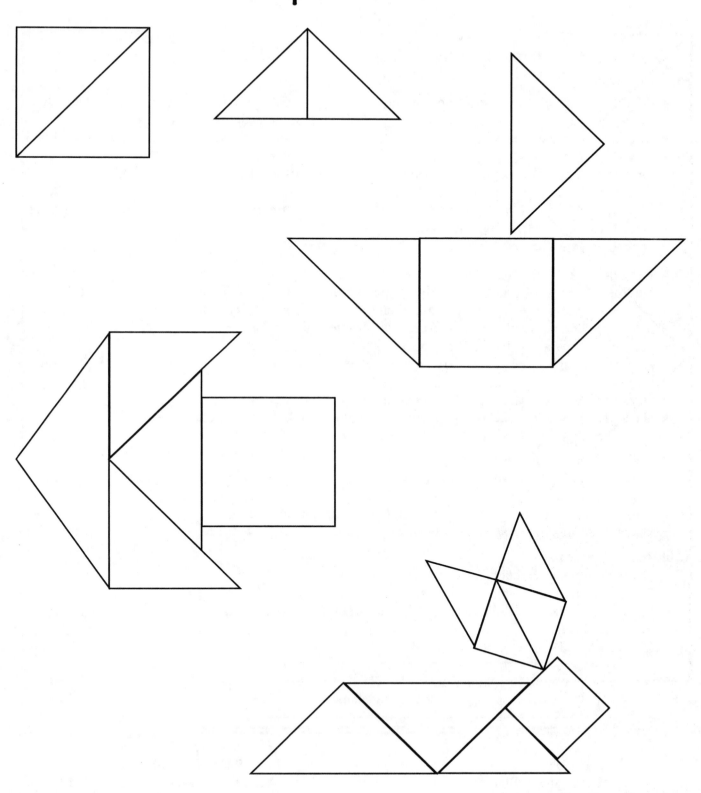

Shape Bus

Activity: Shape Bus
Skills: graphing, identifying shapes

Materials Needed

- duplicating master for shapes to go on the shape graph
- four letter-size envelopes or four resealable plastic bags
- three to six sheets of 12" by 28" (30 cm by 70 cm) colored construction paper
- glue sticks
- one or two boxes of graham crackers (Store opened crackers in a plastic bag.)
- one box of CHEEZ-IT® crackers placed in a large plastic bag
- one box of RITZ BITS® crackers placed in a large plastic bag
- one jar of smooth peanut butter
- paper towels
- plastic knives for spreading the peanut butter

How to Make This Activity

- Do this in groups of four to six at the shape learning center. A volunteer or aide will be needed.
- Reproduce the master sheets of shapes, cut out the shapes, and sort into the envelopes or bags.
- Mark off the construction paper (horizontally) into four sections.
- Glue one shape at the top of each section.
- At the top of the graph, print "My Favorite Shape." Make enough graphs for each group of four to six in the class.
- Lay out four to six paper towels around the table.
- Have plastic bags of crackers, peanut butter, and plastic knives on the table.

Teacher's Directions

- Be sure to use a volunteer to guide the children.
- When all are finished eating and have cleaned up, have them choose their favorite shapes from the shape envelopes.
- Have them glue their favorite shapes on their group's shape graph.
- Discuss the finished graph with the small group.

Children's Directions

1. Take two graham crackers and lay them side by side.
2. Spread peanut butter on the crackers.
3. Put five CHEEZ-IT® crackers (squares) in a straight line. Add four RITZ BITS® crackers (circles) to make wheels.
4. It's a SHAPE BUS—Eat it!

Labels

> **Activity:** Shape Bus
> **Skills:** graphing, identifying shapes   (Tab)

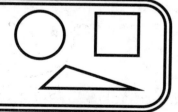

> **Theme:** Shapes
> **Activity:** Shape Bus
> **Skills:** graphing, identifying shapes   (Folder)

Shape Graph Master

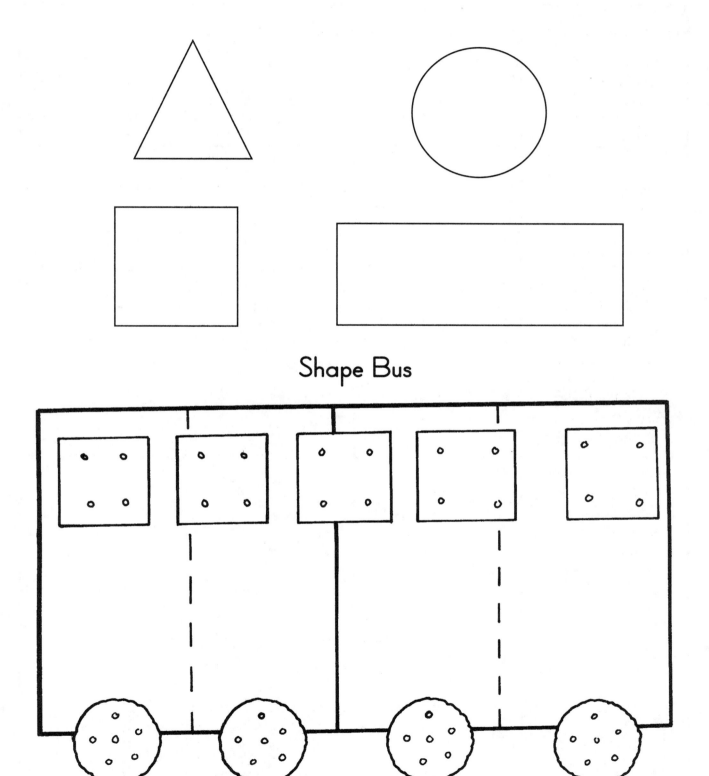

Shape Bus

2 graham crackers, 5 CHEEZ-IT crackers, 4 RITZ BITS crackers

Shape Graph Sample

My Favorite Shape			
◯	▢	△	▭

Hidden Shapes

Activity: Hidden Shapes
Skills: sorting, identifying shapes, small-muscle coordination

Materials Needed

- five red construction paper circles from master sheet
- five green construction paper squares from master sheet
- five yellow construction paper triangles from master sheet
- one sheet of construction paper
- one resealable plastic bag

- tagboard
- clown master
- crayons

How to Make This Activity

- Reproduce one of each shape on the correct colors of construction paper.
- Glue each sheet to tagboard.
- Laminate each sheet.
- Cut out the shapes and place them in the plastic bag. Place the bag in the folder.
- Reproduce the clown master—one for each child and one for the folder.
- Color one clown sheet, following the instructions.
- Glue clown sheet to the construction paper, laminate, and glue it to the back of the folder.
- Place clown sheets in the folder.

Teacher's Directions

To help younger children use the self-checking clown on the back of the folder, read the directions under the name: color all the circles red, all the squares green, and all the triangles yellow.

Self-Checking Feature: The children may look on the back of the folder to remind them of how to color the clown.

Children's Directions

1. Sort the paper shapes by colors.
2. Take one paper and find and color the hidden shapes:
    Circles—red
    Squares—green
    Triangles—yellow

Labels

> **Activity:** Hidden Shapes
> **Skills:** sorting, identifying shapes, small-muscle coordination

(Tab)

> **Theme:** Shapes
> **Activity:** Hidden Shapes
> **Skills:** sorting, identifying shapes, small-muscle coordination

(Folder)

Shape Master—Circles

Red

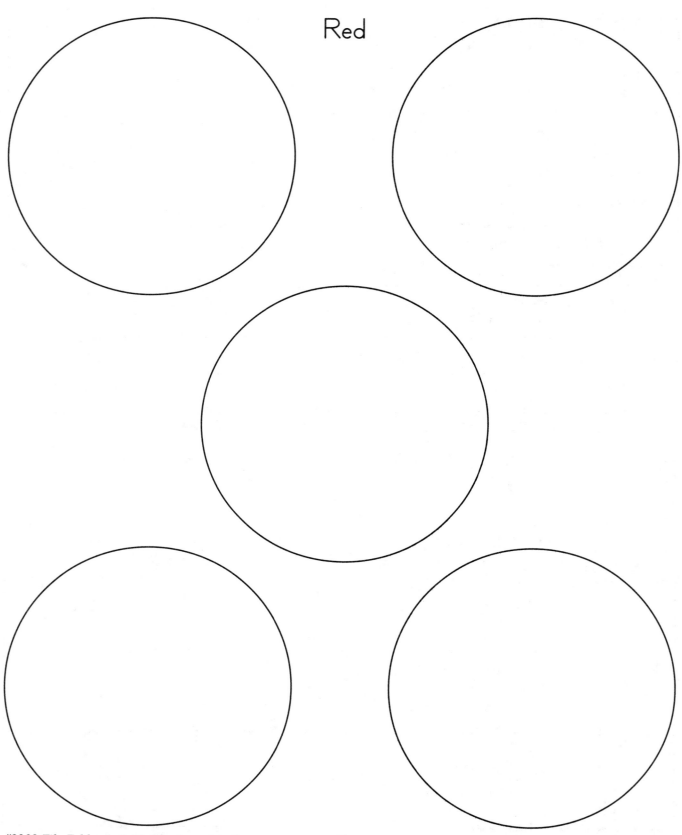

Shape Master—Squares

Green

Shape Master—Triangles

Yellow

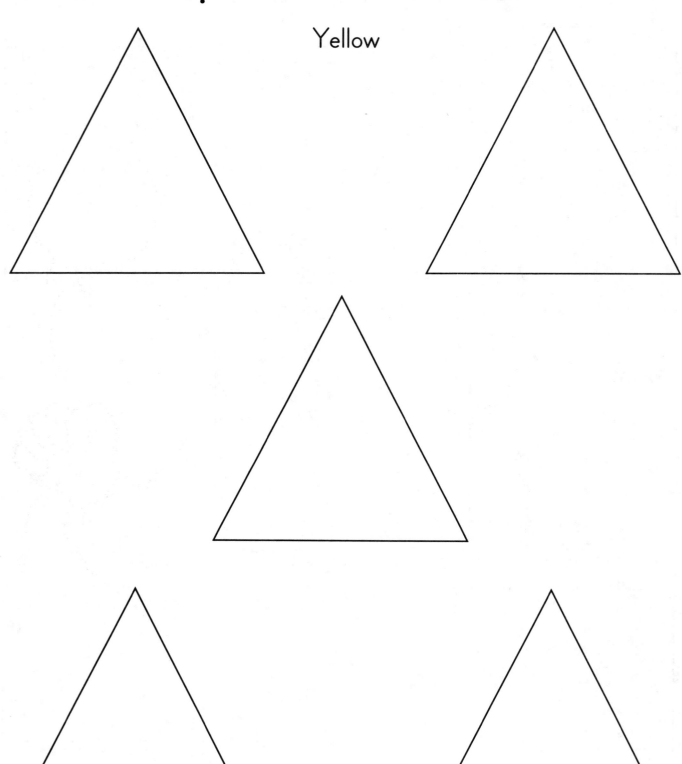

Shape Master—Clown

Name _____

Find the hidden shapes in the picture of the clown.
Color all the circles red. Color all the squares green. Color all the
triangles yellow.

Wormy Apples

An apple theme is fun to use to begin school or introduce the fall season. Use the flannelboard story "Little Bear's Star" to introduce this theme. The children love this story and will love to sample various kinds of apples.

Activity: Wormy Apples
Skill: sequencing

Materials Needed

- duplicating master of apples
- 9" by 12" (22 cm by 30 cm) red construction paper
- 12" by 18" (30 cm by 46 cm) manila paper or white construction paper cut in strips of 6" by 18" (15 cm by 46 cm)
- glue
- crayons
- contact paper

How to Make This Activity

- Duplicate the apples—four for each child and four for the folder.
- Cut out the apples.
- Accordion-fold the strips into four sections.
- For the folder for self-checking, see the sample on page 55.
- Tear four apples to show a progression of a worm eating an apple. (See the sample.)
- Draw a worm and an apple stem on each apple.
- Glue to the folder, in a row, so the children may check their work.
- Place contact paper on the folder where the apples are glued.
- Place the remaining apples in the folder.

Teacher's Directions

- Demonstrate the sequencing of the worm eating the apple and how it changes.
- Show the children how to tear or cut the worm's bite out of the apple.
- Demonstrate how to draw the stem and the worm.

Self-Checking Feature: Look in the folder to see how the worm eats the apple.

Children's Directions

1. Take four apples.
2. Tear or cut a bite out of each apple.
3. Glue the apples on the paper.
4. Draw a stem and a worm on each apple.

Labels

> **Activity:** Wormy Apples
> **Skill:** sequencing

(Tab)

> **Theme:** Apples
> **Activity:** Wormy Apples
> **Skills:** sequencing

(Folder)

Little Bear's Star

This is a flannelboard story. Before reading the story to the children, have the pieces prepared. Patterns that you will need are on pages 49–56. As you read the story, put the pieces on the flannelboard. You may also choose to have the children put the pieces on the flannelboard.

You might also want to have a big red apple to show to the children. Cut the apple across the middle so the stem is on the top and the blossom end of the apple is on the bottom. This is crosswise from the way an apple is normally cut. The seeds form the star. Do this one time before you show it to the children so you are sure how to do it correctly.

Inside the Bear family's cave lived a lonely little bear.

Little Bear was lonely because all of his friends were in Bear School. Little Bear was too little to go to Bear School.

All day Little Bear followed Mama Bear around while she worked. Mama Bear was a very good mother, and she felt very sorry for Little Bear. She tried very hard to find something different for Little Bear to do each day so he would forget about being lonely.

One day Mama Bear told Little Bear to try to find a little red house with no windows and no doors, a chimney on top, and a star in the middle. Little Bear was very puzzled. He couldn't think of anything that lived in a house with no windows or doors, but he started out to look for the house.

First, he met a mouse. "Have you seen a little red house with no windows and no doors, a chimney on top, and a star in the middle?" asked Little Bear.

"No, no," squeaked the mouse as she scampered away into the field.

Second, he met a butterfly. "Have you seen a little red house with no windows and no doors, a chimney on top, and a star in the middle?" asked Little Bear.

"No, no," whispered the butterfly as he fluttered around the flowers.

Little Bear's Star *(cont.)*

Third, he met a pig. "Have you seen a little red house with no windows and no doors, a chimney on top, and a star in the middle?" asked Little Bear.

"No, no," oinked the pig as she trotted into her pen.

Fourth, he met a frog. "Have you seen a little red house with no windows and no doors, a chimney on top, and a star in the middle?" asked Little Bear.

"No, no," croaked the frog as he jumped into the pond.

Fifth, he met an owl. "Have you seen a little red house with no windows and no doors, a chimney on top, and a star in the middle?" asked Little Bear.

"Whooooo, me?" asked the wise old owl. "No, but you might ask my friend, Mr. Worm."

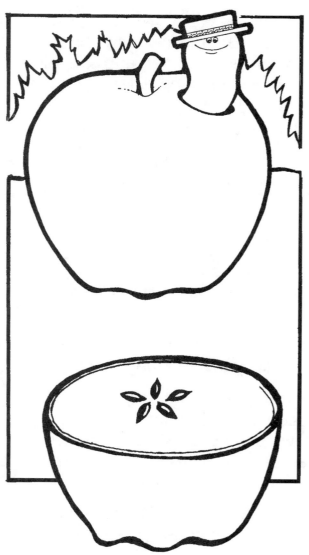

Little Bear looked all over the ground for Mr. Worm, but he couldn't find him anywhere. Finally, he remembered that Mr. Worm really liked apples, so he walked to the apple orchard. There he found Mr. Worm boring his way into a big red apple. "Oh," Little Bear thought, "that nice red apple could be a house and the stem could be a chimney. It doesn't have any windows or any doors."

"Mr. Worm, could there be a star in the middle of that apple?" Little Bear asked.

"Why don't you take a nice big apple home and ask someone?" Mr. Worm replied.

"Oh, thank you, Mr. Worm!" Little Bear cried as he ran home. When Little Bear got home, Mama Bear cut the apple across the middle and found Little Bear's star!

Flannelboard Patterns

Mama Bear

Flannelboard Patterns *(cont.)*

Little Bear

Field Mouse

Flannelboard Patterns (cont.)

Pigpen

Pig

Frog

Flannelboard Patterns *(cont.)*

Flowers

Butterfly

Bear Cave

The Bears

WELCOME

Flannelboard Patterns (cont.)

Tree

Apple Star

Apple

Flannelboard Patterns (cont.)

Owl

Mr. Worm

Apple Orchard

Sample for Folder

Glue to the folder in a row.

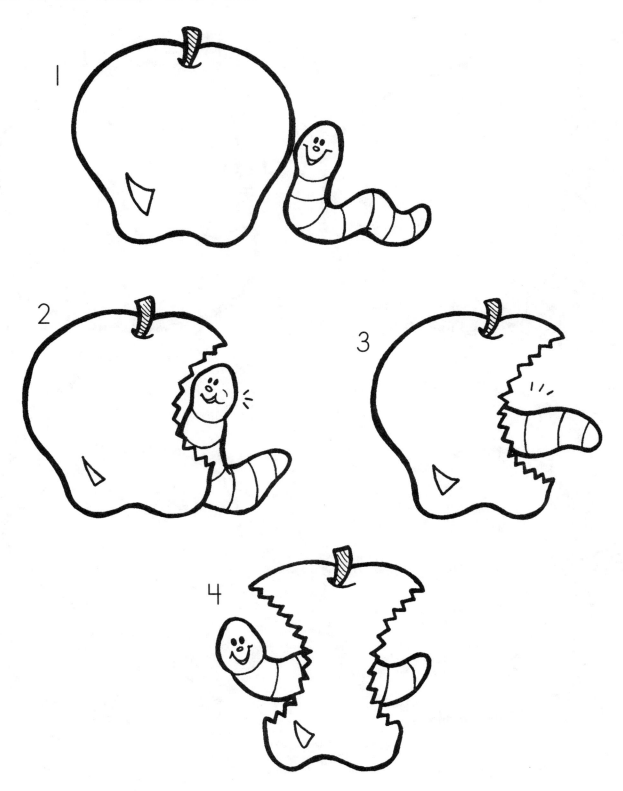

Apple Master

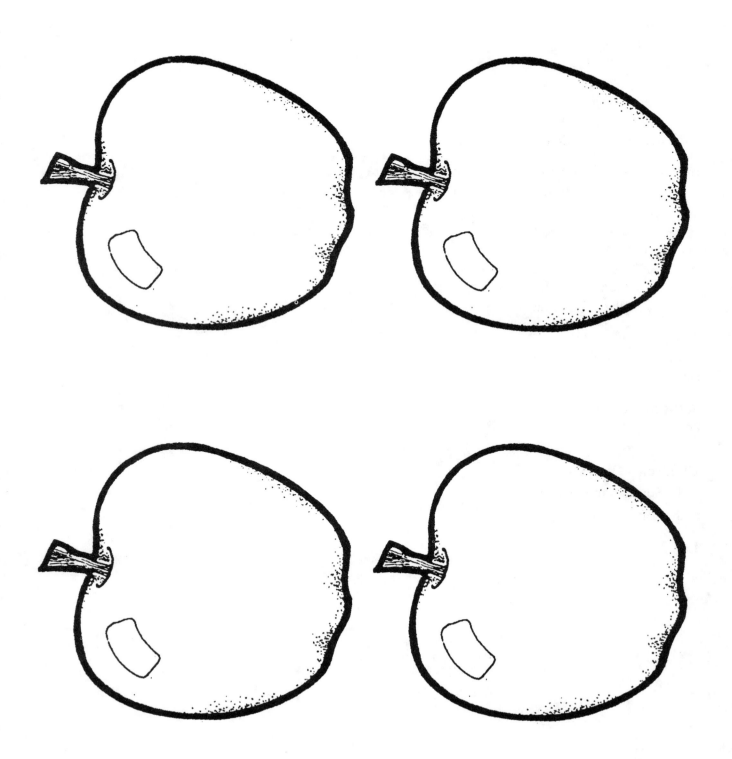

Apple Sorting

Activity: Apple Sorting
Skills: recognizing colors, recognizing sizes

Materials Needed

- duplicating masters of apples
- 9" by 12" (23 cm by 30 cm) construction paper—red, yellow, green
- scissors
- glue
- contact paper
- resealable plastic bag

How to Make This Activity

- Reproduce the apple master on the various colors of construction paper—three to six sheets, depending on how many apples you wish the children to sort.
- Cut out the apples.
- For the folder for self-checking:
  - ✓ Cut out one large red apple, one medium green apple, and one small yellow apple and glue them to the folder. Cover with contact paper.
  - ✓ Place the remaining apples in a plastic bag.

Teacher's Directions

Demonstrate to the children how to sort the colors and then how to mix them up again and sort by sizes.

Self-Checking Feature: *The children may match the colored apples to the apples on the folder both by colors and then by sizes.*

Children's Directions

1. Sort the apples by colors.
2. Sort the apples by sizes.

Labels

> **Activity:** Apple Sorting
> **Skills:** recognizing colors and sizes   (Tab)

> **Theme:** Apples
> **Activity:** Apple Sorting
> **Skills:** recognizing colors and sizes      (Folder)

Large Apples

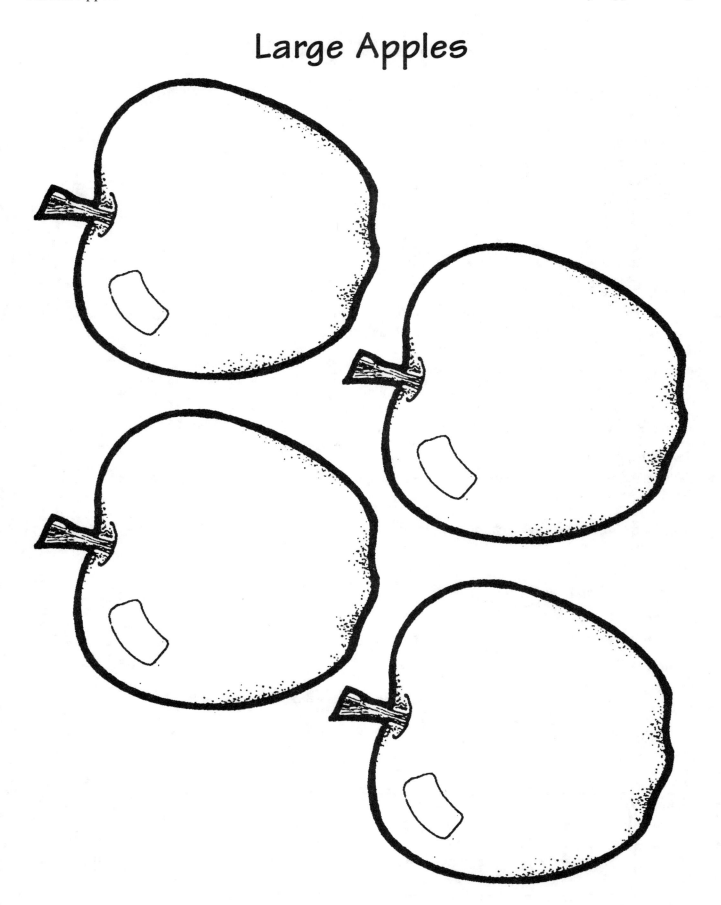

Medium Apples

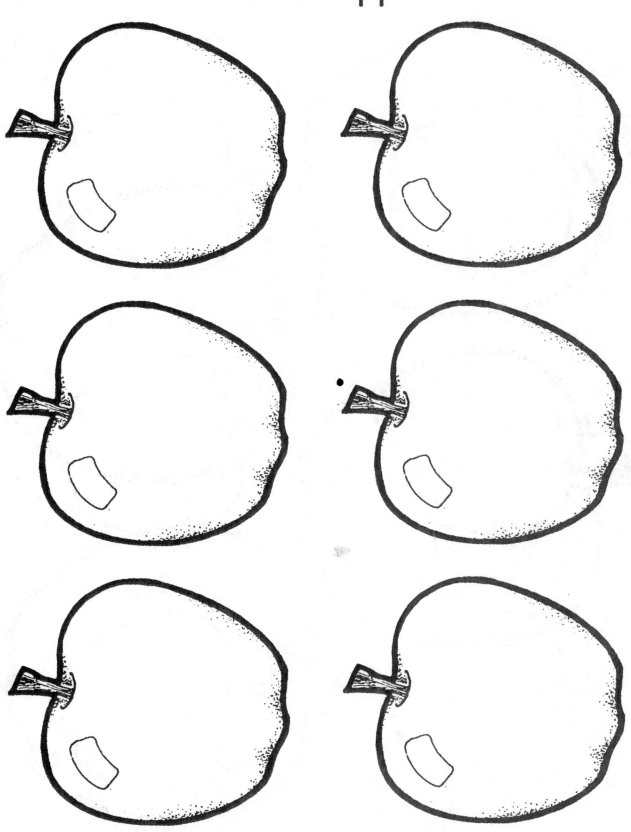

Small Apples

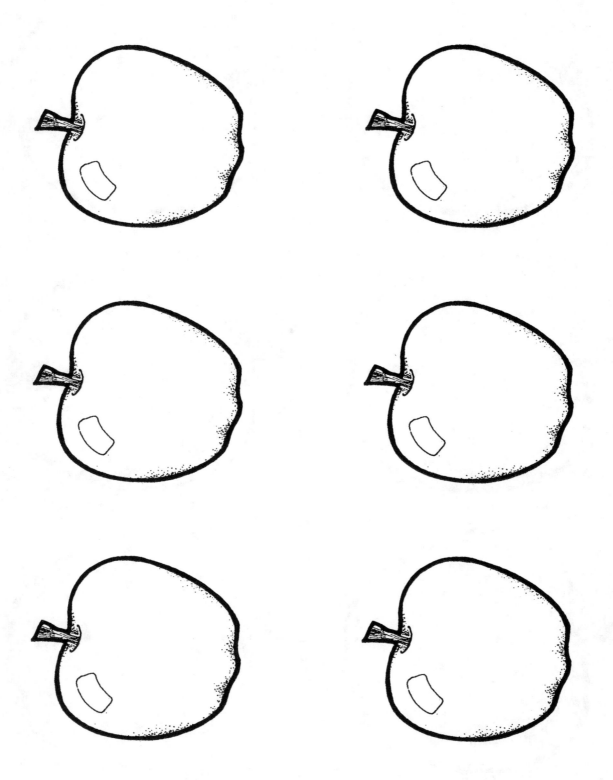

Apple Trees

Activtiy: Apple Trees
Skill: number order

Materials Needed

- 11 sheets of 9" by 12" (23 cm by 30 cm) construction paper
- duplicating masters of apple trees
- laminate or contact paper

How to Make This Activity

- Duplicate the apple tree masters.
- Glue each tree to one sheet of construction paper.
- Laminate or cover with contact paper.
- For the folder for self-checking:
  - ✓ Duplicate the master of the small trees.
  - ✓ Glue the sheet on the folder.
  - ✓ Cover with contact paper.

Teacher's Directions

- Demonstrate to the children how to put the trees in number order.
- This activity may be extended to include matching sets and numbers by adding cutout apples to the folder. The children may then place the correct number of apples on each tree.

Self-Checking Feature: The children may look in the folder to see the trees in number order.

Children's Directions

Put the apple trees in number order.

Labels

Activity: Apple Trees
Skill: number order   (Tab)

Theme: Apples
Activity: Apple Trees
Skill: number order   (Folder)

Apple Tree Master

Apple Tree Numbers

Apple Tree Numbers (cont.)

Apple Tree Numbers *(cont.)*

Apple Tree Numbers (cont.)

Apple Tree Numbers (cont.)

Apple Tree Numbers (cont.)

Apple Tree Numbers (cont.)

Apple Tree Numbers (cont.)

Apple Tree Numbers *(cont.)*

Apple Tree Numbers *(cont.)*

Apple Tree Numbers (cont.)

Apple Book

Activity: Apple Book
Skills: color word recognition, writing

Materials Needed

- duplicating masters of apple book
- crayons or markers
- color words—red, yellow, and green printed in the folder
- contact paper
- pencils

How to Make This Activity

- Reproduce enough copies of the apple book for each child and staple each book together.
- For the folder for self-checking:
  - ✓ Print the color words in red, yellow, and green on one side of the folder.
  - ✓ Print the color words in black on the other side of the folder.

Teacher's Directions

- Demonstrate how to trace over words.
- Show how to find the color words in the folder.

Self-Checking Feature: *The children may look in the folder to find the color words.*

Children's Directions

1. Take one color book.
2. Read the color word.
3. Trace over the color word with a pencil.
4. Color the apple the same color.

Labels

> **Activity:** Apple Book
> **Skills:** color word recognition, writing   (Tab)

> **Theme:** Apples
> **Activity:** Apple Book
> **Skills:** color word recognition, writing   (Folder)

I Like Apples

by

_____

I Like Apples (cont.)

I like red apples.

I Like Apples *(cont.)*

I like green apples.

I Like Apples (cont.)

I like yellow apples.

I Like Apples *(cont.)*

I like the one with the worm the best!

The Worm and the Apple

Activity: The Worm and the Apple
Skills: position words, cooperative learning

Materials Needed

- two real apples or pictures of apples
- glue
- laminate or contact paper
- construction paper
- tagboard
- directions master
- duplicating master of apple and worm, showing position word actions
- a small pretend worm or picture of a worm (See duplicating master.)

How to Make This Activity

- Duplicate the worm on construction paper, cut it out, glue it on tagboard, and laminate. Make two worms.
- Duplicate the apple and worm position word master. (page 82)
- Cut out each section of the apple and worm sheet.
- Glue to the folder.
- Cover with contact paper.
- Duplicate the directions master. Make two copies.
- Glue each set of directions to a piece of tagboard.
- Laminate each set of directions.

Teacher's Directions

- This activity is for children who are reading.
- Demonstrate the activity to the children first.
- Show the children how to find a partner and how to take turns reading the directions.

Self-Checking Feature: Look in the folder to see where the worm is for each apple.

Children's Directions

1. Find a partner.
2. Take a worm, an apple, and a paper telling you what to say.
3. Take turns reading the directions to your partner.
4. Help your partner if he or she has trouble.

Labels

> **Activity:** The Worm and the Apple
> **Skills:** position words, cooperative learning   (Tab)

> **Theme:** Apples
> **Activity:** The Worm and the Apple
> **Skills:** position words, cooperative learning   (Folder)

The Worm Master

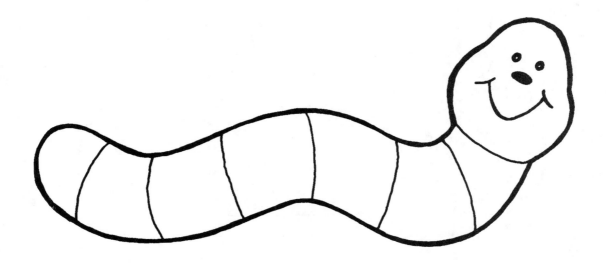

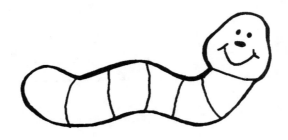

Sample for Folder

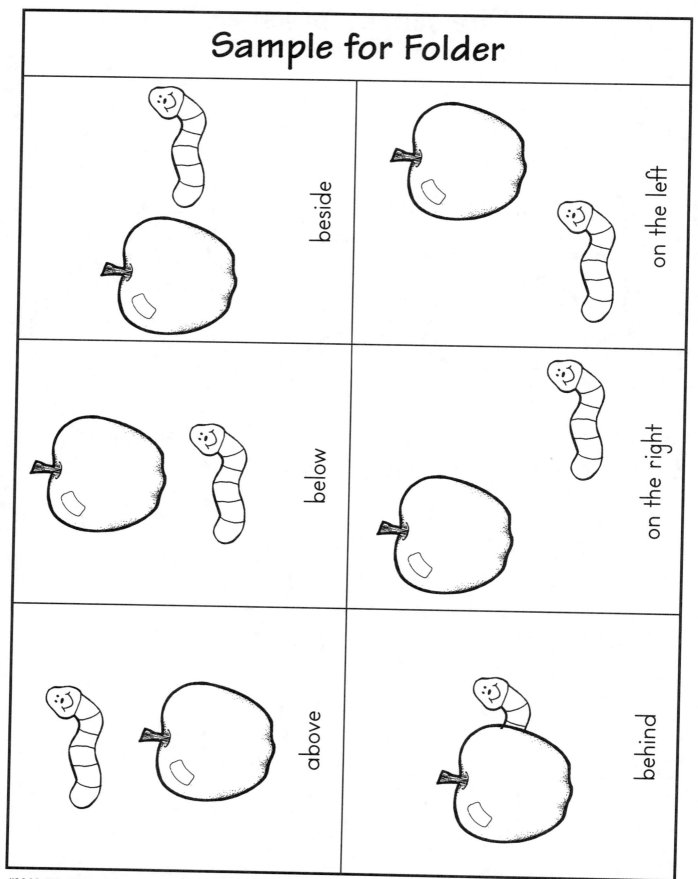

beside

on the left

below

on the right

above

behind

Directions Master

Directions

1. Hold the worm above the apple.

2. Hold the worm below the apple.

3. Put the worm beside the apple.

4. Put the worm behind the apple.

5. Put the worm on the right side of the apple.

6. Put the worm on the left side of the apple.

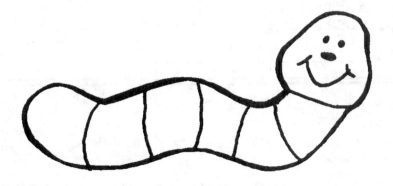

Family Sizes

The family is a theme all children can relate to, however their family is configured. Begin the unit developing the many varied family units in the class. The children may wish to draw pictures of their own families to put on the bulletin board. Ask the children to bring in a picture of something their family likes to do together. Mount their pictures with their family drawings. To encourage discussion, bring in posters of many types of families.

Activity: Family Sizes
Skills: counting, writing numbers, recognizing a variety of ethnic groups

Materials Needed

- duplicating master of families
- pencils
- glue stick
- crayons
- contact paper

How to Make This Activity

- Duplicate the family master—one per child and one for the folder.
- Complete the page for the folder; color and glue it on the folder.
- Cover the completed page with clean contact paper.
- Place duplicated copies in the folder.

Teacher's Directions

- Demonstrate how to count the individual families and write the number in the box.
- Discuss the variety of ethnic families and how everyone is both alike and different.

Self-Checking Feature: The children may look in the folder to check the numbers in the families.

Children's Directions

1. Take one family picture.
2. Count the number of people in each family.
3. Write the correct number in each box.
4. Color each family.

Labels

> **Activity:** Family Sizes
> **Skills:** counting, writing numbers, recognizing a variety of ethnic groups

(Tab)

> **Theme:** Families
> **Activity:** Family Sizes
> **Skills:** counting, writing numbers, recognizing a variety of ethnic groups

(Folder)

Family Master

Family Fun

Activity: Family Fun
Skill: graphing

Materials Needed

- 18" by 24" (46 cm by 61 cm) white construction paper
- duplicating master of circles
- glue sticks
- crayons
- pencils
- marker
- contact paper

How to Make This Activity

- Duplicate the master of circles—one per child.
- Cut out the circles and place them in the folder.
- Glue a sample graph master in the folder.
- Cover the graph sample with contact paper.
- Divide the white paper into five sections (see the sample).
- Print the title at the top of the graph (see the sample).

Teacher's Directions

- Demonstrate how to color a family on the circle.
- Demonstrate how to glue the circle under the picture chosen.
- Discuss the graph when completed.

Children's Directions

1. Choose a circle.
2. Draw and color your family.
3. Glue your circle under what your family likes to do.

Labels

> **Activity:** Family Fun
> **Skill:** graphing

(Tab)

> **Theme:** Families
> **Activity:** Family Fun
> **Skill:** graphing

(Folder)

Family Master

Graph Sample

What does your family like to do?

Beach	Movies	Games	Mountains	Park

Families Do Things Together

Activity: Families Do Things Together
Skill: sequencing

Materials Needed
- three duplicating masters
- three different colors of tagboard
- duplicating master for the folder
- contact paper
- glue stick
- three resealable plastic bags
- laminate

How to Make This Activity
- Duplicate each master on a different color of paper.
- Color each sheet of pictures.
- Glue each sheet on a different color of tagboard.
- Laminate.
- Cut each sheet apart on the lines and place the sections in a plastic bag.
- Duplicate the master for the folder, color, and glue in the folder. Cover with contact paper.

Teacher's Directions
- Discuss activities the children may do as a family.
- Show the various activities in each plastic bag in the folder.
- Demonstrate how to put them in the correct order by words or pictures.

Self-Checking Feature: *The children may look in the folder to see the correct order of the pictures.*

Children's Directions
1. Take one plastic bag.
2. Put the pictures in the correct order.

Labels

> **Activity:** Families Do Things Together
> **Skill:** sequencing

(Tab)

> **Theme:** Families
> **Activity:** Families Do Things Together
> **Skill:** sequencing

(Folder)

Sample for Folder

eating together

children playing in a clean room

family playing at a lake

cooking together

children cleaning room

family getting in the car

shopping together

children's messy room

family packing

Theme: Families   Activity: Families Do Things Together

Doing Things Together

		eating together
		cooking together
		shopping together

© *Teacher Created Materials, Inc.*   91   *#2209 File Folder Activities for Learning Centers*

Doing Things Together (cont.)

		children playing in a clean room
		children cleaning room
		messy room

Doing Things Together *(cont.)*

family packing	family getting in the car	family playing at a lake

"One, Two, Buckle My Shoe"

A unit of nursery rhymes is fun for the children to participate in. They are already familiar with many nursery rhymes, and they love to say and sing them. Introduce nursery rhymes by reading various ones the children know and then move on to unfamiliar ones. Bring in posters or pictures that go with the particular rhymes.

Activity: "One, Two, Buckle My Shoe"
Skills: tracing numbers, recognizing numbers 1–10, repeating a nursery rhyme, matching pictures and rhymes

Materials Needed

- pencils
- contact paper
- duplicating master of "One, Two, Buckle My Shoe"
- glue

How to Make This Activity

- Duplicate the master—one per child and one for the folder.
- Complete the master for the folder sample, glue it to the folder, and cover with contact paper.
- Place children's copies in the folder.

Teacher's Directions

- Review the rhyme with the children.
- Act the rhyme out.
- Demonstrate how to trace the numbers.
- Using a pencil, demonstrate how to match the numbers and the pictures.

Self-Checking Feature: The children may check the folder to see how the words, numbers, and pictures match.

Children's Directions

1. Take one paper and pencil.
2. Trace the numbers.
3. Draw a line to match the numbers with the correct picture.
4. Say the rhyme as you work.

Labels

> **Activity:** "One, Two, Buckle My Shoe"
> **Skills:** tracing numbers, recognizing numbers 1–10,
> repeating a nursery rhyme, matching pictures and rhymes

(Tab)

> **Theme:** Nursery Rhymes
> **Activity:** "One, Two, Buckle My Shoe"
> **Skills:** tracing numbers, recognizing numbers 1–10,
> repeating a nursery rhyme, matching pictures and rhymes

(Folder)

"One, Two, Buckle My Shoe" *(cont.)*

Buckle my shoe.

Shut the door.

Pick up sticks.

Lay them straight.

A big fat hen.

"Humpty Dumpty"

Activity: "Humpty Dumpty"
Skill: recognizing size from largest to smallest

Materials Needed

- duplicating master of eggs
- strips of manila paper
- contact paper
- crayons
- 9" by 12" (23 cm by 30 cm) white construction paper
- glue sticks
- scissors

How to Make This Activity

- Duplicate the master of eggs—one per child and one for the folder sample.
- Cut strips of manila paper for children to glue the eggs on—one per child.
- Cut out the eggs for the folder sample.
- Glue the eggs in the folder from largest to smallest.
- Cover the eggs with contact paper.
- Place children's copies and strips of manila paper in the folder.

Teacher's Directions

- Review the nursery rhyme.
- Demonstrate how to cut the eggs out and glue them on the manila strip in order of largest to smallest.

Self-Checking Feature: *The children may check the folder to see the correct order.*

Children's Directions

1. Take one Humpty Dumpty paper and one strip of paper.
2. Cut out each egg.
3. Glue the eggs on the paper—largest to smallest.
4. Color the eggs.

Labels

> **Activity:** "Humpty Dumpty"
> **Skill:** recognizing size from largest to smallest　(Tab)

> **Theme:** Nursery Rhymes
> **Activity:** "Humpty Dumpty"
> **Skill:** recognizing size from largest to smallest 　(Folder)

"Humpty Dumpty" *(cont.)*

Humpty Dumpty sat on a wall,

Humpty Dumpty had a great fall;

All the king's horses and all the king's men,

Couldn't put Humpty together again.

"Jack and Jill"

Activity: "Jack and Jill"
Skill: number sequencing (0–10)

Materials Needed

- duplicating master of "Jack and Jill"
- pencils
- contact paper
- glue
- crayons

How to Make This Activity

- Duplicate the master—one per child and one for the folder.
- Folder sample: Complete the dots, glue the sample in the folder, and cover with contact paper.
- Place children's copies in the folder.
- Place folder, pencils, and crayons at the nursery rhyme center.

Teacher's Directions

- Review and discuss the nursery rhyme.
- Discuss where the water came from.
- Demonstrate how to complete the dot-to-dot paper.

Self-Checking Feature: *The children may look in the folder to see how to complete the dot-to-dot paper.*

Children's Directions

1. Take one dot-to-dot paper.
2. Follow the numbers to connect the dots with a pencil.
3. Color the picture.
4. Say the rhyme.

Labels

```
┌─────────────────────────────────────┐
│  Name: "Jack and Jill"              │   (Tab)
│  Skill: number sequencing (0–10)    │
└─────────────────────────────────────┘
```

```
┌─────────────────────────────────────────────┐
│                                             │
│  Theme: Nursery Rhymes                      │   (Folder)
│  Activity: "Jack and Jill"                  │
│  Skill: number sequencing (0–10)            │
│                                             │
└─────────────────────────────────────────────┘
```

"Jack and Jill" *(cont.)*

Jack and Jill went up the hill

To fetch a pail of water.

Jack fell down and broke his crown,

and Jill came tumbling after.

10

9

1   2

7   8

3

6

4

5

"Hey Diddle, Diddle"

Activity: "Hey Diddle, Diddle"
Skill: sequencing

Materials Needed

- duplicating master of sequencing pictures
- 9" by 12" (23 cm by 30 cm) white construction paper
- glue
- laminate or contact paper
- stapler
- crayons

How to Make This Activity

- Duplicate the master—one per child and one for a folder sample.
- Folder sample: Color, cut out on the lines, glue in the folder in order, and cover with contact paper.
- Cut the children's copies on the lines and place in four stacks.

Teacher's Directions

- Review and discuss the nursery rhyme.
- Demonstrate how to take one paper off each stack.
- Demonstrate how to put pages in order.
- Demonstrate how to staple the book together.

Self-Checking Feature: *The children may look in the folder to see the correct story order.*

Children's Directions

1. Take four nursery rhyme papers.
2. Put the pages in the correct order.
3. Staple together.
4. Color the book.
5. Say the rhyme.

Labels

> **Activity:** "Hey Diddle, Diddle"
> **Skill:** sequencing   (Tab)

> **Theme:** Nursery Rhymes
> **Activity:** "Hey Diddle, Diddle"
> **Skill:** sequencing      (Folder)

"Hey Diddle, Diddle" *(cont.)*

Hey Diddle, Diddle
The cat and the fiddle,

The cow jumped over the moon.

The little dog laughed to
see such sport,

And the dish ran away
with the spoon.

"Pease Porridge"

Activity: "Pease Porridge"
Skill: opposites—hot and cold

Materials Needed
- duplicating master of opposites
- crayons
- glue
- contact paper
- cold items—ice cube, can of soda, etc.
- pictures of hot items

How to Make This Activity
- Duplicate the master—one per child and one for the folder sample.
- Glue one paper in the folder, color, and cover with contact paper.
- Place children's copies and hot and cold items on a counter at the center.

Teacher's Directions
- Discuss hot and cold items.
- Let the children touch the cold items and look at the pictures of the hot items.
- Demonstrate how to color the opposites paper.

Self-Checking Feature: *The children may look in the folder to check their coloring of the paper.*

Children's Directions
1. Touch the cold items.
2. Look at the pictures of the hot items.
3. Take one paper and read the nursery rhyme.
4. Color cold picture blue.
5. Color hot pictures red.

Labels

> **Activity:** "Pease Porridge"
> **Skill:** opposites—hot and cold

(Tab)

> **Theme:** Nursery Rhymes
> **Activity:** "Pease Porridge"
> **Skill:** opposites—hot and cold

(Folder)

"Pease Porridge" *(cont.)*

Pease porridge hot,

Pease porridge cold,

Pease porridge in the pot, nine days old.

Some like it hot,

Some like it cold,

Some like it in the pot, nine days old.

◆   ◆   ◆

Color cold pictures blue.   Color hot pictures red.

ice cube

soup

ice–cream cone

sun

candle

snowman

"Jack Be Nimble"

Activity: "Jack Be Nimble"
Skills: recognizing the letter J, recognizing the sound of J

Materials Needed

- duplicating master of the letter J
- crayons
- glue
- contact paper

How to Make This Activity

- Duplicate the J master—one per child and one for the folder.
- Complete (color) the folder sample, glue it in the folder, and cover with contact paper.
- Place children's copies and crayons at a center, counter, or table.

Teacher's Directions

- Review the nursery rhyme.
- Act out the nursery rhyme.
- Discuss fire safety.
- Demonstrate how to complete the paper.

Self-Checking Feature: *The children may look in the folder to see if they colored the correct pictures.*

Children's Directions

1. Color the pictures that begin with J.
2. Say the rhyme.

Labels

> **Activity:** "Jack Be Nimble"
> **Skills:** recognizing the letter J, recognizing
>   the sound of J

(Tab)

> **Theme:** Nursery Rhymes
> **Activity:** "Jack Be Nimble"
> **Skills:** recognizing the letter J, recognizing the sound of J

(Folder)

"Jack Be Nimble" *(cont.)*

Jack be nimble,

Jack be quick,

Jack jump over the candlestick.

Color the pictures that begin with J.

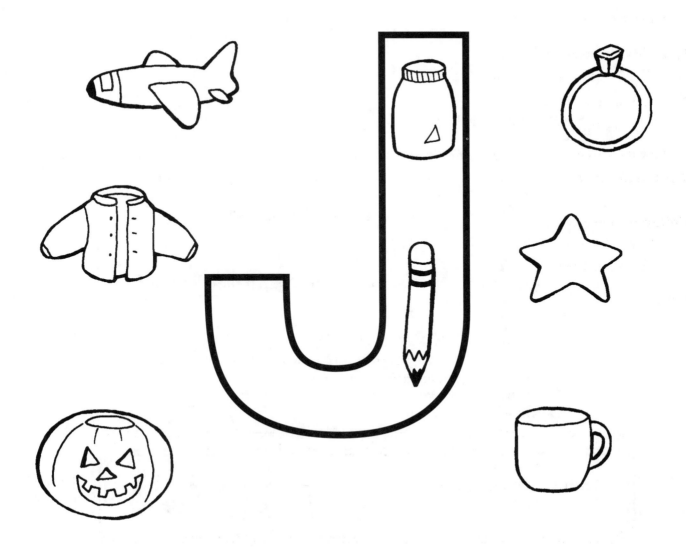

How We Travel

Transportation is great fun as a theme for the early grades. Introduce this theme using Raffi's (or another version) song "The Wheels on the Bus." Gather posters of various means of transportation to discuss with the children. Use big blocks to help the children build a variety of ways people move. Bring in a variety of books the children may wish to read on transportation. Brainstorm with the children the various ways they have traveled and how they travel to school.

Activity: How We Travel
Skill: classification

Materials Needed

- tagboard
- master—classification pictures
- masters of pictures of land, water, air
- three 9" by 12" (23 cm by 30 cm) pieces of construction paper
- resealable plastic bags
- crayons or markers
- laminate or contact paper
- glue

How to Make This Activity

- Run off master of classification pictures.
- Color the pictures.
- Glue pictures on tagboard, laminate, and cut them out on the straight lines. Place the cut pictures in a plastic bag.
- Duplicate pictures of land, water, and air.
- Color the pictures, mount on construction paper, and laminate them.
- Place all in a folder.

Teacher's Directions

Demonstrate this to younger children who may not be ready to read the instructions.

Children's Directions

Place each vehicle on the picture that shows where it moves.

Labels

> **Activity:** How We Travel
> **Skill:** classification   (Tab)

> **Theme:** Transportation
> **Activity:** How We Travel
> **Skill:** classification      (Folder)

Classification Pictures

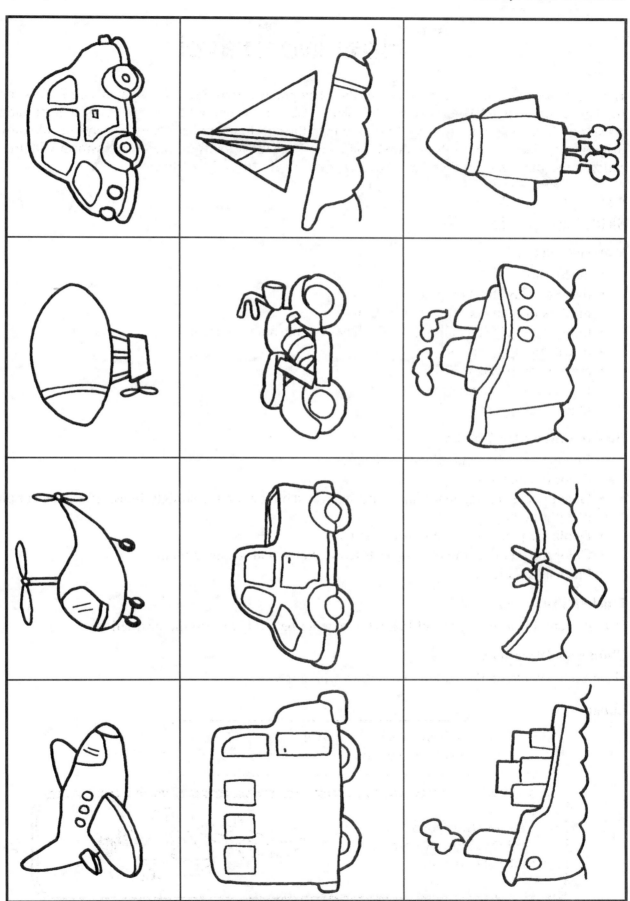

On Land

On Water

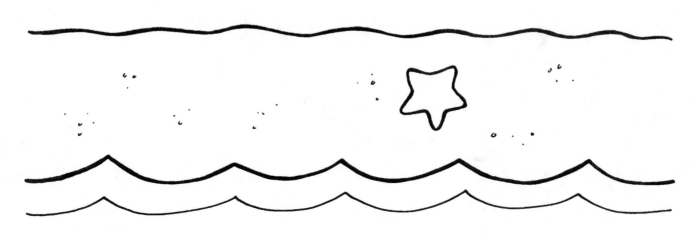

In Air

Our Travel Graph

Activity: Our Travel Graph
Skill: graphing

Materials Needed

- one 18" by 24" (46 cm by 61 cm) white construction paper
- master pictures of a car, bus, bike, shoe
- crayons
- markers
- resealable plastic bag
- glue sticks

How to Make This Activity

- Duplicate the master, running off enough to give the children choices.
- Cut out the pictures. If the children are old enough, they may cut out their choice of picture.
- Place the pictures in the plastic bag and place in the folder.
- Mark the construction paper, vertically, into four sections.
- Print "How We Travel to School" at the top of the paper.
- Glue one car, one bus, one bike, and one shoe at the top of each section of the graph.

Teacher Directions

- Demonstrate how to complete the activity to younger children.
- Discuss the completed graph with the children.

Children's Directions

1. Choose the picture that tells how you come to school.
2. Print your name on the front of the picture.
3. Color the picture.
4. Glue the picture on the graph under how you come to school.

Labels

> **Activity:** Our Travel Graph
> **Skill:** graphing   (Tab)

> **Theme:** Transportation
> **Activity:** Our Travel Graph
> **Skill:** graphing   (Folder)

How We Travel to School

car picture	bus picture	bike picture	shoe picture

Transportation Master

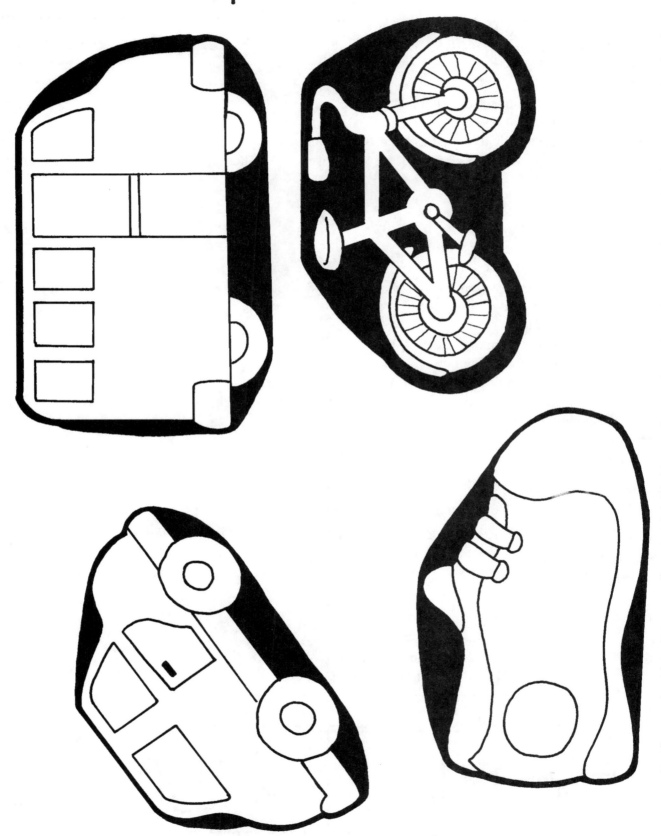

Number Convoy

Activity: Number Convoy
Skill: matching numbers to sets

Materials Needed

- master of truck with sets and numbers
- construction paper
- a variety of small stickers such as stars, hearts, animals, etc.
  (These may be purchased at any teacher supply store. An alternative would be to use a marker to draw the pictures.)
- laminate or contact paper
- glue
- resealable plastic bag

How to Make This Activity

- Duplicate the truck pattern on construction paper—enough for the numbers 0 to 10 or as high as the children are ready for.
- Cut out each truck.
- Cut the cab apart from the trailer.
- Place one number on each tab.
- Place the corresponding stickers (or draw a small picture) on the trailer side.
- For the folder for self-checking: Mark the cab (on the back) with stickers to match the corresponding number. Do the same for the trailer.
- Laminate the sets.
- Place in the plastic bag.

Teacher's Directions

- This activity may also be made to match letters and beginning sounds.
- Place a letter on the cab and a picture that begins with that letter on the trailer.

Children's Directions

Match the number cab with the correct trailer of sets.

Labels

> **Activity:** Number Convoy
> **Skill:** matching numbers to sets

(Tab)

> **Theme:** Transportation
> **Activity:** Number Convoy
> **Skill:** matching numbers to sets

(Folder)

Truck Master

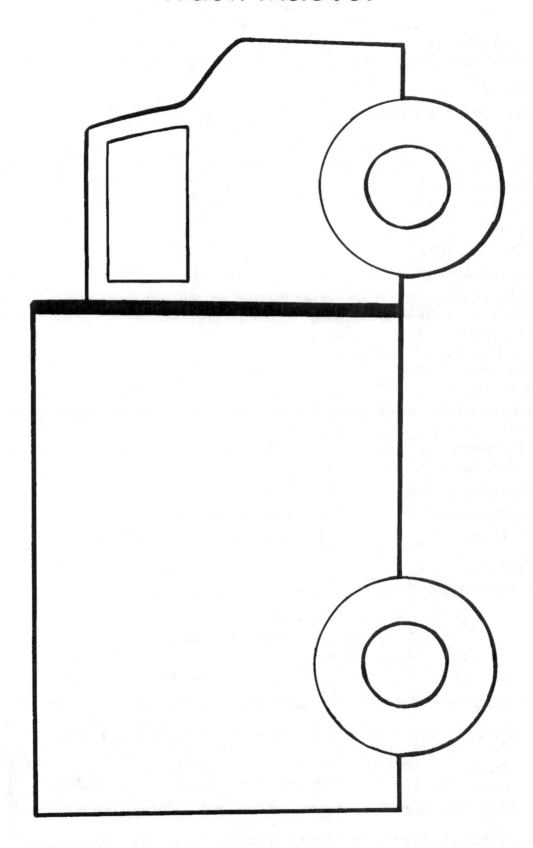

Going Places

Activity: Going Places
Skills: eye-hand coordination, small-muscle control, recognizing shapes

Materials Needed

- masters of a rocket, truck, boat
- tagboard
- glue
- scissors
- crayons
- laminate or contact paper

How to Make This Activity

- Duplicate masters—one for each child and one for the folders.
- For the folder: Cut out the shapes and glue onto the picture.
- Color the pictures. Glue the completed picture inside the folder cover. Laminate or cover with contact paper. The children may use the completed picture to self-check their work.
- Place duplicated pictures in each folder.

Teacher's Directions

- For younger children, demonstrate how to cut, match, and glue the shapes to the pictures.

Children's Directions

1. Cut out the shapes.
2. Match the shapes to the pictures.
3. Glue the shapes to the pictures.
4. Color your picture.

Labels

Activity: Going Places
Skills: eye-hand coordination, small-muscle control, recognizing shapes

(Tab)

Theme: Transportation
Activity: Going Places
Skills: eye-hand coordination, small-muscle control, recognizing shapes

(Folder)

Truck Master

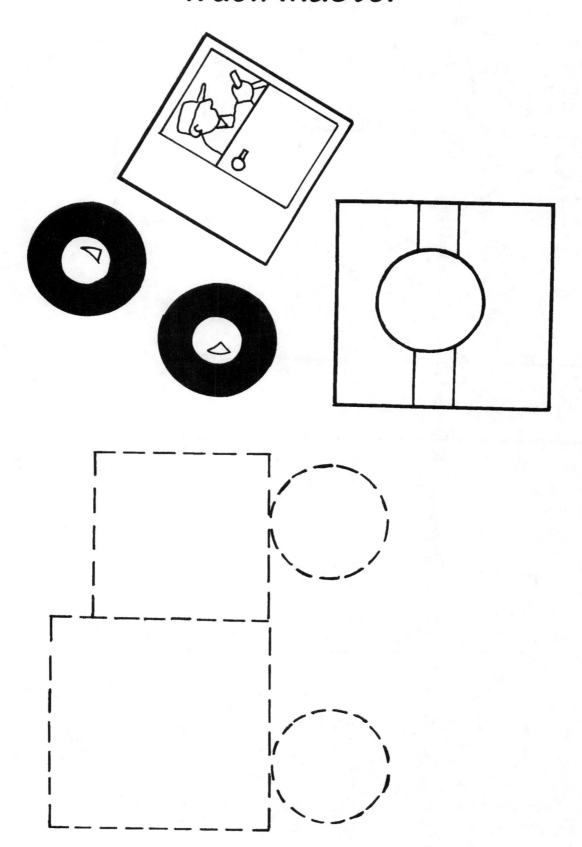

Boat Master

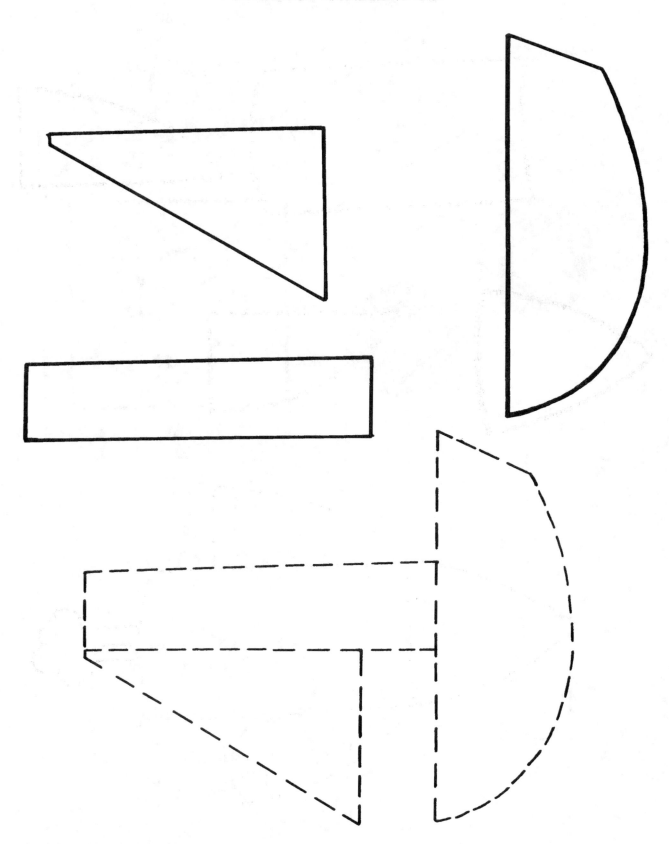

Rocket Master

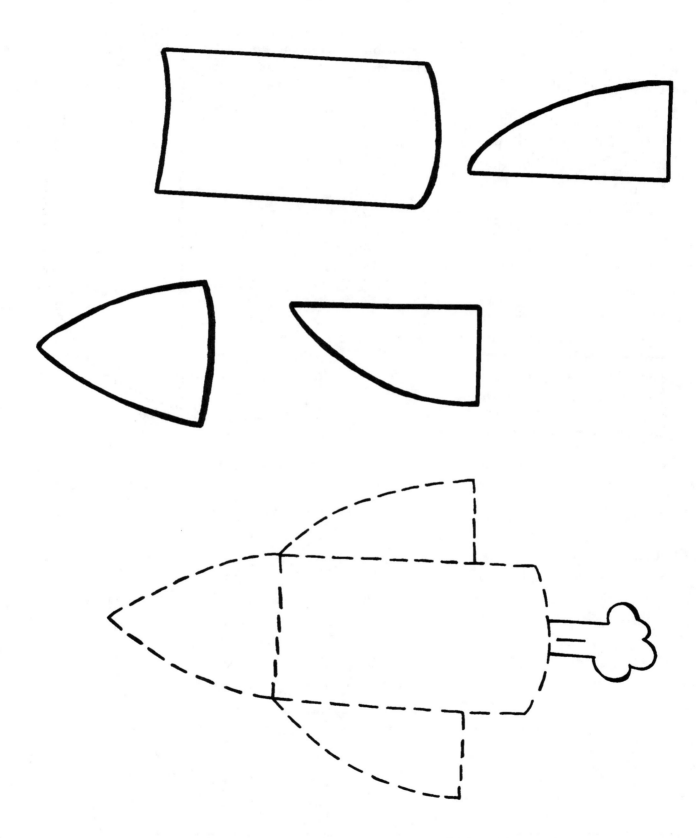

Snowman Buttons

Introduce the theme of winter, using the much loved story *The Snowman* by Raymond Briggs (Random House, Inc., 1988). There is also a video available based on this book. Discuss the many varied aspects of winter, such as snow, cold, types of clothing worn, animals in winter, etc. Brainstorm with the children for words that relate to winter and print them on chart paper for the children to refer to later.

Activity: Snowman Buttons
Skills: matching numbers to sets, small-muscle control

Materials Needed

- duplicating masters of snowmen for the children and the folder
- small packages of stickers (Snowflakes, happy faces, colored dots, etc., may be purchased at a teacher supply store, drug store, or variety store.)
- laminate
- contact paper
- glue
- pencils
- markers
- resealable plastic bags

How to Make This Activity

- Duplicate snowmen masters 0–10. Run off enough for one set per child.
- Staple each set of 0–10 together.
- Duplicate master of small snowmen, glue it to the folder, and cover with contact paper.
- Place stapled snowmen sets in the folder.
- Place the various kinds of stickers in different plastic bags and place bags in the folder.

Teacher's Directions

- Demonstrate to the children how to trace over the numbers on the hats.
- Demonstrate how and where to put the stickers on the snowmen. Show the variety of stickers.

Self-Checking Feature: Children may check the folder for correct number of dots on each snowman.

Children's Directions

1. Take one snowman book.
2. Read the numbers on each hat.
3. Trace over the numbers on each hat.
4. Place the correct number of stickers on the snowmen.

Labels

> **Activity:** Snowman Buttons
> **Skills:** matching numbers to sets, small-muscle control

(Tab)

> **Theme:** Winter
> **Activity:** Snowman Buttons
> **Skills:** matching numbers to sets, small-muscle control

(Folder)

Snowman Buttons Master

Snowman Buttons Master (cont.)

122

Snowman Buttons Master (cont.)

Snowman Buttons Master (cont.)

124

Snowman Buttons Master *(cont.)*

Snowman Buttons Master (cont.)

Snowman Buttons Master (cont.)

Snowman Buttons Master (cont.)

Snowman Buttons Master (cont.)

Snowman Buttons Master (cont.)

Snowman Buttons Master *(cont.)*

Snowman Buttons Master *(cont.)*

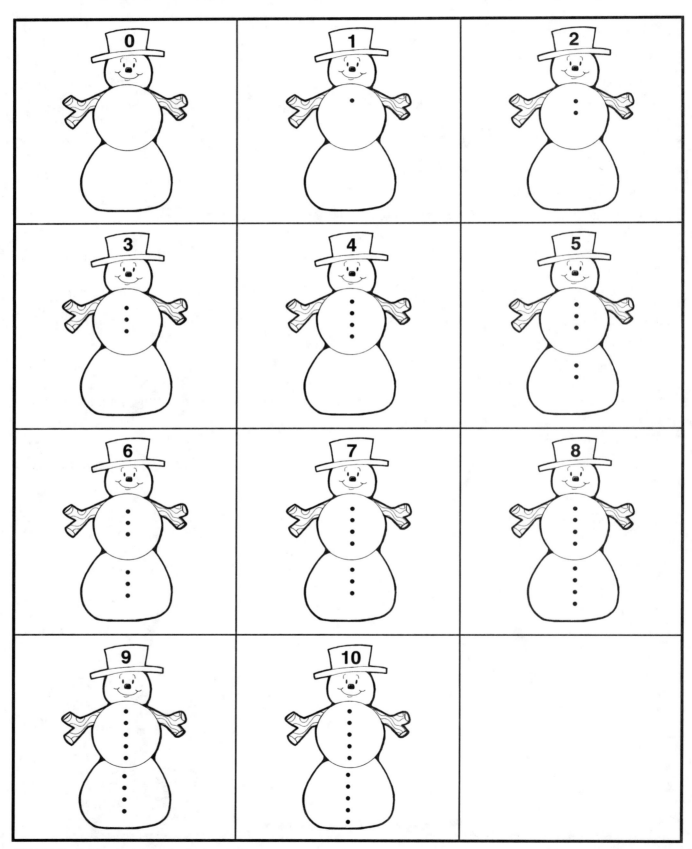

Snowman Book

Activity: Snowman Book
Skills: following directions, sequencing, reading sentences

Materials Needed

- manila paper—8" by 11" (20 cm by 28 cm)
- crayons (including white)
- stapler
- children's scissors—two or three pairs
- duplicating master of the snowman book
- white chalk
- paper clips

How to Make This Activity

- Duplicate the snowman book pages on manila—one set per child.
- Paper-clip each snowman book set together.
- Color one snowman book, cut it out, and staple together with the cover. Place the completed book in the folder for a sample.
- Place the folder, stapler, scissors, crayons, chalk, and snowman books at the winter center.

Teacher's Directions

- Demonstrate how to read and color the book page by page.
- Demonstrate how to cut the pages apart on the lines.
- Demonstrate how to put the pages in the correct order.
- Brainstorm ideas to make the cover—show how to trace over the title and draw a winter picture.
- Demonstrate how to staple the book together.
- A volunteer would be helpful for this activity.

Self-Checking Feature: *Children may look in the folder for a sample of a completed book and ideas to complete the book cover.*

Children's Directions

1. Take one snowman book.
2. Read each sentence.
3. Color the picture.
4. Cut out the pages on the lines.
5. Put the pages in the correct order.
6. Trace and color your book cover.
7. Staple your book.
8. Read your book to a friend.

Labels

> **Activity:** Snowman Book
> **Skills:** following directions, sequencing, reading sentences

(Tab)

> **Theme:** Winter
> **Activity:** Snowman Book
> **Skills:** following directions, sequencing, reading sentences
>
>

(Folder)

I Made a Snowman

Directions

1. Read the sentence.

2. Color each picture.

3. Cut out the pages on the lines.

4. Put the pages in order.

5. Make a cover.

6. Staple your book.

7. Read your book to a friend.

I Made a Snowman

Snowman Master *(cont.)*

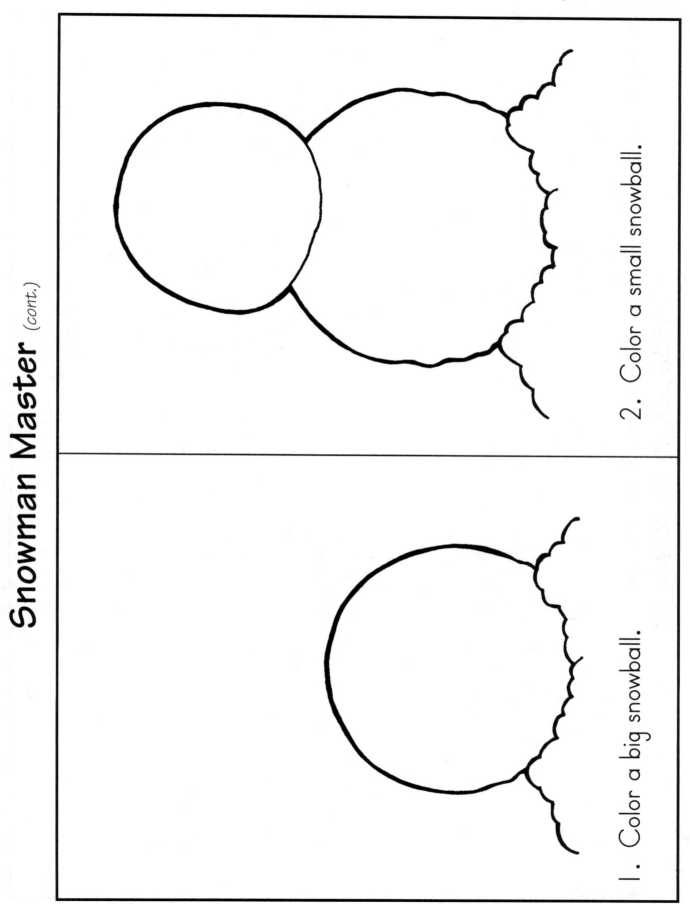

2. Color a small snowball.

1. Color a big snowball.

Snowman Master *(cont.)*

4. Color a hat.

3. Color a snowman face.

Snowman Master *(cont.)*

6. Color a broom.

5. Color buttons and a scarf.

Sample for Folder *(sequence order)*

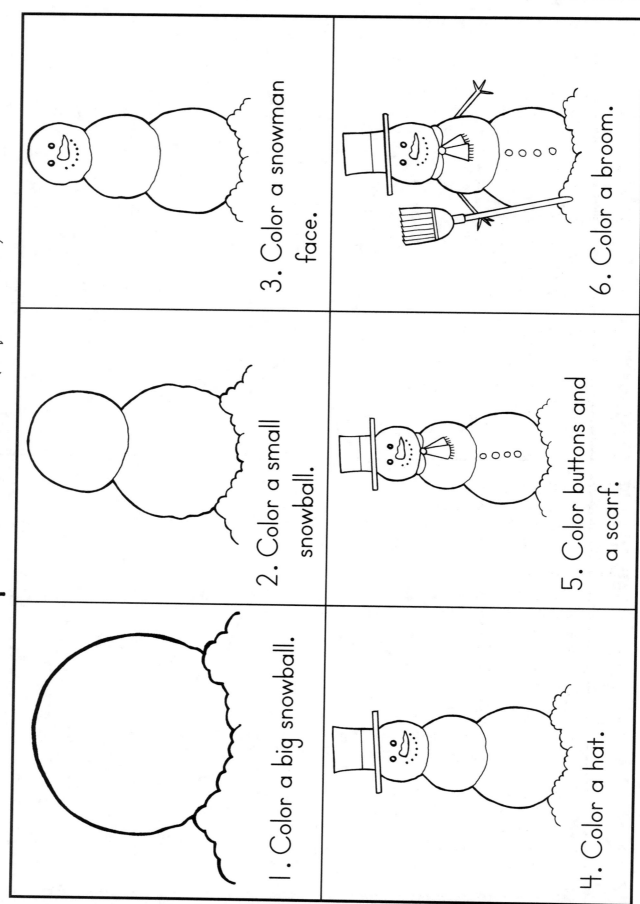

1. Color a big snowball.

2. Color a small snowball.

3. Color a snowman face.

4. Color a hat.

5. Color buttons and a scarf.

6. Color a broom.

Crystal Painting

To introduce this activity to the class, sprinkle a few grains of table salt on black paper. Each grain is a crystal. Shake the paper gently so the grains will spread apart. Show the children how to look at the crystals with a magnifying glass and discuss shapes, likenesses, and differences.

Activity: Crystal Painting
Skills: measurement, learning about crystals

Materials Needed

- 8" by 11" (20 cm by 28 cm) manila paper—one per child
- 9" by 12" (23 cm by 31 cm) black construction paper—three sheets
- table salt
- magnifying glass—two or three
- water
- Epsom salt (buy at the grocery store)
- plastic measuring cup (one-cup size)

- two sets of measuring spoons
- teaspoons for mixing—two or three
- paintbrushes—two or three
- little butter tubs for mixing—two or three
- crayons, white chalk
- towels for cleanup
- contact paper
- glue

How to Make This Activity

- At the winter center, demonstrate to children how to complete each step of the activity.
- Color and glue the winter picture samples to the folder. Place contact paper over the pictures.

Teacher's Directions

- Demonstrate how to mix the water and Epsom salt.
- Brainstorm what to color on a winter picture.
- Demonstrate how to paint "thickly" on the picture and dry it flat.

Children's Directions

1. Sprinkle a little salt on black paper.
2. Look at the crystals with a magnifying glass and discuss what you see.
3. Color a winter picture.
4. Measure into a butter tub: $1/2$ cup (120 mL) water, 6 teaspoons (30 mL) Epsom salt.
5. Mix together with a spoon.
6. Paint your picture.

Labels

> **Activity:** Crystal Painting
> **Skills:** measurement, learning about crystals

(Tab)

> **Theme:** Winter
> **Activity:** Crystal Painting
> **Skills:** measurement, learning about crystals
>

(Folder)

Winter Pictures

Snowman Guess

Activity: Snowman Guess
Skill: estimating

Materials Needed

- duplicating master of snowman
- 9" by 12" (23 cm by 30 cm) blue construction paper—one per child
- crayons
- cotton balls
- glue sticks
- pencils

How to Make This Activity

- Duplicate the snowman master on blue construction paper—one per child.
- Make one sample for the folder with cotton balls glued on and coloring added.
- Place all in the folder.

Teacher's Directions

- Demonstrate how to estimate the number of cotton balls that might be needed to cover the snowman.
- Demonstrate where to write your guess.
- Demonstrate how to glue on the "snow balls."
- Count the cotton balls and demonstrate where to write the number of cotton balls counted.
- Demonstrate adding arms, a hat, a broom, shoes, mittens, etc., to the snowman.

Children's Directions

1. Take one snowman paper.
2. Guess how many snowballs will be needed to cover the snowman.
3. Write the number in the box.
4. Glue on the snowballs.
5. Count the snowballs.
6. Write the number in the box.
7. Add arms, a hat, a broom, mittens, and shoes to the snowman.

Labels

Activity: Snowman Guess
Skill: estimating   (Tab)

Theme: Winter
Activity: Snowman Guess
Skill: estimating      (Folder)

Cotton Ball Master

I guessed . . . .

I counted . . . .

Number Beans

The theme of numbers is best used when incorporated all through the curriculum every day. Displaying the calendar and weather chart, counting children at school every day, counting days the children have been in school, and counting treats and snacks are just some of the ways numbers may be used in the classroom. As the concept of numbers becomes more highly developed, the children are ready to enjoy more activities using what they learn.

Activity: Number Beans
Skills: learning numbers and sets 0–6, writing numbers 0–6

Materials Needed

- Popsicle sticks—seven per child
- beans—any kind that may be glued on
- 12" by 18" (30 cm by 46 cm) light colored construction paper—one per child
- glue sticks
- pencils
- duplication master for the folder sample
- containers to hold the beans and the sticks
- contact paper

How to Make This Activity

- Section the construction paper into seven sections (see the folder sample).
- Print the numbers 0–6 as in the sample. This activity may be adapted for any series of numbers.
- Duplicate the master, glue the sample inside the folder, and cover with contact paper.
- Place construction paper copies, glue sticks, beans, and pencils at a center or table.

Teacher's Directions

- Demonstrate how to trace over the numbers.
- Demonstrate how to glue the sticks on the paper in each column.
- Demonstrate how to glue the correct number of beans on each stick.

Self-Checking Feature: *The children may look in the folder to check how many beans to glue on for each number or to check their work.*

Children's Directions

1. Take one paper.
2. Trace over the numbers.
3. Glue one stick above each number.
4. Glue the correct number of beans on each stick.

Labels

> **Activity:** Number Beans
> **Skills:** learning numbers and sets 0–6, writing numbers 0–6   (Tab)

> **Theme:** Numbers
> **Activity:** Number Beans
> **Skills:** learning numbers and sets 0–6, writing numbers 0–6   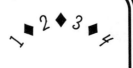   (Folder)

Bean Master

Wrapping Paper Count

Activity: Wrapping Paper Count
Skills: estimating, writing numbers

Materials Needed

- tagboard—white 9" by 12" (23 cm by 30 cm)
- a variety of gift wrap with large animals, airplanes, letters, butterflies, dinosaurs, etc.
- large resealable plastic bag
- laminate or contact paper

- grease pencils or crayons
- small rag for cleaning
- marker
- scissors

How to Make This Activity

- Cut wrapping paper to display the numbers the class is working on—e.g., three dinosaurs, four airplanes, etc.
- Glue the pictures on the tagboard (see the samples).
- Label each page—e.g., Dinosaurs, Airplanes (see the samples).
- Draw two squares across from the picture (see the samples).
- Label the squares "Guess" and "Check" (see the samples).
- Laminate.
- Print the numbers 0–10 in the folder.

Teacher's Directions

- Demonstrate how to guess how many are in the picture.
- Demonstrate how to write the guess in the box.
- Demonstrate how to count the items in the picture and write the number.
- Show the children how to wipe off the numbers with the rag.

Self-Checking Feature: The children may look in the folder to check how to write the numbers.

Children's Directions

1. Take one board.
2. Guess how many are in the picture.
3. Write your guess.
4. Count how many are in the picture.

5. Write how many are in the picture.
6. Check to see if your guess was correct.
7. Wipe off the numbers.

Labels

Activity: Wrapping Paper Count
Skills: estimating, writing numbers

(Tab)

Theme: Numbers
Activity: Wrapping Paper Count
Skills: estimating, writing numbers

1 ■ 2 ◆ 3 ■ 4

(Folder)

Guess

Check

Dinosaurs

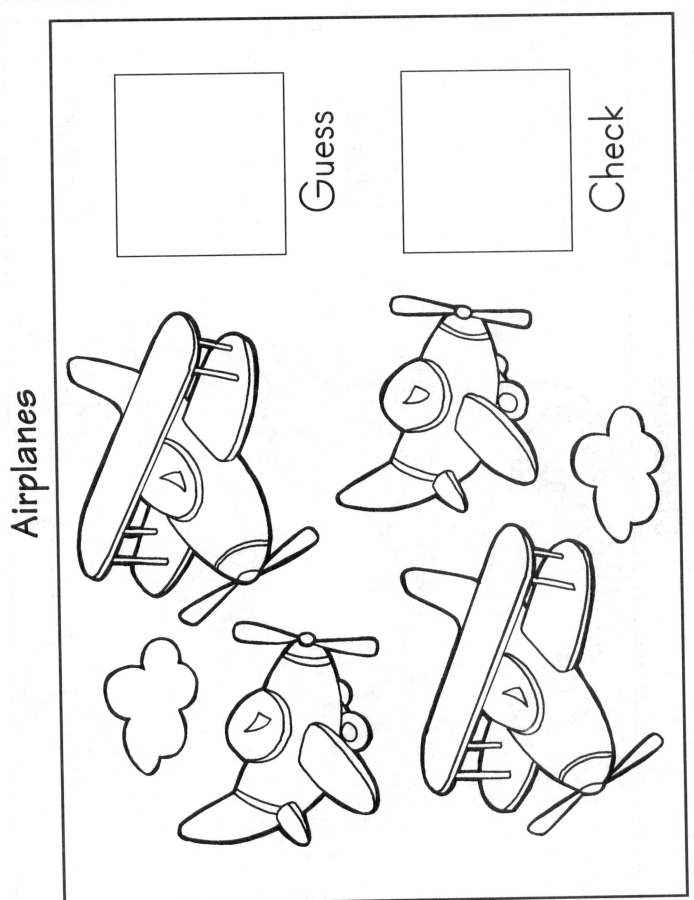

Guess

Check

Airplanes

Guess

Check

Letters

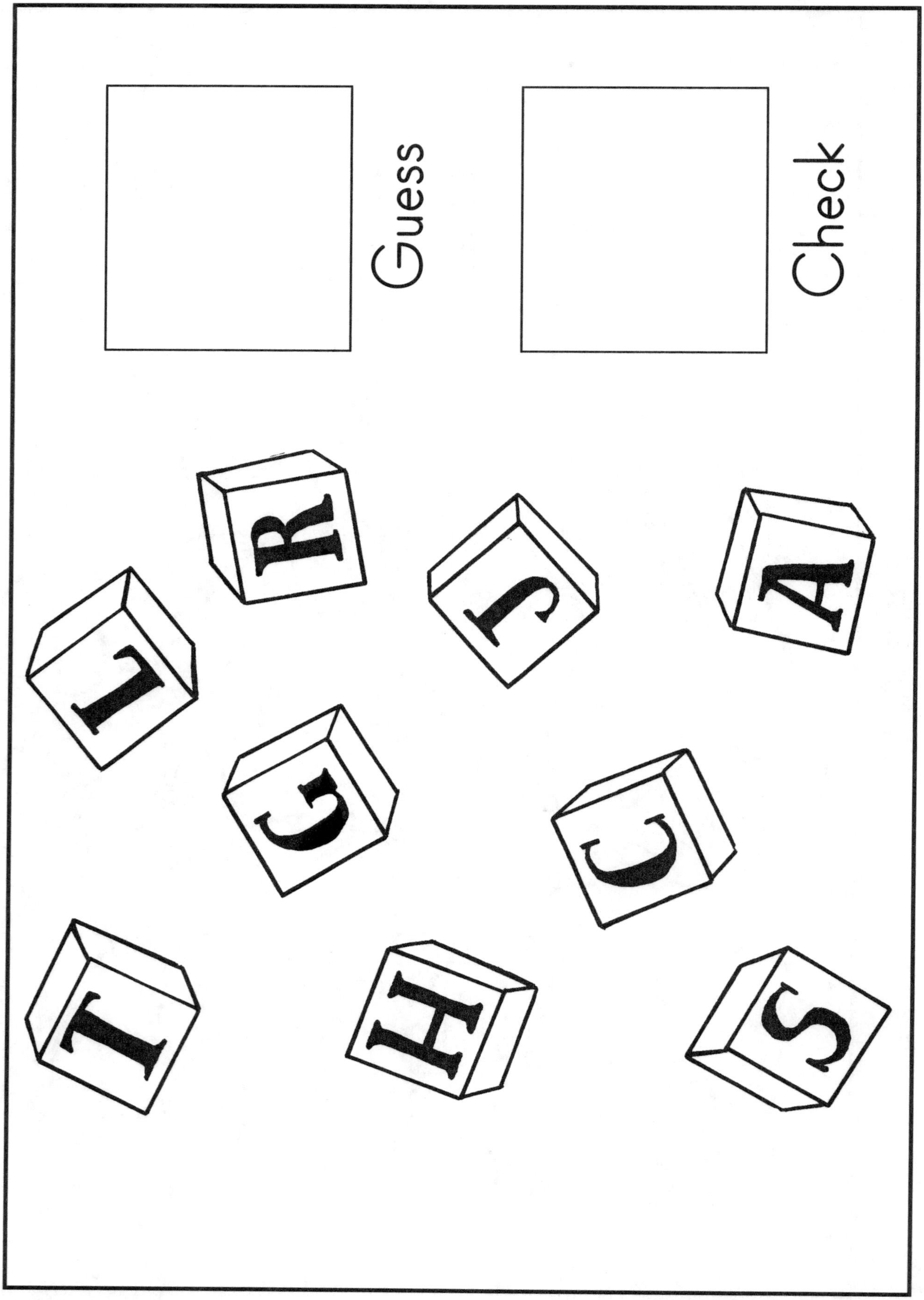

R

J

A

L

G

C

T

H

S

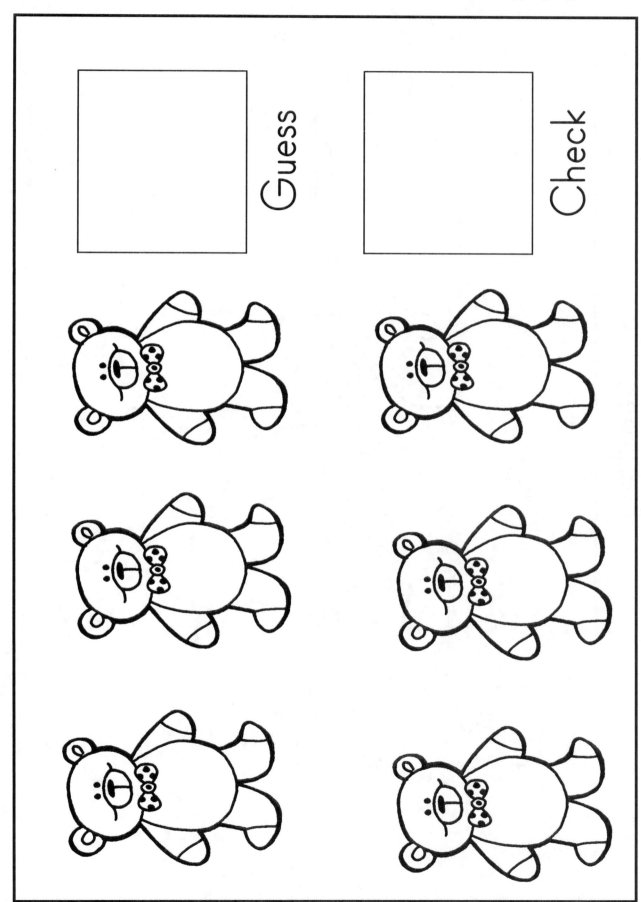

Bears

Guess

Check

Guess

Check

Elephants

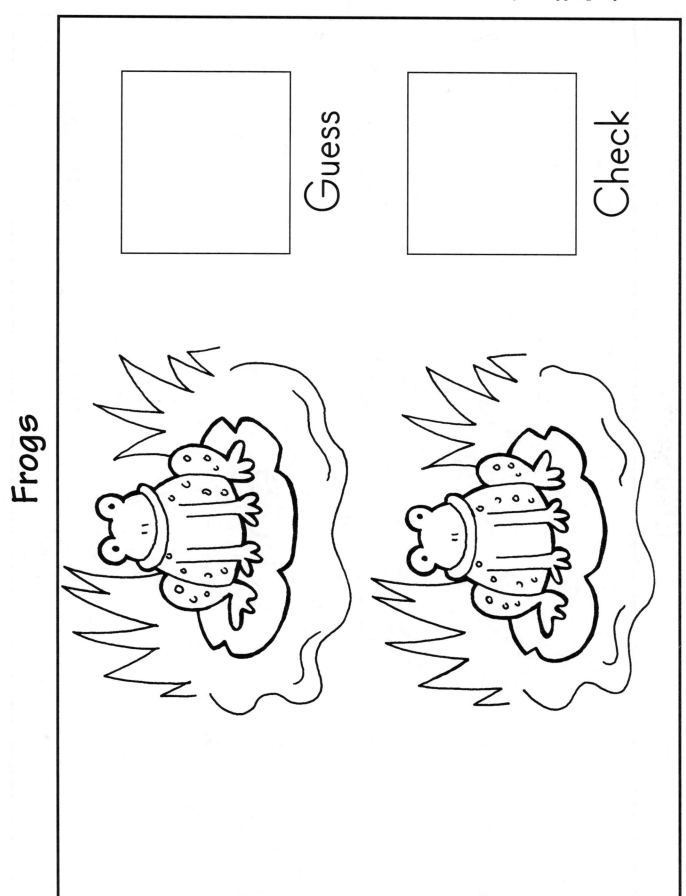

Frogs

Guess

Check

Theme: Numbers

Activity: Wrapping Paper Count

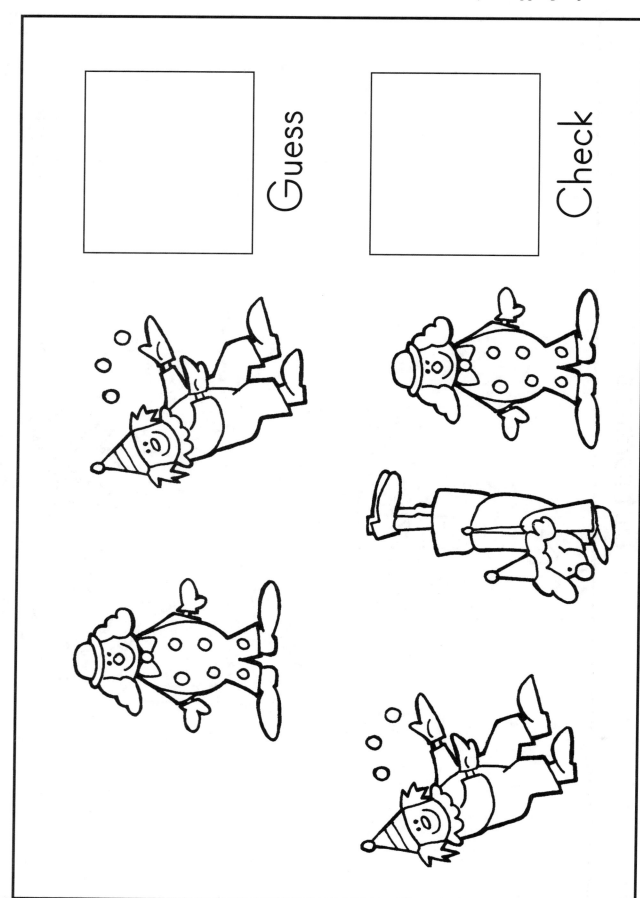

Butterflies

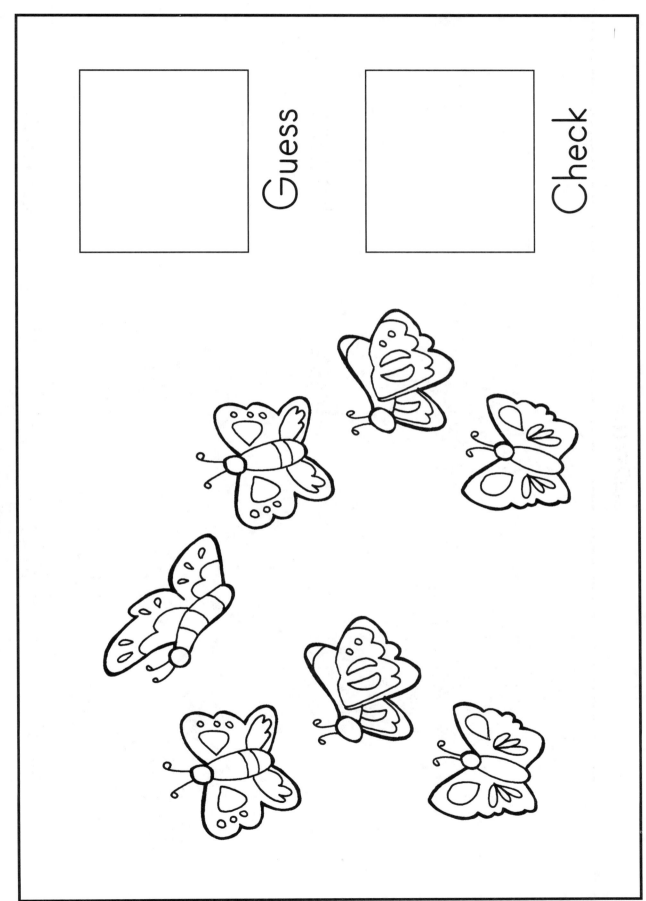

Guess

Check

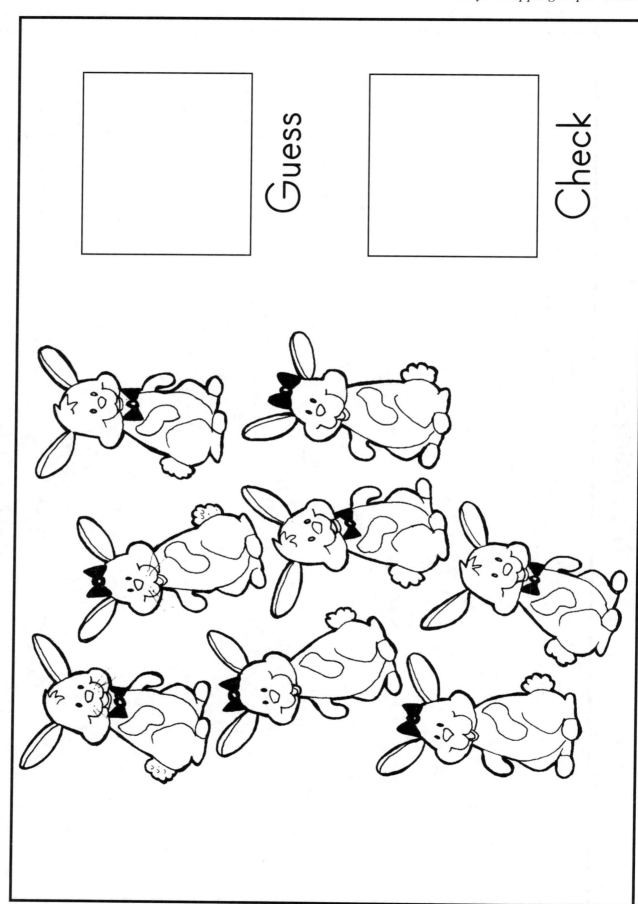

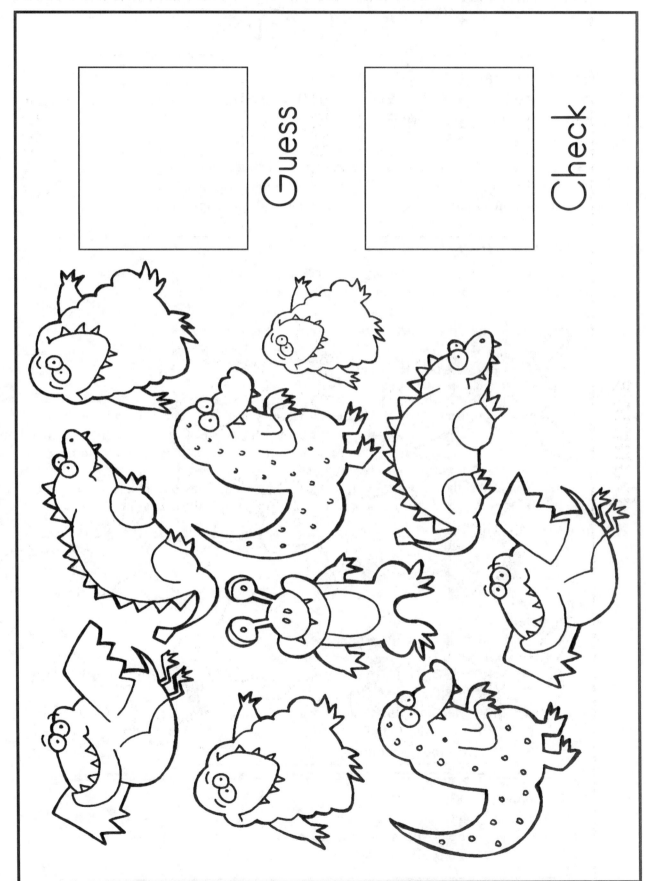

Monsters

Guess

Check

Frog Count

Activity: Frog Count
Skills: counting 0–10 in order, counting 0–10 backwards, counting 0–10 mixed up, cooperative learning—partners

Materials Needed

- four light colors of 9" by 12" (23 cm by 30 cm) construction paper
- frog award duplicating masters
- lily pad duplicating masters, 0–10
- laminate or contact paper
- resealable plastic bags—four
- markers
- scissors

How to Make This Activity

- Duplicate lily pad masters on one color—one of each number.
- Laminate the lily pads, cut them out, and place them in a plastic bag.
- Duplicate frog awards, each type of award on a separate color—one per child per color.
- Place each set of the frog award colors in a separate plastic bag.
- Print the numbers 0–10 in order on one side of the folder and backwards on the other side.
- Cover the numbers with contact paper.

Teacher's Directions

- Demonstrate how to find a partner for the activity and how to decide who will go first.
- Demonstrate how one partner lays the lily pads on the floor in order, backwards, or mixed up.
- Demonstrate how to pretend to be a frog and jump over a lily pad and say the number.
- Explain how the other partner watches and listens.
- Show the frog award they get if they jump over lily pads and say the numbers correctly.
- It would be helpful to have a volunteer at this activity to help the children.

Self-Checking Feature: Children may check the folder for numbers in order or backwards.

Children's Directions

1. Choose a partner.
2. Decide who will go first.
3. Lay out the lily pads.
4. Hop over the lily pads and say the number.
5. Take a frog award if you are correct.

Labels

> **Activity:** Frog Count
> **Skills:** counting 0–10 in order, counting 0–10 backwards, counting 0–10 mixed up, cooperative learning—partners

(Tab)

> **Theme:** Numbers
> **Activity:** Frog Count
> **Skills:** counting 0--10 in order, counting 0–10 backwards, counting 0–10 mixed up, cooperative learning—partners
>
> 1 ■ 2 ◆ 3 ■ 4

(Folder)

Frog Award

I hopped and counted the numbers 0–10 in order!

Frog Award *(cont.)*

I hopped and counted the numbers 0–10 backwards!

Frog Award *(cont.)*

I hopped and counted the
numbers 0–10 mixed up!

Lily Pad Master

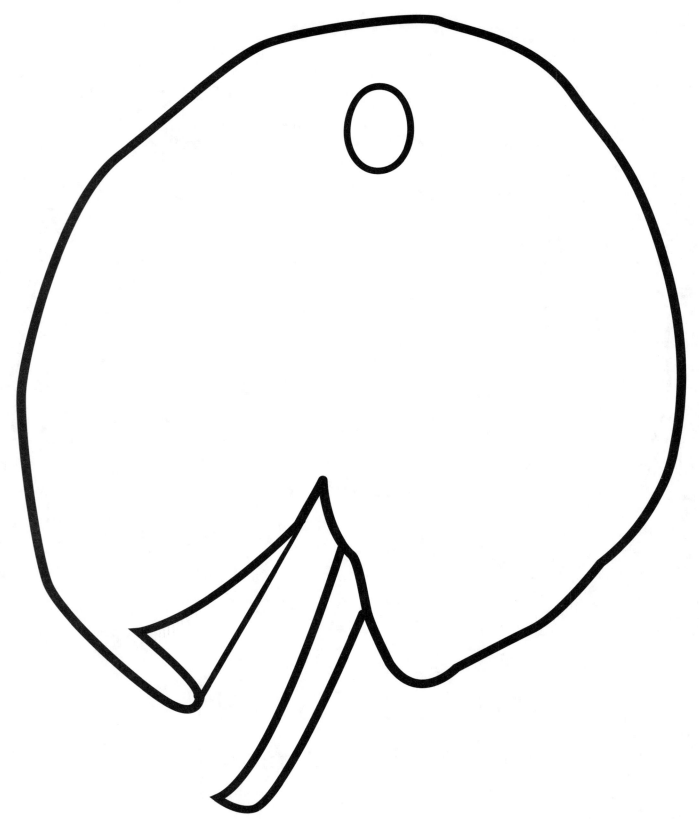

Lily Pad Master (cont.)

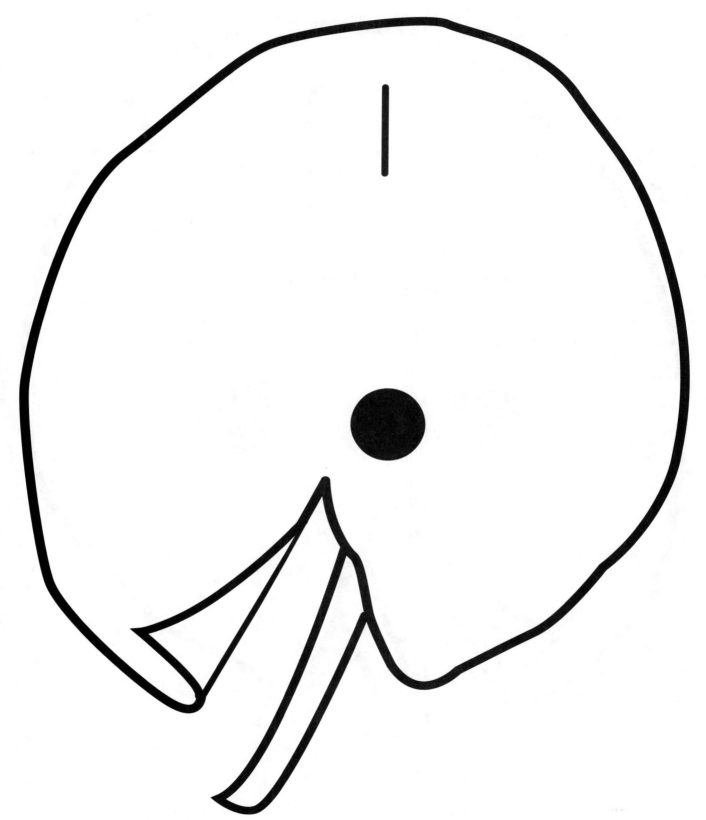

Lily Pad Master *(cont.)*

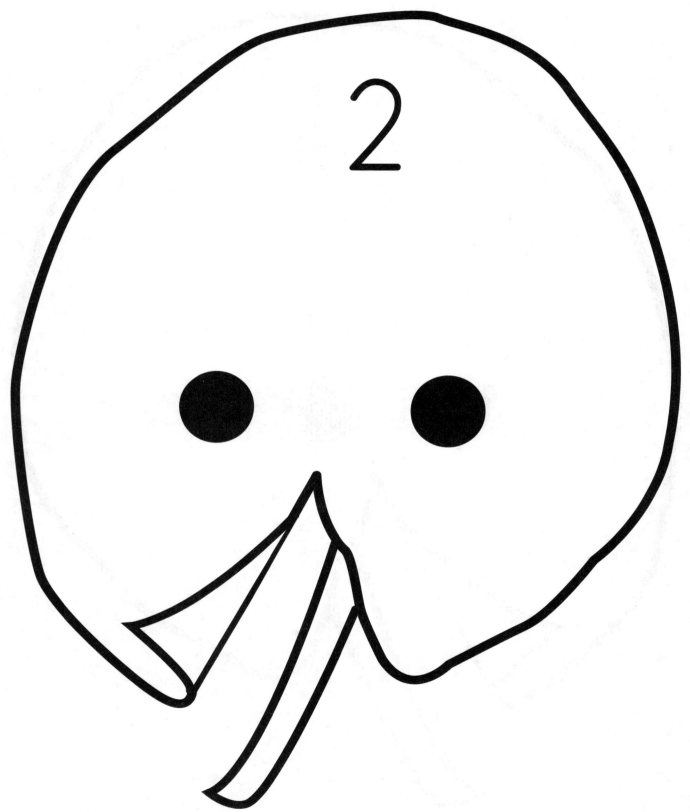

Lily Pad Master (cont.)

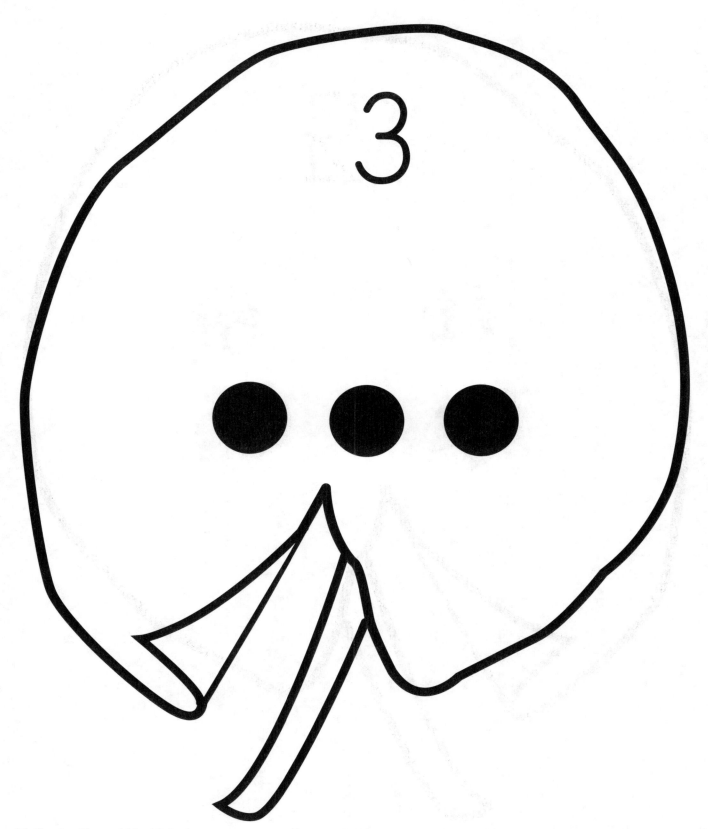

Lily Pad Master *(cont.)*

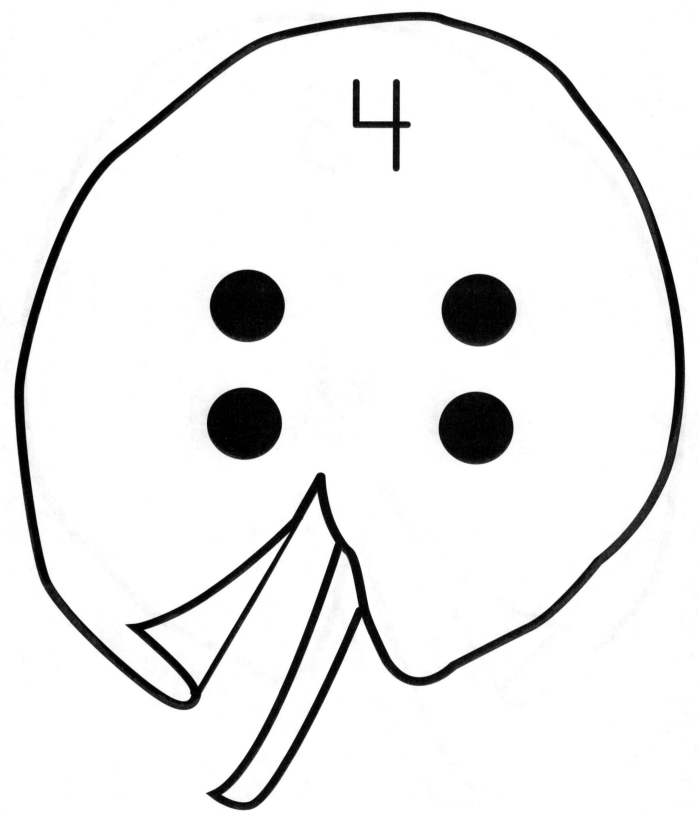

Lily Pad Master (cont.)

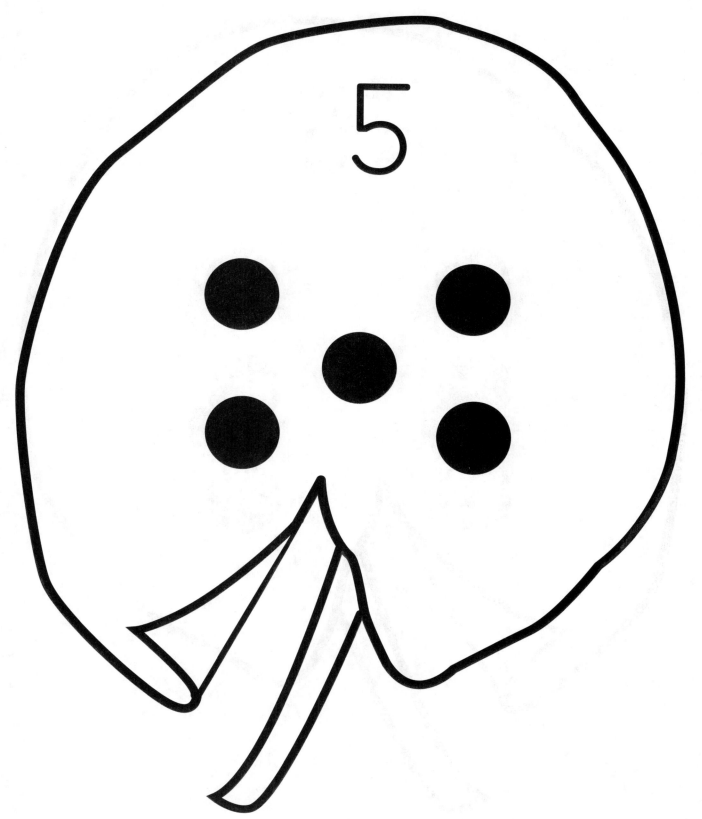

Lily Pad Master (cont.)

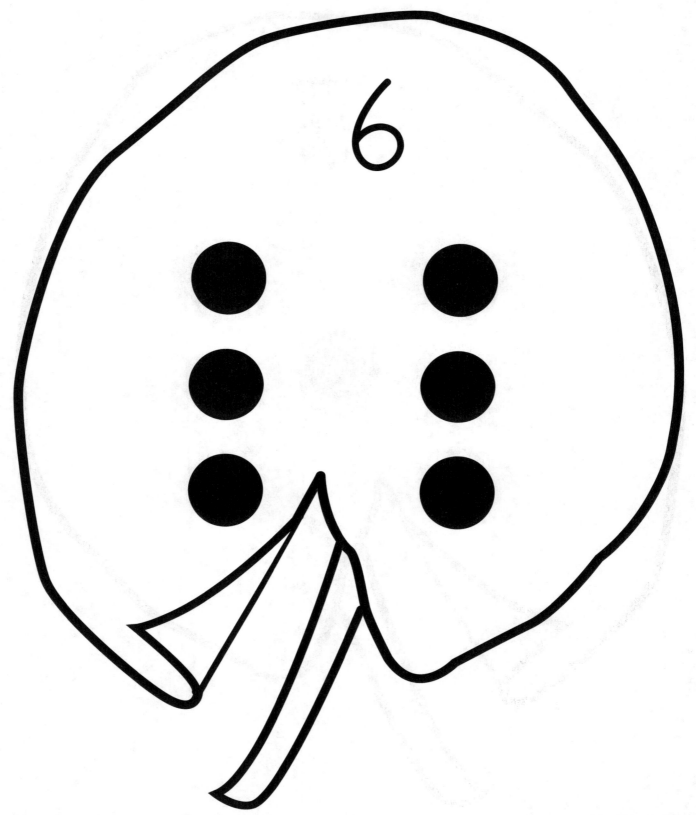

Lily Pad Master (cont.)

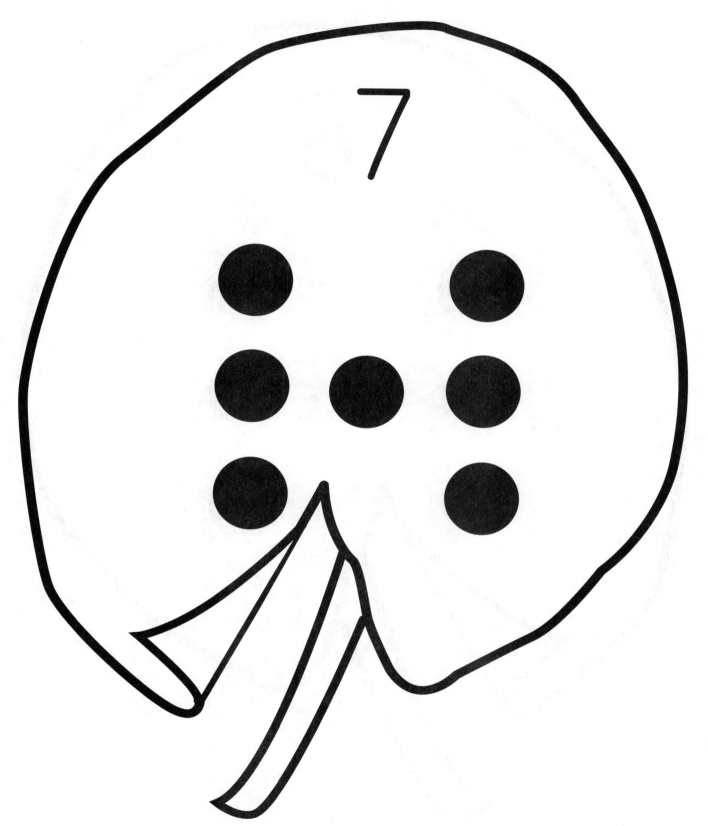

Lily Pad Master (cont.)

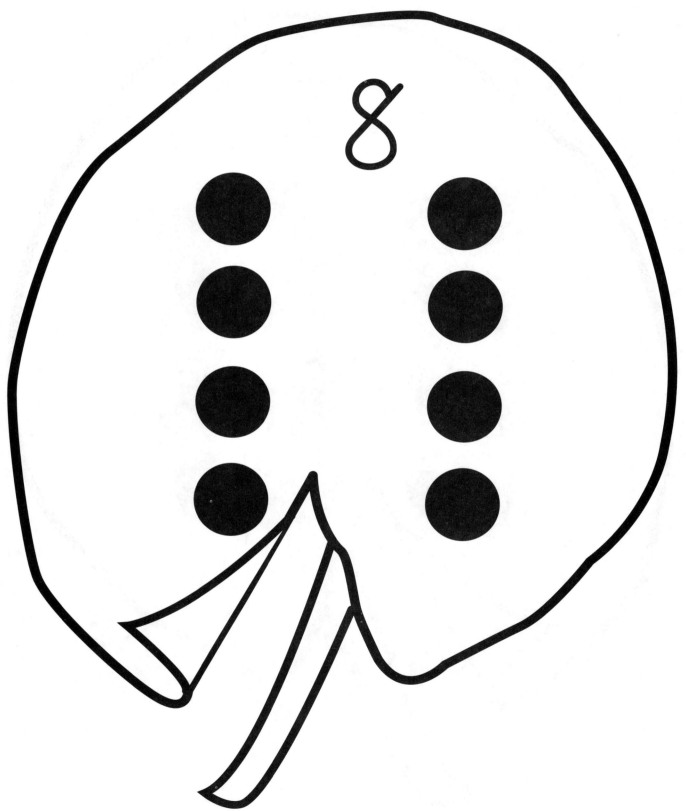

Lily Pad Master (cont.)

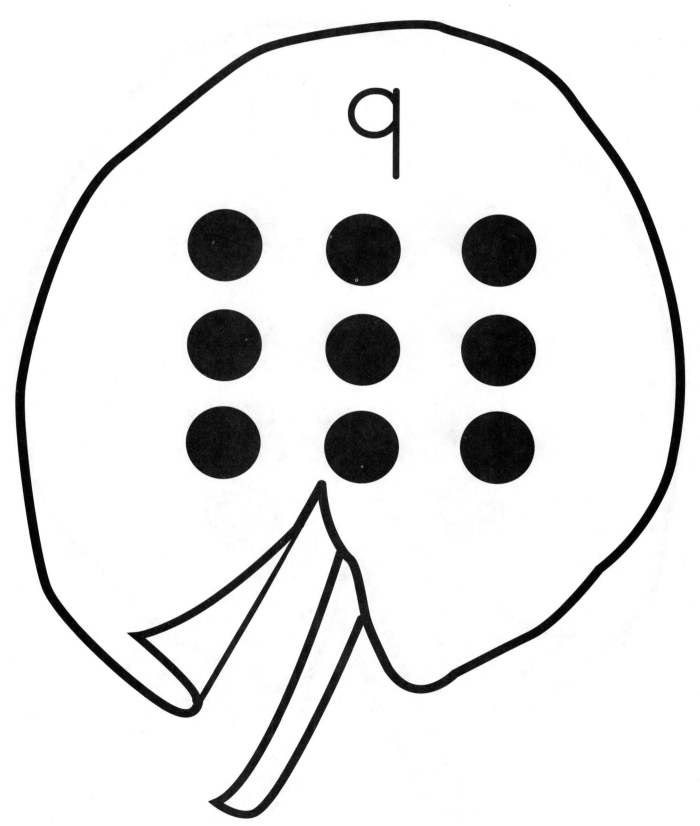

Lily Pad Master (cont.)

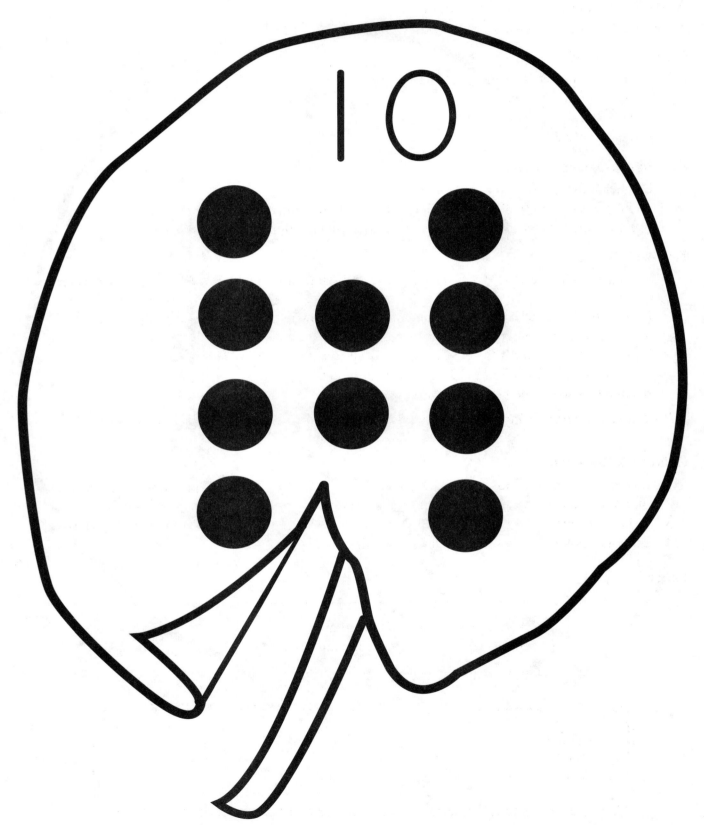

Chocolate Chip Numbers

Activity: Chocolate Chip Numbers
Skills: estimating, counting, number writing

Materials Needed

- book—*If You Give a Mouse a Cookie*
- duplicating master
- paper towels—one per child
- contact paper
- chocolate chip cookies—one per child
- pencils
- marker

How to Make This Activity

- Duplicate the master—one per child.
- Write the numbers 0–30 in the folder and cover with contact paper.
- Place cookies, paper towels, pencils, the folder, and the duplicated papers at a center.

Teacher's Directions

- Read the book *If You Give a Mouse a Cookie* by Laura Joffe Numeroff (Scholastic, 1985) and discuss it.
- Demonstrate how to look at a cookie and estimate how many chocolate chips are in it.
- Show the children where to write their estimates on their paper.
- Demonstrate how to eat the cookie and count the chocolate chips as it is eaten.
- Show the children where to write the number of chocolate chips.
- A volunteer would be helpful at this center.

Self-Checking Feature: The children may look in the folder to see how to write the numbers.

Children's Directions

1. Take one paper, one cookie, and one paper towel.
2. Guess how many chocolate chips are in your cookie.
3. Write your guess.
4. Eat your cookie and count your chocolate chips.
5. Write the number of chocolate chips in your cookie.
6. Throw your paper towel away.

Labels

> **Activity:** Chocolate Chip Numbers
> **Skills:** estimating, counting, number writing

(Tab)

> **Theme:** Numbers
> **Activity:** Chocolate Chip Numbers
> **Skills:** estimating, counting, number writing

(Folder)

Estimate Master

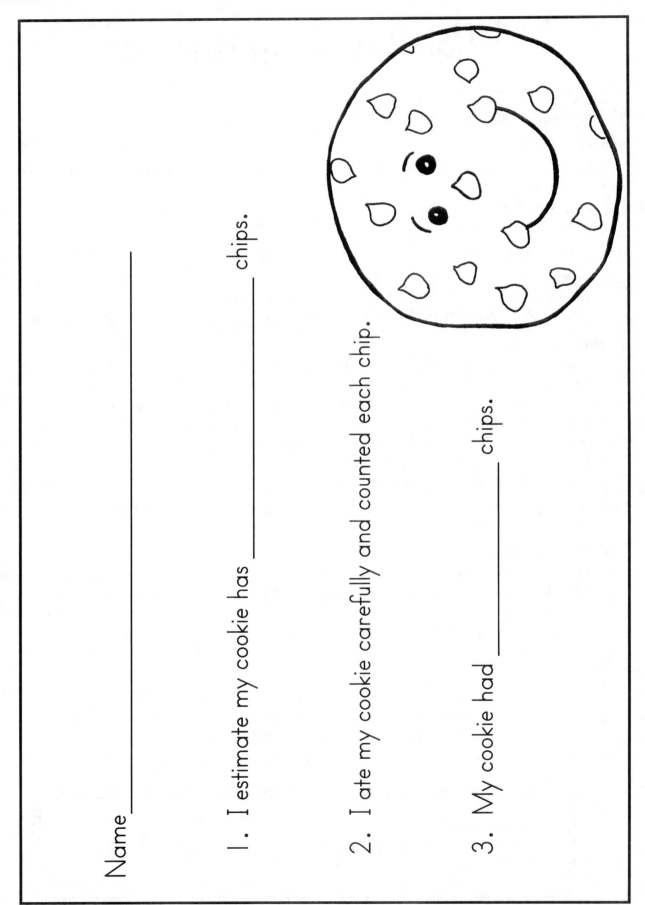

Name _____

1. I estimate my cookie has _____ chips.

2. I ate my cookie carefully and counted each chip.

3. My cookie had _____ chips.

Number Clay

Activity: Number Clay
Skills: learning numbers 0–10, writing numbers 0–10

Materials Needed

- two clay containers (margarine tubs with lids or Cool Whip tubs with lids)
- two clay boards
- numbers masters 0–10
- 9" by 12" (23 cm by 30 cm) light-colored construction paper
- glue or glue sticks
- clay
- pencils
- yarn—any color
- children's scissors

How to Make This Activity

- Duplicate the number masters—one set of 0–10 per child.
- Place number papers, pencils, clay, yarn, scissors, and glue sticks at a center.

Teacher's Directions

- Pre-cut the yarn for young children.
- Demonstrate how to trace over the numbers.
- Demonstrate how to roll out the clay to place on the numbers and then remove the clay.
- Demonstrate cutting a piece of yarn to fit a number and then gluing the yarn on the number.
- A volunteer would be helpful at this center.

Children's Directions

1. Take a paper with the numbers on it.
2. Trace over the numbers.
3. Roll out the clay to fit on top of your numbers.
4. Take off the clay.
5. Cut a piece of yarn to fit each number.
6. Glue the yarn to each number.

Labels

> **Activity:** Number Clay
> **Skills:** learning numbers 0–10, writing numbers 0–10

(Tab)

> **Theme:** Numbers
> **Activity:** Number Clay
> **Skills:** learning numbers 0–10, writing numbers 0–10
>
>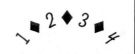

(Folder)

Number Master

Number Master *(cont.)*

Number Master (cont.)

176

Alphabet Hopscotch

There are many options in deciding how to incorporate alphabet activities into the curriculum. Activities may be included according to a particular theme, or activities may be set out in conjunction with the letter or letters the class is currently working on. There are many literature books which also revolve around the alphabet. Use a variety of methods to introduce these activities to the children.

Activity: Alphabet Hopscotch
Skill: letter recognition

Materials Needed

- chalk
- markers
- Scotch tape
- glue stick
- master of hopscotch ideas
- butcher paper
- contact paper

How to Make This Activity

- Duplicate the master of hopscotch ideas and glue in the folder. Cover with contact paper.
- Using the chalk, draw the hopscotch ideas on the floor of the classroom (in a corner) or on the sidewalk outside the room.
- Another option is to draw (with markers) the hopscotch ideas on butcher paper and tape the butcher paper to the floor.

Teacher's Directions

- Demonstrate how to jump in the hopscotch grid and say the letters aloud as you jump.
- Either uppercase or lowercase letters may be marked in the hopscotch diagram.

Children's Directions

1. Hop in each space and say the letter to a friend.
2. Try not to jump on a line.

Labels

> **Activity:** Alphabet Hopscotch
> **Skill:** letter recognition

(Tab)

> **Theme:** Alphabet
> **Activity:** Alphabet Hopscotch
> **Skill:** letter recognition
>
> A ☆ B ✧ C ☆ D

(Folder)

Hopscotch Patterns

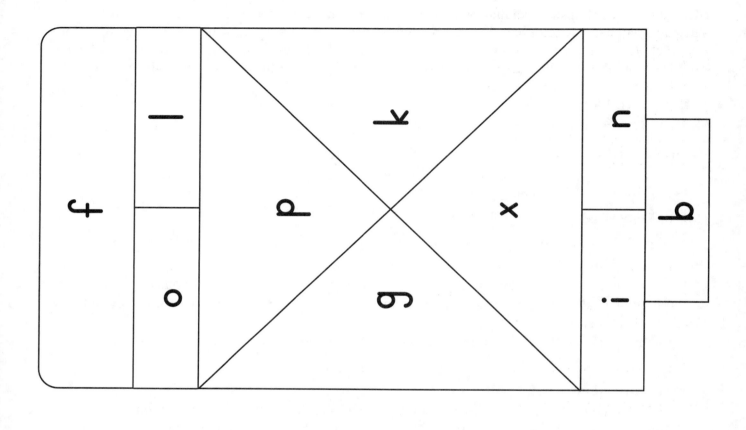

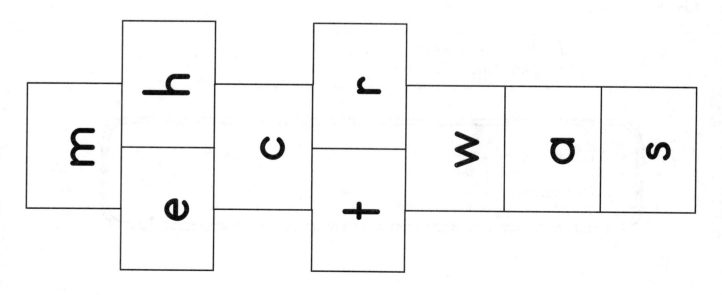

Flannelboard Alphabet

Activity: Flannelboard Alphabet
Skill: alphabetical order

Materials Needed

- flannel letters: uppercase and lowercase (These may be purchased at a teacher supply store.)
- flannelboard
- duplicating master of the alphabet in order
- contact paper
- two resealable plastic bags

How to Make This Activity

- Duplicate the alphabet master, glue in the folder, and cover it with contact paper.
- Place the flannel letters in the plastic bags, separating the uppercase and lowercase letters.
- Place the folder, letters, and the flannelboard at a center or a counter.

Teacher's Directions

- Demonstrate how to place the letters in order on the flannel board.
- Demonstrate how to choose a friend to help decide on the order.

Self-Checking Feature: The children may look in the folder to check the order of the letters.

Children's Directions

1. Place the letters on the flannelboard in order.
2. Choose a friend to help you.

Labels

> **Activity:** Flannelboard Alphabet
> **Skill:** alphabetical order

(Tab)

> **Theme:** Alphabet
> **Activity:** Flannelboard Alphabet
> **Skill:** alphabetical order
>
> A ☆ B ✧ C ☆ D

(Folder)

Sample for Folder

A B C D E F G H I

J K L M N O P Q R

S T U V W X Y Z

a b c d e f g h i

j k l m n o p q r

s t u v w x y z

ABC Feel and Guess

Activity: ABC Feel and Guess
Skills: matching letters to beginning sounds, cooperative learning—partners

Materials Needed

- small items that start with letters the class has been learning—e.g., Aa—Ff
  - Aa—apple, small airplane
  - Bb—little ball, basket
  - Cc—cat, car, clay
  - Dd—dish, doll, dog
  - Ee—envelope, eraser, egg
  - Ff—flower, feather

- small bag
- 3" by 5" (8 cm by 13 cm) cards
- markers
- resealable plastic bag

How to Make This Activity

- Print the ABC's on the cards—uppercase on one side and lowercase on the other side, one letter per card. Place the cards to be used in a plastic bag.
- Place one item for each letter in the bag.
- To make this self-checking, print the letters and a picture of the item chosen for each letter in the folder and cover with contact paper.

Teacher's Directions

- Demonstrate choosing a partner to play this activity.
- Demonstrate how the children need to close their eyes, reach in the bag, and remove one item.
- Demonstrate telling your partner what item you have and what letter it begins with.
- Demonstrate finding that letter on the card.
- Younger children will need a volunteer to help with this activity.

Self-Checking Feature: *The children may look in the folder to match the letter and the items.*

Children's Directions

1. Find a partner.
2. Close your eyes, reach in the bag, and choose one item.
3. Tell your partner what you have and what letter it starts with.
4. Find the card with that letter on it.

Labels

> **Activity:** ABC Feel and Guess
> **Skills:** matching letters to beginning sounds, cooperative learning—partners

(Tab)

> **Theme:** Alphabet
> **Activity:** ABC Feel and Guess
> **Skills:** matching letters to beginning sounds, cooperative learning—partners

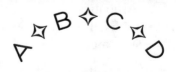

(Folder)

ABC Follow Directions

Activity: ABC Follow Directions
Skills: letter recognition, following directions

Materials Needed

- masters of directions on various figures
- 9" by 12" (23 cm by 30 cm) construction paper, various colors
- marker that writes on laminate
- scissors
- resealable plastic bag
- laminate

How to Make This Activity

- Duplicate the masters on construction paper and laminate.
- Cut out each figure.
- Print the letters on the back of each figure—one letter (Aa, etc.) per cutout figure. The directions will be on one side and the letter on the other side.
- Place cutout figures in the plastic bag.

Teacher's Directions

- Demonstrate how to draw a figure from the bag and name the letter.
- Demonstrate how to turn over the figure and read the directions to a friend.
- Demonstrate how to follow the directions.
- Demonstrate how to take turns choosing a figure.
- A volunteer would be helpful for younger children.

Children's Directions

1. Find a partner to play this activity with.
2. Choose a figure from the bag.
3. Say the letter.
4. Turn over the figure and read the directions.
5. Follow the directions.
6. Take turns with your partner.

Labels

Activity: ABC Follow Directions
Skills: letter recognition, following directions   (Tab)

Theme: Alphabet
Activity: ABC Follow Directions
Skills: letter recognition, following directions   (Folder)

Directions Master

Do a silly dance to the door.

Jump back.

Count to 10.

Touch your right hand to your nose.
Touch your left hand to your toes.
Jump five times.

Walk backwards to the door.

Hop back to your desk.

Sing the ABC song.

Find a friend.
On paper, write the ABC's.
Who did it faster?

Directions Master

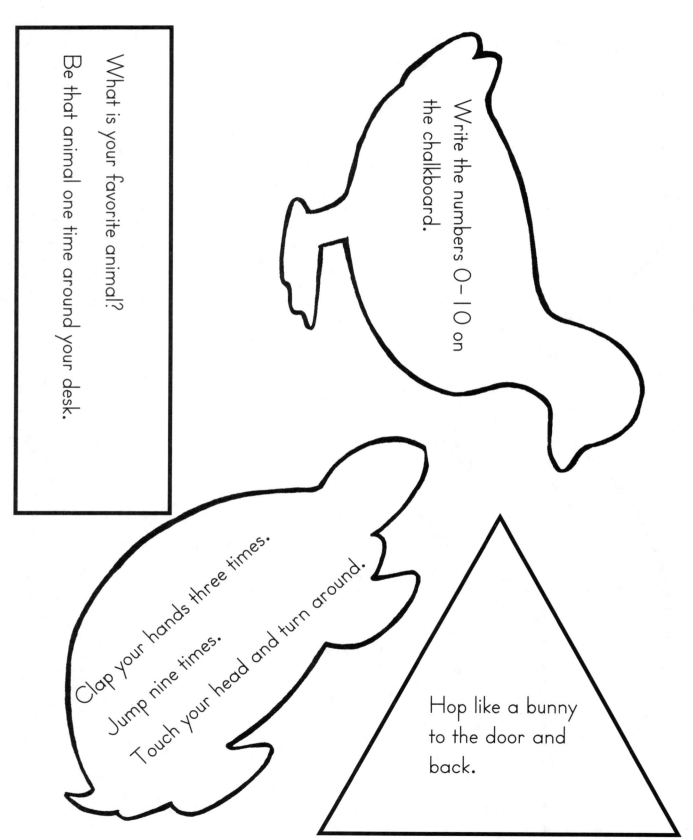

What is your favorite animal?
Be that animal one time around your desk.

Write the numbers 0–10 on the chalkboard.

Clap your hands three times.
Jump nine times.
Touch your head and turn around.

Hop like a bunny to the door and back.

Directions Master *(cont.)*

Touch and count all the doors in the room.

How many are there?

Jump that many times.

Reach to the sky and then touch the floor six times.

Skip to the door.

Knock three times.

Walk slowly to a chair and sit down.

Find a friend.

Be an elephant one time around the room.

Directions Master *(cont.)*

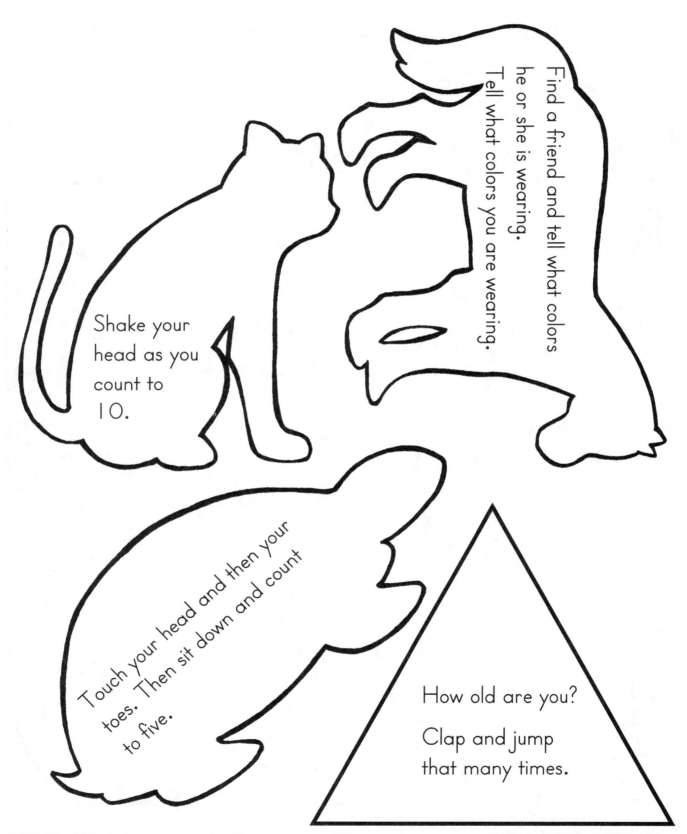

Find a friend and tell what colors
he or she is wearing.
Tell what colors you are wearing.

Shake your
head as you
count to
10.

Touch your head and then your
toes. Then sit down and count
to five.

How old are you?

Clap and jump
that many times.

Directions Master *(cont.)*

Walk across the room on your tiptoes and say the ABC's.

Find a friend who has black shoes and walk around the room with him or her one time.

Skip around the room one time and then clap your hands four times.

Find a friend who is taller.

Find a friend who is shorter.

Directions Master *(cont.)*

Touch your toes.

Touch your knees.

Sit down and
count to three.

Hop on your left foot and
clap seven times.

Count the legs on a table.

Count the legs on a friend.

Are they are same or
different?

Find one book.

Place the book on top of a shelf.

Directions Master (cont.)

Find your favorite book.

Read your book to a friend.

Draw a picture of
your family.

Who is the oldest?

Who is the youngest?

Fossil Search

Children never seem to tire of dinosaurs. There are many books, songs, videos, posters, and activities on dinosaurs. Plan to spend a few weeks developing this unit across the curriculum. Develop the areas of fossils and paleontology, what dinosaurs ate, the land they lived in, the different kinds of dinosaurs, and various theories on how they died out. It will be an enjoyable and interesting unit.

Activity: Fossil Search
Skills: critical thinking, writing

Materials Needed

- duplication master of "Dinosaur Fossil discovered . . ." (Add name of your school or town.)
- two clay boards
- two magnifying glasses
- toothpicks in a container
- small balls of clay—one per child
- pencils and marker
- small shells, small beans, small seeds—one of each per child
- contact paper
- container to hold the balls of clay

How to Make This Activity

- Duplicate the master of Fossil Discovery—one per child.
- Fill each ball of clay with one shell, one bean, one seed (one filled ball of clay per child).
- Place the clay balls, toothpicks, magnifying glasses, clay boards, and duplicated papers at a dinosaur center with crayons or pencils.
- Print dinosaur words in the folder, cover with contact paper, and place at the dinosaur center.

Teacher's Directions

- Review how paleontologists carefully dig to find dinosaur bones (fossils).
- Demonstrate how to "pretend to be a fossil hunter."
- Using a clay ball, toothpick, and clay board, carefully dig in the clay to find "fossils."
- Children may put the "fossils" back in the clay ball to take home.
- Demonstrate writing a story about your "find."

Self-Checking Feature: *The children may look in the folder for dinosaur idea words for their story.*

Children's Directions

1. Take one clay ball, one toothpick, one clay board.
2. Pretend to be a fossil hunter.
3. Dig apart the clay to find the "fossils."
4. Put the "fossils" back in your clay to take home.
5. Write a story about your "fossil discovery" and draw a picture.

Labels

> **Activity:** Fossil Search
> **Skills:** critical thinking, writing

(Tab)

> **Theme:** Dinosaurs
> **Activity:** Fossil Search
> **Skills:** critical thinking, writing

(Folder)

Fossil Discovery

Dinosaur fossil
discovered in . . .

Sample Words for Folder

- eggs
- dinosaur
- claws
- bones
- spikes
- teeth
- meat eater
- fossil
- plant eater
- skeleton

- coldblooded
- Tyrannosaurus Rex
- Apatosaurus
- Allosaurus
- Stegosaurus
- Triceratops
- Diplodocus
- Brachiosaurus
- Ankylosaurus
- Pteranodon

Dinosaur Sorting

Activity: Dinosaur Sorting
Skills: sorting, counting, color words

Materials Needed

- gummy dinosaurs (from the store)
- container for the plastic eggs
- duplicating master of dinosaurs
- plastic eggs that open
- resealable plastic bag
- paper towels
- pencils and markers
- contact paper

How to Make This Activity

- Fill each plastic egg with varying amounts of four colors of the gummy dinosaurs—red, green, orange, and yellow. (One color should be for two or three dinosaurs, one color for three or four, one color for four or five, one color for five or six—all in one egg.)
- Place extra gummy dinosaurs in the plastic bag for a treat for children to eat when they finish.
- Duplicate the dinosaur master.
- Print the color words in black and also in the colors in the folder and cover with contact paper.
- Place the duplicated dinosaur papers in the folder with the children's directions.
- Place eggs, paper towels, pencils, plastic eggs, and the folder at the dinosaur center or a table.

Teacher's Directions

Demonstrate how to . . .

- open the plastic egg and sort the gummy dinosaurs on a paper towel into four colors.
- count each color and write the number in the correct box.
- count all the gummy dinosaurs and write in the total.
- put the dinosaurs back in the plastic egg and take one dinosaur from the plastic bag to eat.

Self-Checking Feature: Children may check the folder to read color words in color or in black.

Children's Directions

1. Take 1 egg and 1 paper towel.
2. Open the egg.
3. Sort the dinosaurs into their own colors.
4. Count how many are in each dinosaur color group.
5. Write how many dinosaurs are in each color group.
6. Count all the dinosaurs and write the number.
7. Put all the dinosaurs back in the egg.
8. Eat one dinosaur from the plastic bag.

Labels

> **Activity:** Dinosaur Sorting
> **Skills:** sorting, counting, color words

(Tab)

Theme: Dinosaurs
Activity: Dinosaur Sorting
Skills: sorting, counting, color words

(Folder)

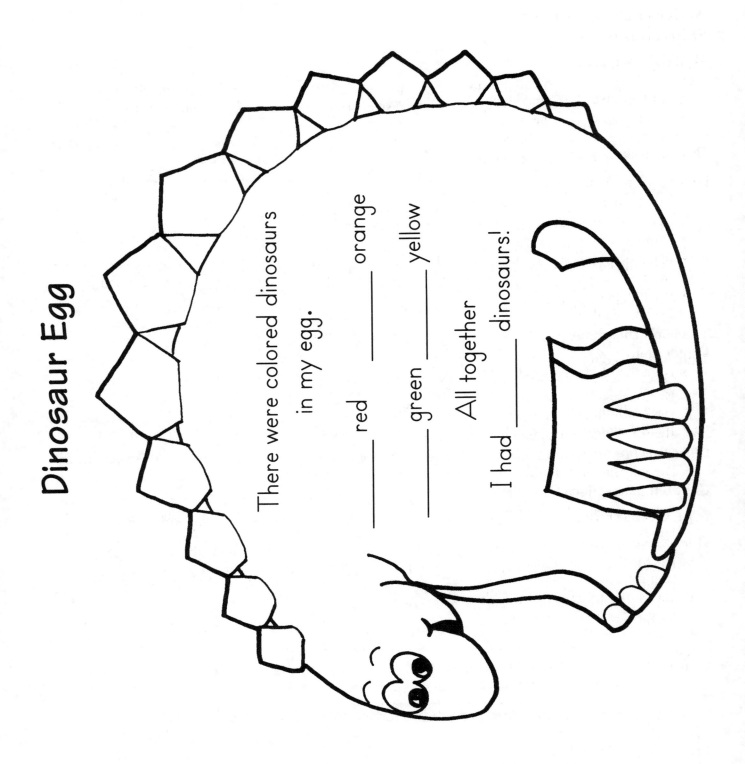

Dinosaur Egg

There were colored dinosaurs in my egg.

_____ red

_____ orange

_____ green

_____ yellow

All together

I had _____ dinosaurs!

Dinosaur Food

Activity: Dinosaur Food
Skill: critical thinking

Materials Needed

- bread and tuna or bologna
- plastic knives for spreading
- two containers for the tuna (bologna) and tomatoes
- duplicating masters of dinosaurs to cut apart
- duplicating masters of plant and meat eaters

- tomatoes and mayonnaise
- crayons and glue sticks
- paper towels and contact paper
- dinosaur pictures, small and large

How to Make This Activity

- Mix up the tuna (or bologna) and place in a container.
- Slice the tomatoes and place them in a container.
- Duplicate the masters.
- Place small pictures of meat-eating dinosaurs on one side of the folder and small pictures of plant-eating dinosaurs on the other side of the folder. Label each side. Cover with contact paper.
- Place duplicated papers, bread, tuna (or bologna), tomatoes, knives, paper towels, and crayons at the dinosaur center.
- Place large posters of dinosaurs around the dinosaur center.

Teacher's Directions

- Discuss plant- and meat-eating dinosaurs and show pictures.
- Demonstrate how to choose being a plant eater or a meat eater.
- Demonstrate making a sandwich: tuna (or bologna) for a meat eater, tomato for a plant eater, two slices of bread, spreading the mayonnaise.
- Demonstrate drawing a picture of the kind of dinosaur chosen or cutting out the dinosaur chosen.
- Demonstrate how to glue on the dinosaur chosen and color it.
- A volunteer would be helpful at this center to oversee the making of the sandwiches.

Self-Checking Feature: *Children may check the folder for plant- and meat-eating dinosaurs.*

Children's Directions

1. Decide if you are a meat-eating or a plant-eating dinosaur.
2. Take a paper towel and two slices of bread.
3. Spread the mayonnaise on the bread.
4. Choose tuna (bologna) or tomato.

5. Eat your sandwich.
6. Draw a picture of the kind of dinosaur you chose or cut out and glue on the dinosaur picture you chose.

Labels

> **Activity:** Dinosaur Food
> **Skill:** critical thinking   (Tab)

> **Theme:** Dinosaurs
> **Activity:** Dinosaur Food
> **Skill:** critical thinking   (Folder)

Meat Eater

Plant Eater

Sample for Folder

P = plant eating   M = meat eating

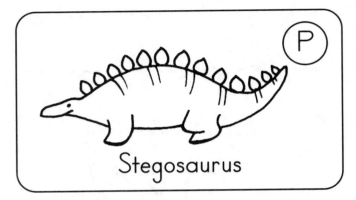

Stegosaurus

Brachiosaurus

Ankylosaurus

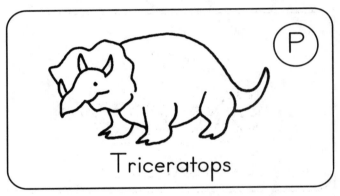

Triceratops

Pteranodon

Allosaurus

Tyrannosaurus

Apatosaurus

Dinosaur Master

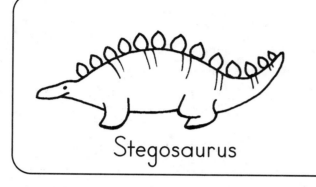

Stegosaurus

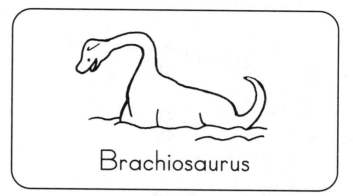

Brachiosaurus

Ankylosaurus

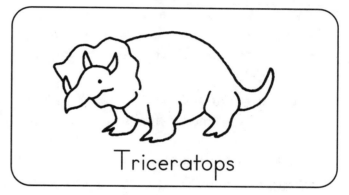

Triceratops

Pteranodon

Allosaurus

Tyrannosaurus

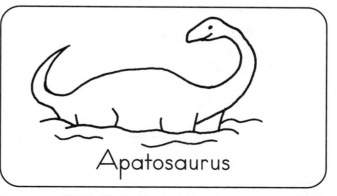

Apatosaurus

Dinosaur Puzzles

Activity: Dinosaur Puzzles
Skill: visual discrimination

Materials Needed:

- tagboard cut to 9" by 12" (23 cm by 30 cm) in two colors
- duplicating masters of dinosaurs
- glue
- children's scissors
- laminate or contact paper
- four large resealable plastic bags
- crayons

How to Make This Activity

- Duplicate the dinosaur masters—two of each.
- Glue one of each dinosaur to a different color tagboard for color coding.
- Laminate and cut apart.
- Place each puzzle in a plastic bag.
- Place the four pictures of the uncut dinosaurs in the folder for self-checking.
- Duplicate additional copies of the dinosaur masters if the children are going to take a dinosaur home.

Teacher's Directions

- Demonstrate how to put the puzzles together and to put them back in each bag.
- If the children are to take a picture home, demonstrate how to color the picture, cut it into fourths, and then put it together in a completed puzzle.

Self-Checking Feature: *The children may check the folder to see how the finished puzzles will look.*

Children's Directions

1. Take one puzzle.
2. Put it together to make a dinosaur.
3. Put the puzzle back in the bag.

Labels

> **Activity:** Dinosaur Puzzles
> **Skill:** visual discrimination   (Tab)

> **Theme:** Dinosaurs
> **Activity:** Dinosaur Puzzles
> **Skill:** visual discrimination      (Folder)

Puzzle Master

Color. Cut into four squares. Put the puzzle together to make a dinosaur.

Puzzle Master (cont.)

Color. Cut into four squares. Put the puzzle together to make a dinosaur.

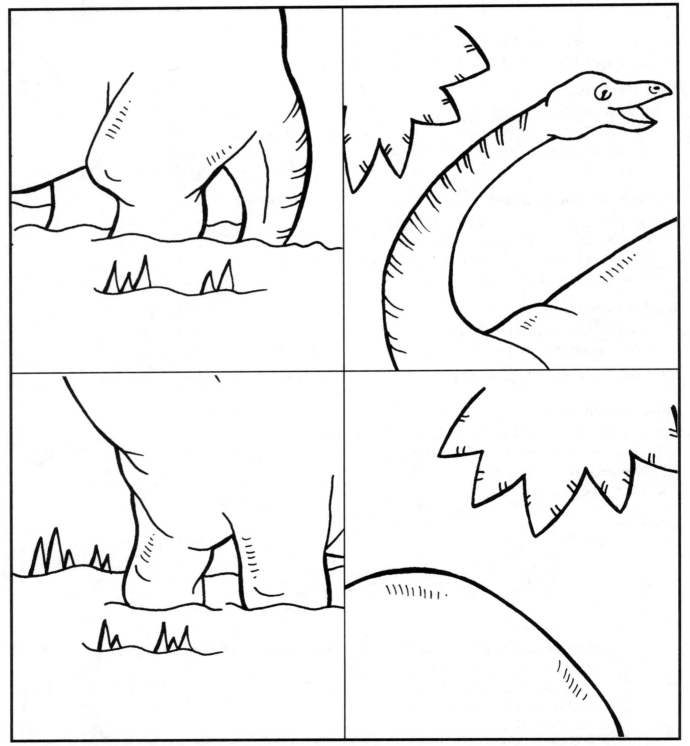

Caterpillar Number Puzzle

Caterpillars and butterflies make a great unit to study in the springtime. Introduce the unit by reading *The Very Hungry Caterpillar* by Eric Carle (Putnam Publishing, 1986). Be sure the children are very familiar with the story before presenting the folder activities to them. Develop this theme over a few weeks, exploring topics such as eggs, butterfly life cycles, caterpillars turning into butterflies, frog life cycles, etc. It's a good science unit that easily lends itself to across-the-curriculum activities.

Activity: Caterpillar Number Puzzle
Skills: matching numbers 0–10, number order 1–10

Materials Needed

- two duplicating masters
- 9" by 12" (23 cm by 30 cm) construction paper in spring colors
- glue sticks
- scissors
- crayons
- contact paper

How to Make This Activity

- Duplicate the masters—one for each per child.
- Cut out puzzle pieces for one caterpillar and complete a sample for the folder. Glue the completed sample in the folder and place contact paper over it.
- Place folder and copies at the butterfly center.

Teacher's Directions

- Demonstrate how to cut the puzzle pieces.
- Demonstrate how to glue the pieces to the uncut caterpillar matching the numbers.

Self-Checking Feature: The children may look in the folder to see a completed caterpillar.

Children's Directions

1. Cut carefully around the number puzzle pieces.
2. Glue cut puzzle pieces to the matching numbers.
3. Say the numbers in order to a friend.
4. Color your caterpillar.

Labels

> **Activity:** Caterpillar Number Puzzle
> **Skills:** matching numbers 0–10, number order 1–10

(Tab)

> **Theme:** Caterpillars and Butterflies
> **Activity:** Caterpillar Number Puzzle
> **Skills:** matching numbers 0–10, number order 1–10

(Folder)

Sample for Folder

Number Puzzle Master

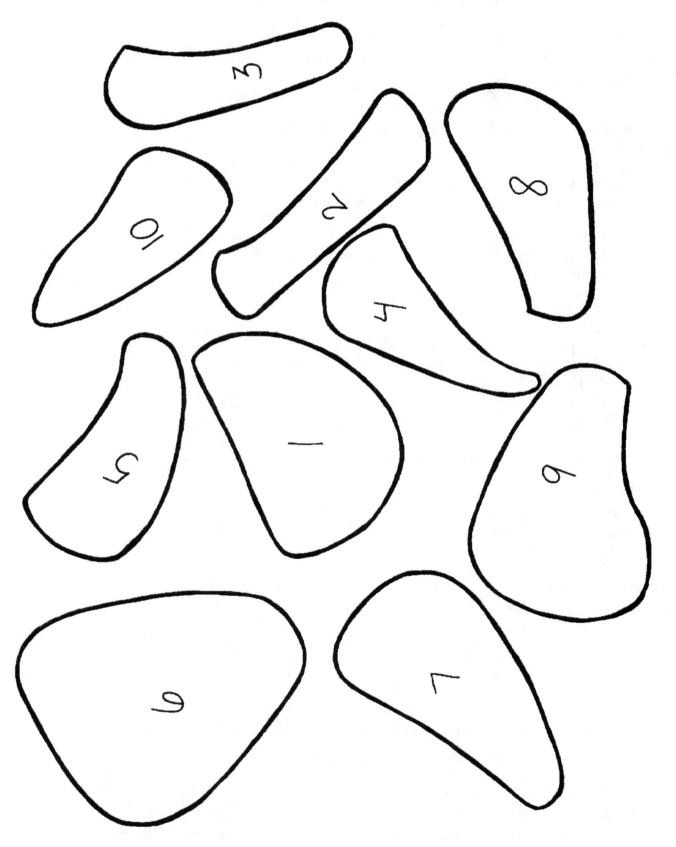

Hungry Caterpillar Sock Book

Activity: Hungry Caterpillar Sock Book
Skills: oral language development, cooperative learning—partners

Materials Needed

- caterpillar book duplicating masters—eight
- 9" by 12" (23 cm by 30 cm) light-colored construction paper
- scissors
- crayons
- children's socks—one per child (Children may bring the socks from home.)
- small eyes to glue to the socks (available at a craft store)

How to Make This Activity

- Duplicate the caterpillar book—one book per child. (Do not staple the book pages together.)
- Cut out the center of each page.
- Glue two eyes on each sock.

Teacher's Directions

- Demonstrate how to carefully color the book.
- Demonstrate how to tell the story using the colored pages of the book.
- Put the sock on one hand.
- As the story is told, place the hand with the sock through each page.
- Demonstrate how to tell the story to a partner.
- The children need to be very familiar with the story.
- A volunteer can be used to cut out the centers of each book and glue eyes on the socks.

Children's Directions

1. Take one book and one sock.
2. Color each page carefully.
3. Tell the story to a partner.

Labels

Activity: Hungry Caterpillar Sock Book
Skills: oral language development,
cooperative learning—partners

(Tab)

Theme: Caterpillars and Butterflies
Activity: Hungry Caterpillar Sock Book
Skills: oral language development,
cooperative learning—partners

(Folder)

The Very Hungry Caterpillar

by Eric Carle

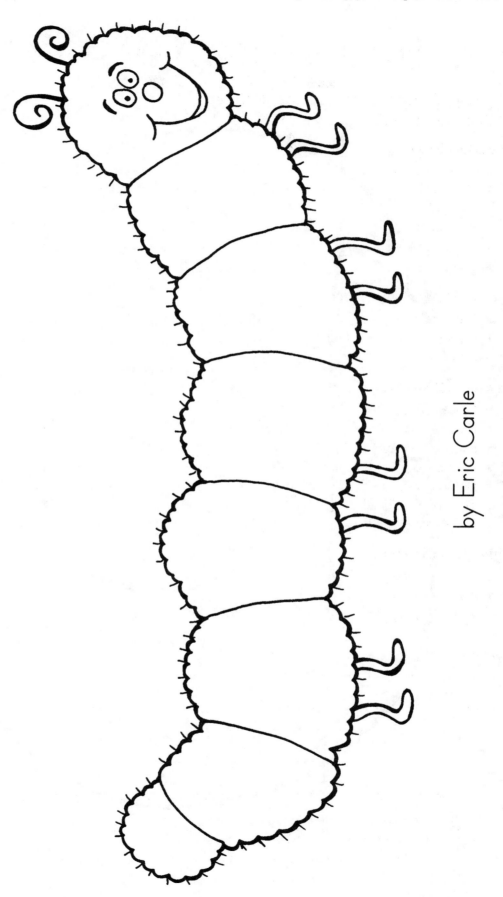

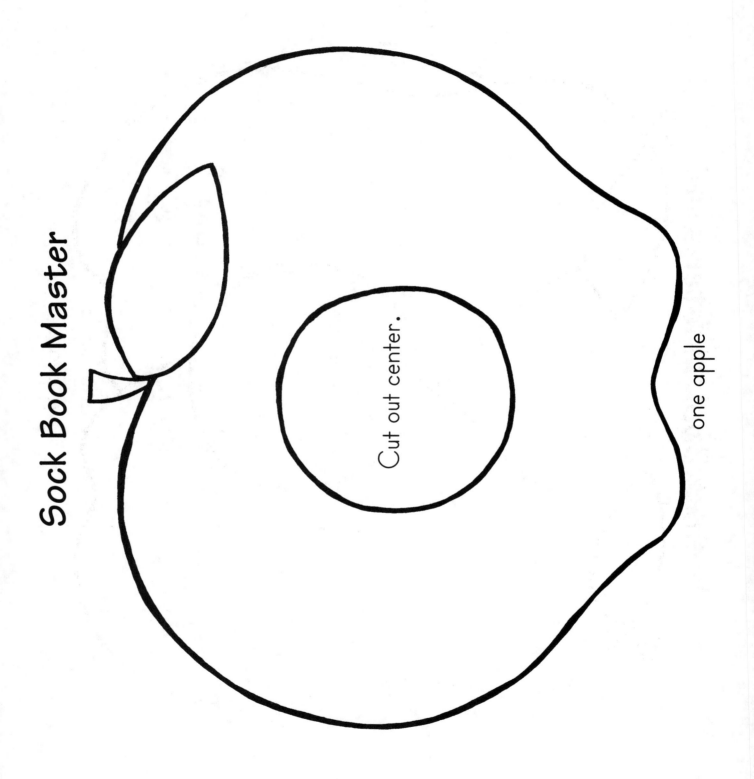

Sock Book Master

Cut out center.

one apple

Sock Book Master (cont.)

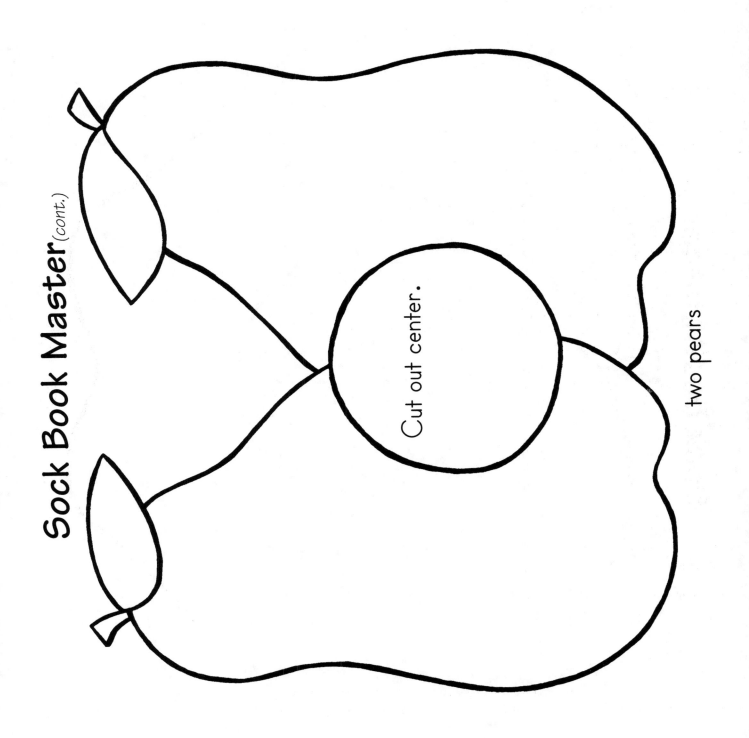

Cut out center.

two pears

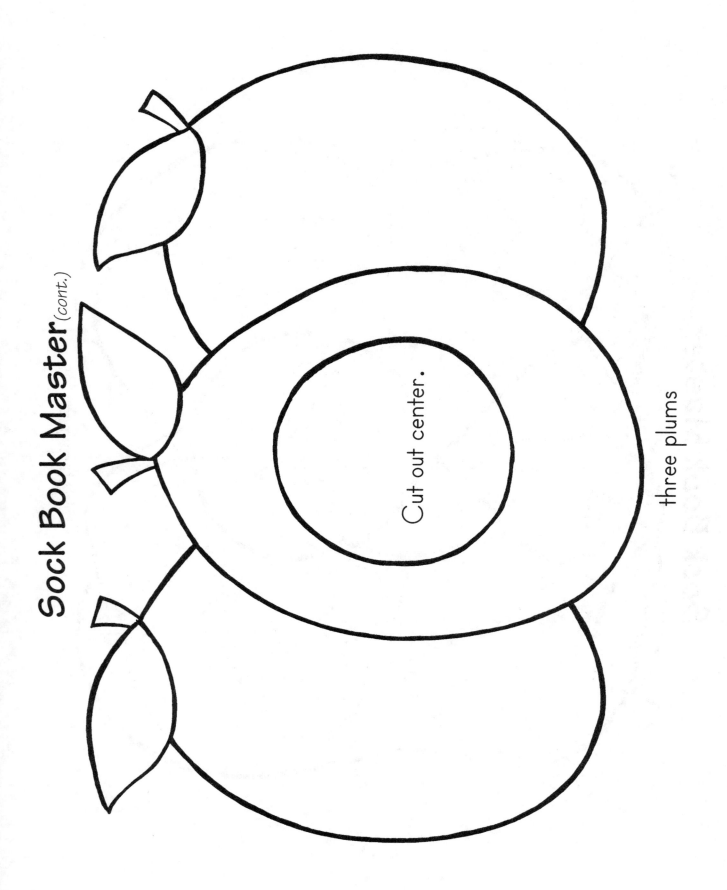

Sock Book Master (cont.)

Cut out center.

three plums

Sock Book Master *(cont.)*

Cut out center.

four strawberries

Sock Book Master (cont.)

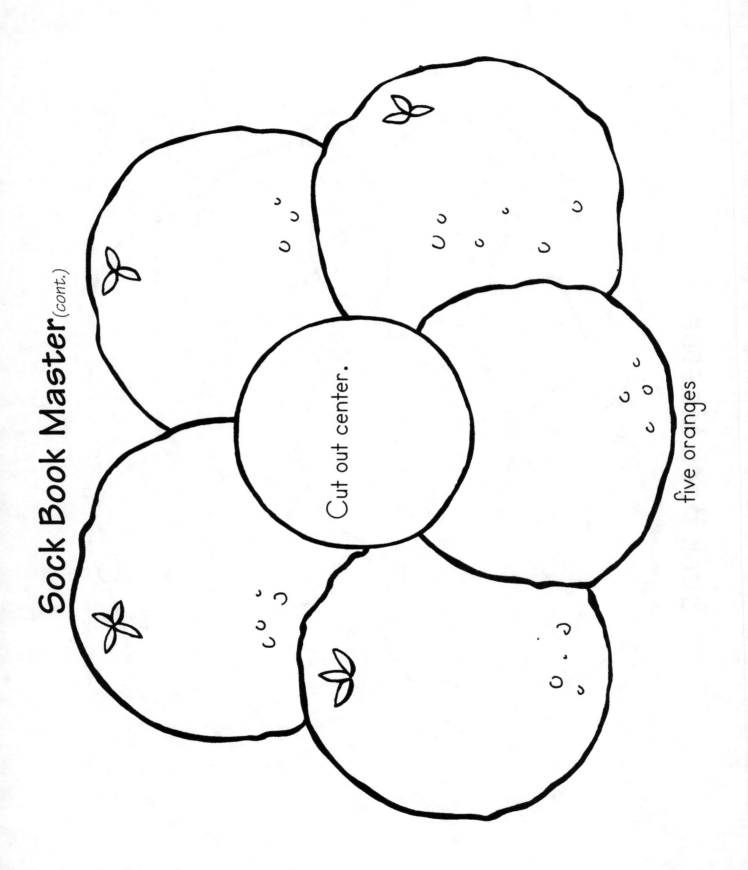

Cut out center.

five oranges

Sock Book Master*(cont.)*

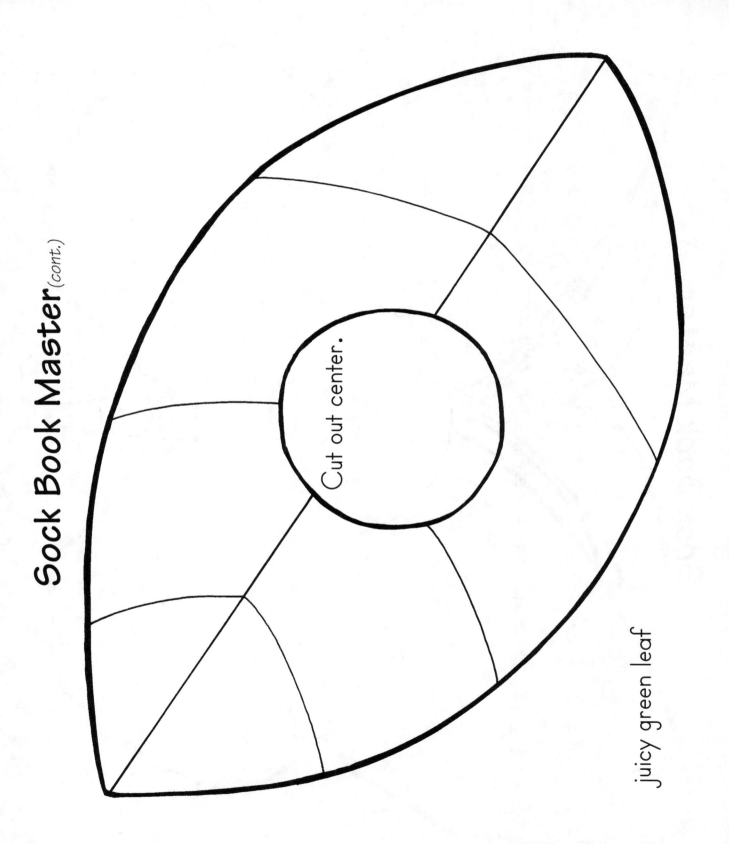

Cut out center.

juicy green leaf

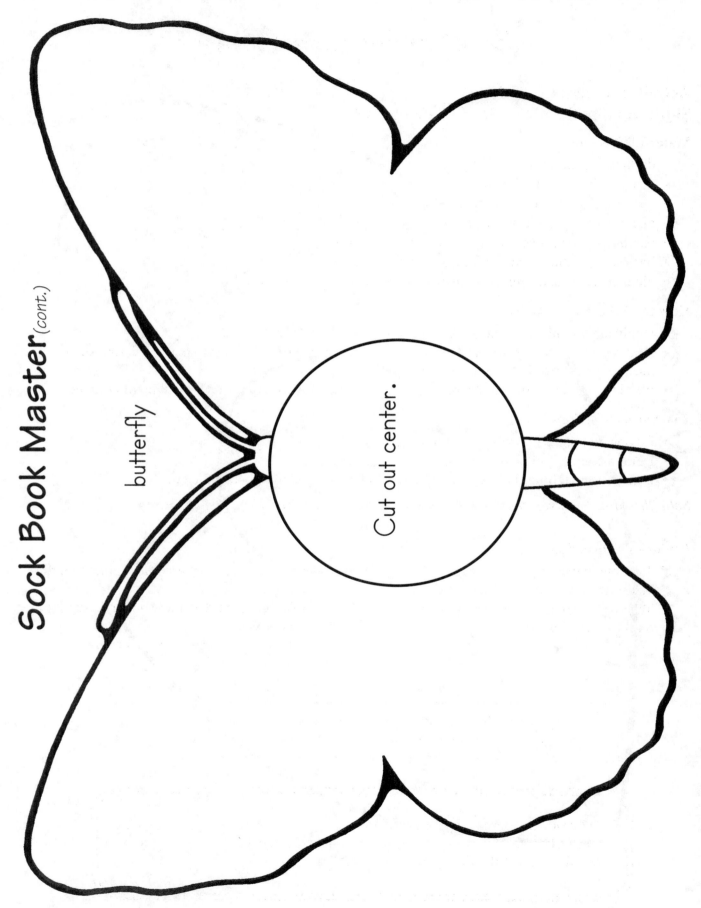

Sock Book Master *(cont.)*

butterfly

Cut out center.

Butterfly Life Cycle

Activity: Butterfly Life Cycle
Skill: learning the life cycle of the butterfly

Materials Needed

- duplicating master of butterfly life cycle
- 9" by 12" (23 cm by 30 cm) white construction paper
- one bag of dried peas (to represent eggs)
- one bag of curly macaroni (to represent a caterpillar)
- one bag of shell macaroni (to represent a cocoon)
- one bag of butterfly macaroni (to represent a butterfly)
- glue, crayons, and four containers to place the peas and macaroni in

How to Make This Activity

- Duplicate the master—one per child and one for the folder.
- Folder sample—color the pictures and then glue on five peas, one curly macaroni, one shell macaroni, and one butterfly macaroni.
- Place the folder, duplicated copies, and all supplies at the butterfly center, table, or counter.

Teacher's Directions

- Review the butterfly cycle with the children.
- Demonstrate coloring and then gluing on each item.
- Demonstrate telling the life cycle to a friend when the picture is completed.

Self-Checking Feature: *The children may check the folder to see a completed sample.*

Children's Directions

1. Take one paper.
2. Take five peas and glue them on the leaf.
3. Take one curly macaroni and glue it on the caterpillar.
4. Take one shell macaroni and glue it on the cocoon.
5. Take one butterfly macaroni and glue it on the butterfly.
6. Tell your butterfly story to a friend.

Labels

> **Activity:** Butterfly Life Cycle
> **Skill:** learning the life cycle of the butterfly   (Tab)

> **Theme:** Caterpillars and Butterflies
> **Activity:** Butterfly Life Cycle
> **Skill:** learning the life cycle of the butterfly      (Folder)

Butterfly Master

Caterpillar Art

Activity: Caterpillar Art
Skill: fine motor control, exposure to various art media

Materials Needed

- sample of caterpillar to trace
- 9" by 12" (23 cm by 30 cm) tagboard—two sheets
- 12" by 18" (30 cm by 46 cm) colored construction paper (various colors—one per child
- crayons   • scissors   • three to four colors of paint

How to Make This Activity

- Trace the caterpillar onto the tagboard and cut out two samples.
- Fold construction paper in half horizontally.
- Place the tagboard caterpillar sample on the fold (the straight edge of the caterpillar sample should rest on the fold).
- Trace around the caterpillar.
- Cut out the caterpillar. DO NOT unfold the paper while cutting.
- Color both sides of the caterpillar without unfolding it.
- Unfold the caterpillar and lay the colored side down so it can't be seen. (Now it's a butterfly.)
- Drip two or three different colors of paint on one side of the opened butterfly.
- Fold the other side of the opened butterfly over carefully and press. Open and let dry.
- Put a completed sample in the folder and place all materials at the butterfly center.

Teacher's Directions

- Demonstrate each step of the above process to the children.
- A volunteer would be helpful for younger children.

Self-Checking Feature: The children may look in the folder for a completed sample.

Children's Directions

1. Fold one sheet of paper in half.
2. Trace the caterpillar.
3. Cut out the caterpillar.
4. Color the caterpillar and then open it.

5. Carefully drip two or three colors of paint on one side of the butterfly.
6. Fold over the other side and press carefully.
7. Open and let dry.

Labels

> **Activity:** Caterpillar Art
> **Skills:** fine motor control, exposure to various art media   (Tab)

> **Theme:** Caterpillars and Butterflies
> **Activity:** Caterpillar Art
> **Skills:** fine motor control, exposure to various art media   (Folder)

Caterpillar Art Master

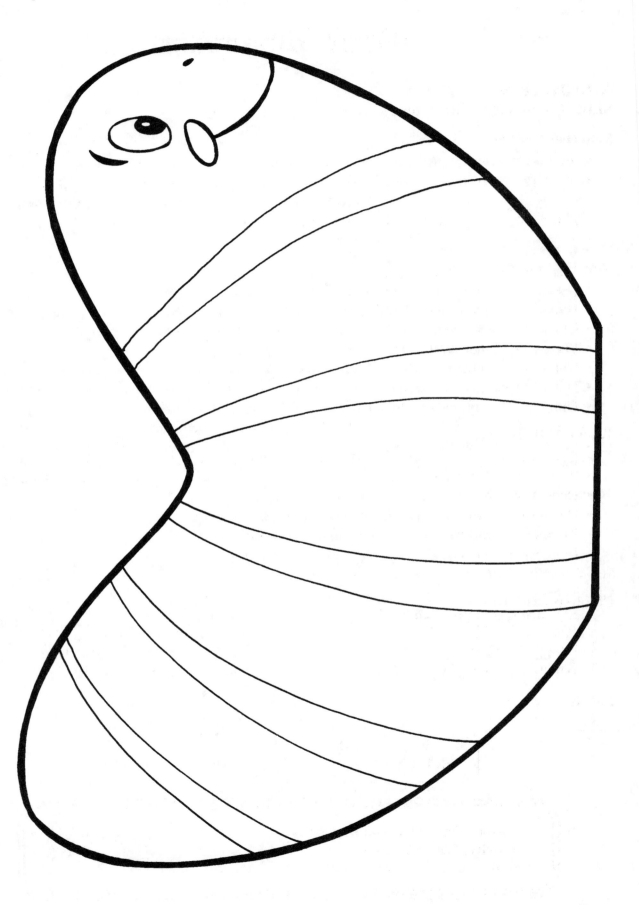

Word Caterpillar

Activity: Word Caterpillar
Skill: vocabulary development

Materials Needed

- master of circles
- vocabulary master
- markers
- glue sticks
- scissors
- master of caterpillar heads
- sample master of finished word caterpillar for the folder
- 9" by 12" (23 cm by 30 cm) various colors of construction paper
- contact paper
- resealable plastic bag

How to Make This Activity

- Duplicate the circle master on construction paper—one per child.
- Duplicate the master of caterpillar heads.
- Cut around each head so the children can still cut out each head on the circle line.
- Place all the heads in the plastic bag.
- Duplicate and glue vocabulary words in the folder and cover them with contact paper.
- Duplicate and glue the sample word caterpillar in the folder. Cover with contact paper.
- Place all materials and the folder at the butterfly center or a table.

Teacher's Directions

- Demonstrate how to brainstorm caterpillar and butterfly words. (See vocabulary master.)
- Place charts of vocabulary words generated around the room in addition to the folder sample.
- Demonstrate how to print one word on each circle.
- Demonstrate how to glue each circle to the proceeding circle.
- Demonstrate cutting out and gluing on the caterpillar's head.
- Demonstrate reading the word caterpillar to a friend.

Self-Checking Feature: Children may check the folder for vocabulary and a sample word caterpillar.

Children's Directions

1. Take one sheet of circles and cut out each circle.
2. Print one word on each circle.
3. Cut out the caterpillar's head.
4. Glue the head and each circle together.
5. Read your word caterpillar to a friend.

Labels

> **Activity:** Word Caterpillar
> **Skill:** vocabulary development   (Tab)

> **Theme:** Caterpillars and Butterflies
> **Activity:** Word Caterpillar      (Folder)
> **Skill:** vocabulary development

Circle Master

Circle Master (cont.)

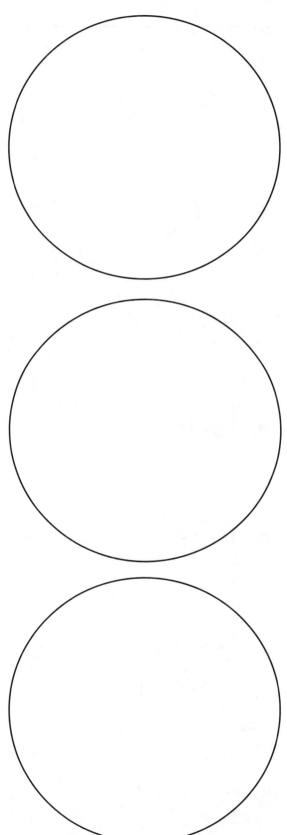

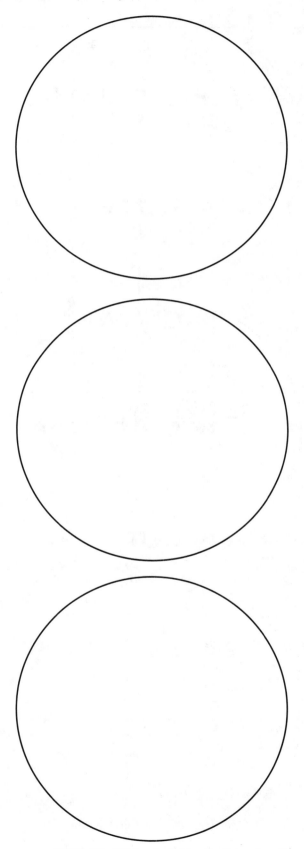

Vocabulary Master

- caterpillar
- fuzzy
- crawl
- butterfly
- eat
- fly
- egg

- head
- wings
- cocoon
- leaves
- legs
- body

Sample for Folder

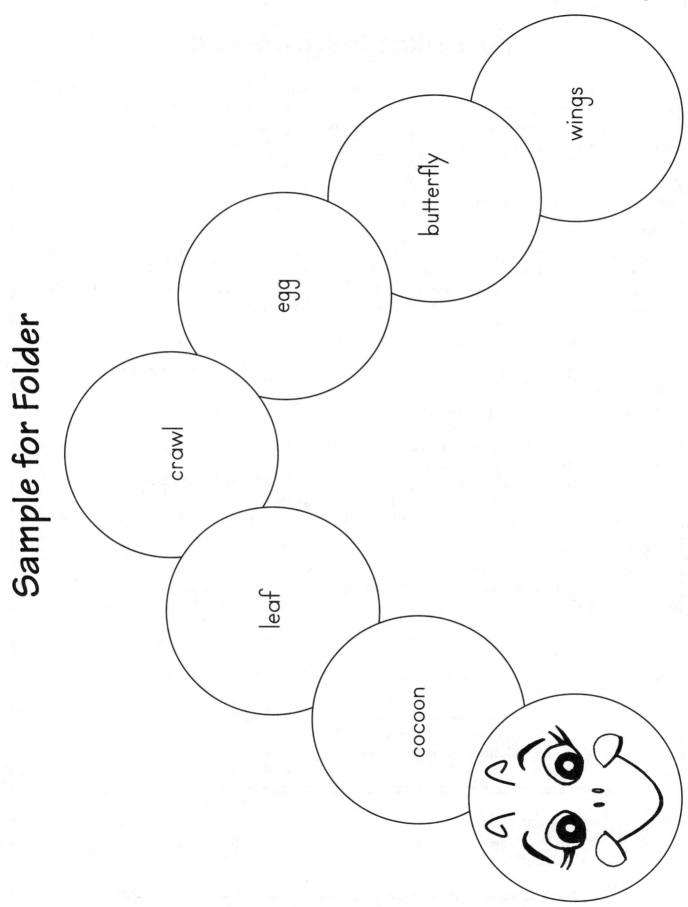

Pumpkin Sequencing

For a total group literature experience, use *Pumpkin Pumpkin* by Jeanne Titherington (Mulberry Books, 1990). The teacher will read and discuss the book with the children. Discuss the seasonal holiday of Halloween and what grows and is harvested at this time. Introduce the following file folder activities on succeeding days.

Activity: Pumpkin Sequencing
Skills: sequencing, visual discrimination

Materials Needed

- pumpkin pictures to duplicate and cut out in squares (four for each child in the class if you wish children to take home a completed copy of the activity)
- 3" by 12" (8 cm by 30 cm) manila paper folded in fourths (Use 12" by 18" [30 cm by 46 cm] and cut one strip for each child if you wish them to have copies to take home.)
- glue sticks at the center or the table
- crayons at the center or the table
- tagboard

How to Make This Activity

- Duplicate the sequence pictures on construction paper or copier paper.
- Color two sets of each picture.
- Mount one set of four pictures on tagboard, laminate, and cut into four squares. This set goes in the folder for the children to put in order.
- Cut and glue one set of pictures in order on the back of the folder for self-checking.
- After children have been successful in putting the pictures in order, they may make their own pictures with the extra pumpkin pictures that the teacher reproduced and placed in the folder.

Teacher's Directions

- Have the children put the pictures in the correct order.
- The children may then glue the pictures in proper sequence and color them.

Self-Checking Feature: *planting the pumpkin seeds, leaves sprouting, the pumpkin growing, jack-o-lantern face*

Children's Directions

1. Put the pictures in the correct order.   2. Glue the pictures in order and color them.

Labels

> **Activity:** Pumpkin Sequencing
> **Skills:** sequencing, visual discrimination   (Tab)

> **Theme:** Halloween
> **Activity:** Pumpkin Sequencing
> **Skill:** sequencing, visual discrimination   (Folder)

Sequencing Master

Pumpkin Faces

Activity: Pumpkin Faces
Skill: graphing

Materials Needed
- four different pumpkin faces duplicated—size 3" by 3" (8 cm by 8 cm)
- title for class pumpkin graph to go on a sentence strip or the top of the construction paper graph
  Suggestions: "What face will your pumpkin have?" "What face should we carve on our class pumpkin?"
- class graph to put at the learning center (white 18" by 24" [46 cm by 61 cm] construction paper)
- glue sticks
- crayons or markers

How to Make This Activity
- Reproduce pumpkin faces and cut them out in squares.
- Place the pumpkin faces in the file folder.
- Make a graph to place at the Halloween learning center.
- Print the title at the top of a sentence strip or on the construction paper.
- Section the white paper vertically into four columns. Use a black marker.
- Glue one colored pumpkin face at the top of each section.
- Mount the graph on a wall by the learning center so the children will be able to reach it.

Teacher's Directions
When all the children have colored and glued on a pumpkin face, discuss the graph. What does it show—more, less, the same, equal number? Count the faces.

Children's Directions
1. Choose one pumpkin face to color.
2. Glue your pumpkin face under the same face on the big graph.

Labels

> **Activity:** Pumpkin Faces
> **Skill:** graphing   (Tab)

> **Theme:** Halloween
> **Activity:** Pumpkin Faces
> **Skill:** graphing      (Folder)

Pumpkin Master

What type of face will your pumpkin have?

scary

angry

cute

happy

Frozen Pumpkin Squares

Activity: Frozen Pumpkin Squares
Skills: measuring, small-muscle coordination

Materials Needed

- bowls—two large and one small
- pumpkin pudding mix
- Cool Whip
- graham crackers—two squares per child
- cookie sheets and mixing spoons
- two measuring spoons—one teaspoon and one tablespoon
- one spreading spatula
- can opener
- paper towels
- one recipe master sheet for the folder and enough duplicated for each child to take one home
- one 8" by 11" (20 cm by 28 cm) sheet of construction paper
- laminating or contact paper

How to Make This Activity

- Run off recipe master sheet for each child.
- Color the master sheet, mount it on construction paper, laminate and glue it to the folder.
- Place the duplicated copies in the folder.
- Set up a table for this center and have one volunteer guide children in this activity.
- Lay out the paper towels one at a time as the children come to the center.
- Put the pumpkin mix in one large bowl and the Cool Whip in the other large bowl.
- Lay out the measuring spoons, the master recipe sheet, the small bowl, the mixing spoons, the spreading spatula, the graham crackers, and the cookie sheets.

Teacher's Directions

- Freeze all the cracker sandwiches and let the children eat them at snack the next day.
- At snack time, discuss how the cracker sandwiches were made.

Children's Directions

1. Measure one teaspoon (5 mL) of pumpkin mix and put in the bowl.
2. Measure three tablespoons (45 mL) Cool Whip and put in the bowl.
3. Mix together.
4. Spread on one cracker.
5. Lay another cracker on top.
6. Put cracker sandwich on the cookie sheet.
7. Clean up.
8. Take one recipe sheet, color, and take home.

Labels

> **Activity:** Frozen Pumpkin Squares
> **Skills:** measuring, small-muscle coordination

(Tab)

> **Theme:** Halloween
> **Activity:** Frozen Pumpkin Squares
> **Skills:** measuring, small-muscle coordination

(Folder)

Pumpkin Master

We made this in class. Try it at home.

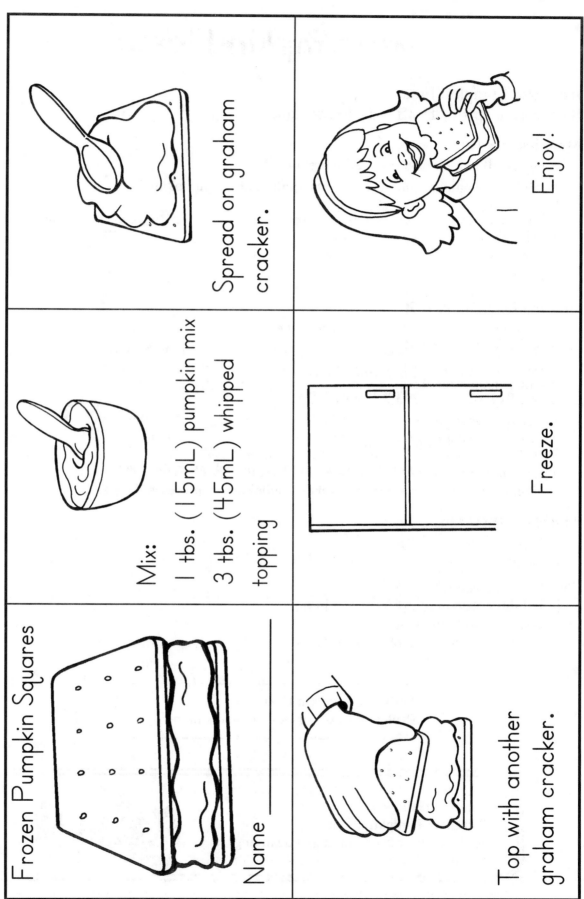

Spread on graham cracker.

Enjoy!

Mix:

1 tbs. (15mL) pumpkin mix

3 tbs. (45mL) whipped topping

Freeze.

Frozen Pumpkin Squares

Name _____

Top with another graham cracker.

Pumpkin Float

Activity: Pumpkin Float
Skills: concepts of floating and sinking

Materials Needed
- one small pumpkin, one larger pumpkin
- one clear container (unbreakable) that will hold the pumpkins
- master sheet
- crayons
- one table
- one towel

How to Make This Activity
- Set up a table at the Halloween learning center.
- Duplicate the master sheet—enough copies for each child to have one.
- Fill a clear container half full of water.
- Put the pumpkins and the towel on the table.

Teacher's Directions
- Have a volunteer/tutor at the table.
- Discuss with the child what happened to the pumpkins in the water.
- Help the children draw their pumpkins in the correct place on the paper.

Children's Directions
1. Take one sheet from the folder.
2. Choose one pumpkin.
3. Guess if the pumpkin will float or sink.
4. Put the pumpkin in the water to check.
5. Draw what happens on your paper.
6. Do the same with the other pumpkin.

Labels

> **Activity:** Pumpkin Float
> **Skills:** concepts of floating and sinking   (Tab)

> **Theme:** Halloween
> **Activity:** Pumpkin Float
> **Skills:** concepts of floating and sinking      (Folder)

Will the Pumpkin Float?

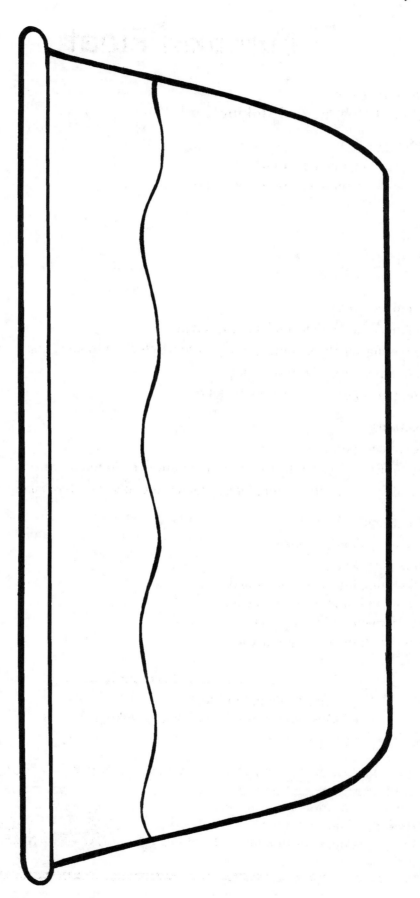

Pilgrim or Indian?

Thanksgiving incorporates a wide variety of topics, such as Pilgrims, the Mayflower, Indians, thankfulness, turkeys, feasting, etc. Children enjoy the different aspects of this holiday. A delightful video to introduce the topic to young children is *The Mouse on The Mayflower*. It may be purchased from Family Home Entertainment, a subsidiary of LIVE Entertainment, Inc.

Activity: Pilgrim or Indian?
Skills: writing words, creative writing

Materials Needed

- duplicating master of story page
- small pictures of a Pilgrim and an Indian
- glue stick
- sentence strips—one per child
- laminate or contact paper
- scissors

How to Make This Activity

- Duplicate the story page master—one per child (decide which level of story page to use).
- Cut sentence strips (see sample).
- Print "a Pilgrim" on one of the cut strips.
- Print "an Indian" on the other cut strip.
- Glue on the small Pilgrim and Indian pictures (see sample).
- Laminate and place in the folder with the duplicate story page.

Teacher's Directions

- Review the story of how the Pilgrims came to America and how the Indians helped them.
- Ask the children to decide if they would like to be Pilgrims or Indians and why.
- Demonstrate how to write the words (or story) and then color a picture about what they wrote.
- Younger children may write the words Pilgrim or Indian and draw a picture. Use story page one.
- Older children may write a story and draw a picture. Use story page two.
- The story pages may be sent home, put in the student's journal, or made into a class book.
- Younger children will need a volunteer at this center.

Self-Checking Feature: Children may check the folder to see how to write Pilgrim *or* Indian.

Children's Directions

1. Take one story page.
2. Choose to be a Pilgrim or an Indian.
3. Write the word. (Or write your story.)
4. Color a picture about your story.

Labels

Activity: Pilgrim or Indian?
Skills: writing words, creative writing

(Tab)

Theme: Thanksgiving
Activity: Pilgrim or Indian?
Skills: writing words, creative writing

(Folder)

Pilgrim or Indian? Master

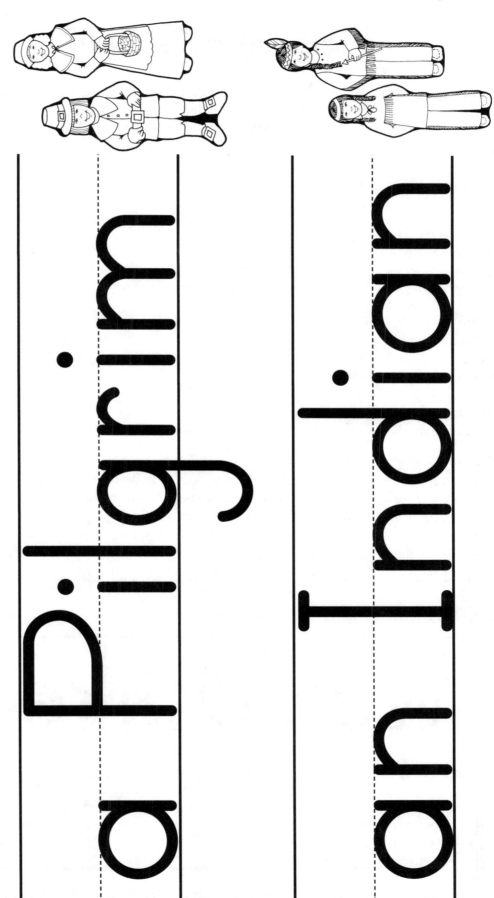

a Pilgrim

an Indian

Story Page One

I would like to
be _____.

Story Page Two

Where Is the Turkey?

Activity: Where Is the Turkey?
Skill: position words

Materials Needed

- duplicating masters of turkey book
- glue sticks
- resealable plastic bag
- duplicating master of small turkeys
- scissors
- crayons
- 9" by 12" (23 cm by 30 cm) construction paper—light color

How to Make This Activity

- Duplicate the turkey book—one book per child.
- Duplicate the turkey master on construction paper—one large or six small turkeys per child.
- Cut out the turkeys and place in a plastic bag. (Older children may cut out their own set of turkeys.)
- Place one completed book in the folder as a sample for self-checking.

Teacher's Directions

- Demonstrate how to read the sentences.
- Demonstrate how to glue on the turkeys.

Self-Checking Feature: *The children may check the completed book in the folder to see where to place the turkeys or to check their work.*

Children's Directions

1. Take one turkey book.
2. Take six turkeys (or cut out six turkeys).
3. Read the sentence.
4. Glue the turkey in the correct place.
5. Color your book.

Labels

> **Activity:** Where Is the Turkey?
> **Skill:** position words

(Tab)

> **Theme:** Thanksgiving
> **Activity:** Where Is the Turkey?
> **Skill:** position words

(Folder)

Turkey Master

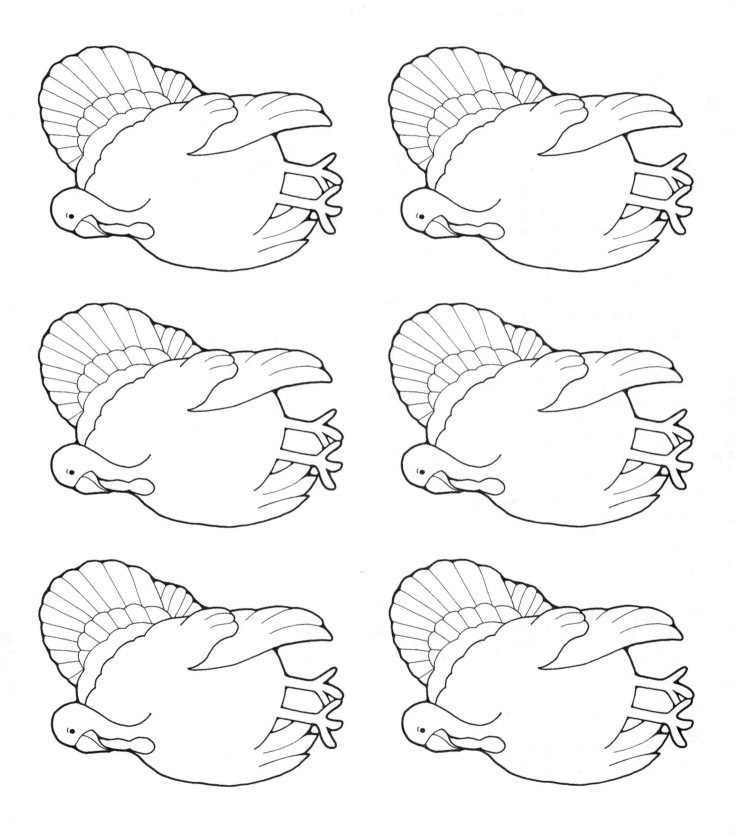

Turkey Master *(cont.)*

Where is the

turkey?

Turkey Master (cont.)

Put the turkey on
the barn.

Turkey Master (cont.)

Put the turkey on the left side of the barn.

Turkey Master *(cont.)*

Put the turkey below the barn.

Turkey Master (cont.)

Put the turkey beside

the barn.

Turkey Master *(cont.)*

Put the turkey above

the barn.

Turkey Master *(cont.)*

Put the turkey on the

right side of the barn.

Indian or Pilgrim Graph

Activity: Indian or Pilgrim Graph
Skill: graphing

Materials Needed

- 18" by 24" (46 cm by 61 cm) white construction paper
- duplicating master of Pilgrims and Indians
- beef jerky (pretend Indian food)
- popcorn cakes (pretend Pilgrim food)
- scissors
- glue sticks
- crayons
- marker
- plastic bag

How to Make This Activity

- Section and label the white construction paper (see the sample).
- Duplicate the master—enough for each child to have a choice of a Pilgrim or an Indian.
- Cut around the Pilgrims and Indians and place in the plastic bag.
- Place the bag in the folder with the children's directions.

Teacher's Directions

- Demonstrate taking a Pilgrim or an Indian, coloring it, and then gluing it on the graph.
- Discuss the graph when all the children have had a turn to choose being a Pilgrim or an Indian.
- For a fun activity, let the children sample some pretend Indian food and Pilgrim food.

Children's Directions

1. Choose a Pilgrim or an Indian.
2. Color your picture.
3. Glue your picture under the Pilgrim or the Indian.
4. Take one taste each of Indian and Pilgrim foods.

Labels

> **Activity:** Indian or Pilgrim Graph
> **Skill:** graphing

(Tab)

> **Theme:** Thanksgiving
> **Activity:** Indian or Pilgrim Graph
> **Skill:** graphing

(Folder)

Sample for Folder

Would you be an Indian or a Pilgrim?

Indian	Pilgrim

Indian or Pilgrim Master

Turkey Fingerprint

Activity: Turkey Fingerprint
Skill: small-muscle control

Materials Needed:

- 9" by 12" (23 cm by 30 cm) white construction paper
- crayons
- colored ink pads
- resealable plastic bag

How to Make This Activity

- Cut white construction paper in half—one per child.
- Place ink pads in the plastic bag for storage.
- Make one completed sample to put in the folder.

Teacher's Directions

- Demonstrate how to lay one hand on the paper and draw around it with a crayon with the other hand.
- Demonstrate how to draw the turkey feet, eye, beak, and the wattle. (See the sample.)
- Demonstrate how to use one finger to stamp the turkey.
- Explain the need to change fingers for each stamp pad color used.
- Demonstrate printing Happy Thanksgiving at the top.

Self-Checking Feature: *The children may look in the folder to see a completed sample of the turkey.*

Children's Directions

1. Take one paper.
2. Use your hand to draw a turkey.
3. Stamp your turkey with your fingertips.
4. Change fingers when you change colors.
5. Print Happy Thanksgiving at the top.

Labels

> **Activity:** Turkey Fingerprint
> **Skill:** small-muscle control   (Tab)

> **Theme:** Thanksgiving
> **Activity:** Turkey Fingerprint
> **Skill:** small-muscle control      (Folder)

Happy Thanksgiving

Christmas Surprise

Introduce this theme by using the calendar and showing the children the various holidays in the season of winter. Discuss the season and then bring in posters and pictures of the many winter holidays that are coming: Christmas, New Year's, Martin Luther King, Jr., Day, Groundhog Day, Abraham Lincoln's Birthday, George Washington's Birthday, Valentine's Day, and St. Patrick's Day.

Activity: Christmas Surprise
Skill: creative writing

Materials Needed

- various sizes of boxes wrapped with Christmas paper and bows.
- one Christmas treat for each child— eg., Christmas stickers, Christmas cookie, etc. (The treats need to be small enough to all fit in one of the wrapped boxes.)
- duplicating master of story page
- Christmas pictures
- pencils, marker, crayons
- contact paper

How to Make This Activity

- Wrap the various boxes, duplicate the story page, and place it in the folder.
- Print Christmas words in the folder with corresponding pictures. (See sample for ideas.)
- Cover the words and pictures with contact paper and place all materials at a center.

Teacher's Directions

- Show the various boxes to the children and let some guess what they think is inside.
- Demonstrate choosing one box, describing what might be inside, writing a story about the guess, and then coloring a picture about the story.
- When all the children have rotated through the center, their stories may be put into a class book.
- Then open all the boxes and find the one with the treats inside to share with the children.

Self-Checking Feature: Children may check the folder for Christmas words to use in their stories.

Children's Directions

1. Take one story page.
2. Choose one Christmas present.
3. Guess what is inside the box.
4. Write a story about your guess.
5. Color a picture about your guess.

Labels

> **Activity:** Christmas Surprise
> **Skill:** creative writing   (Tab)

> **Theme:** Winter Holidays
> **Activity:** Christmas Surprise
> **Skill:** creative writing      (Folder)

Christmas Surprise

Sample for Folder

present	bell
Christmas tree	Santa
star	wreath
candy cane	reindeer
stocking	ornament

Martin Luther King, Jr., Award

Activity: Martin Luther King, Jr., Award
Skills: critical thinking, cooperative learning—partners

Materials Needed

- duplicating master of "I Have a Dream" pledge
- pencils
- duplicating master of "I Have a Dream" award
- crayons
- posters and books of Martin Luther King

How to Make This Activity

- Duplicate both masters—one of each per child—and place in the folder.
- Place the folder at the center with posters and books of Martin Luther King, Jr.

Teacher's Directions:

- Use this holiday to discuss the values that Martin Luther King was trying to communicate. You may wish to read *Happy, Birthday, Martin Luther King* (by Jean Marzollo, Scholastic, Inc., 1993) to the children for background.
- This is a good time to role-play various types of conflict to help children solve problems.
- Discuss and demonstrate a variety of conflict situations.
- Discuss the "I Have a Dream" pledge and the award.
- Show the children how to memorize the pledge.
- Demonstrate how to find a partner and practice saying the pledge to each other.
- Show the pledge award when the pledge is memorized.
- The award may be colored when it is memorized.
- Younger children will need a volunteer to help them remember the pledge.

Children's Directions

1. Find a partner.
2. Read the pledge to yourself until you know it.
3. Sign the pledge.
4. Say the pledge aloud to a partner.
5. Take turns repeating the pledge.
6. Take the pledge award, write your name on it, and color it.
7. Take your pledge and award home and say the pledge to your family.

Labels

> **Activity:** Martin Luther King, Jr., Award
> **Skills:** critical thinking, cooperative
> learning—partners

(Tab)

> **Theme:** Winter Holidays
> **Activity:** Martin Luther King, Jr., Award
> **Skills:** critical thinking, cooperative
> learning—partners

(Folder)

Award

I have a dream . . .

dream

Name _____

Pledge

"I Have a Dream"

I promise to try to find ways to solve problems without fighting and arguing.

I promise to look at people with understanding and appreciation.

Groundhog Pop-Up

Activity: Groundhog Pop-Up
Skill: making shadows

Materials Needed

- flannelboard and flannelboard story
- Dixie cups—one per child
- duplicating master of groundhogs
- 9" by 12" (23 cm by 30 cm) construction paper
- overhead projector
- razor blade or sharp knife and scissors
- Popsicle sticks—one per child
- glue sticks, crayons, and contact paper

How to Make This Activity

- Make up the flannelboard story.
- Duplicate the groundhog master and cut out one groundhog per child.
- Make one slit in the bottom of each Dixie cup.
- Make a completed groundhog, glue it in the folder, and cover with contact paper.
- Set up the overhead projector to focus on a blank wall and place all the materials at the center.

Teacher Directions

- Read the flannelboard story to the children. Then discuss Groundhog Day and the legend.
- Discuss what shadows are and how to make shadows with the overhead projector (see the samples).
- Show children how to manipulate the flannelboard story.
- Demonstrate how to make the groundhog and the Dixie cup "hole."
    1. Cut out and color the groundhog and glue it to the end of a Popsicle stick.
    2. Slip the other end of the Popsicle stick through the slit in the Dixie cup; the groundhog can then be moved up and down in the cup, "his hole."

Self-Checking Feature: *The children may look in the folder to see a sample of the groundhog.*

Children's Directions

1. Tell the story using the flannelboard and pictures.
2. Turn on the projector and make shadows.
3. Take one cup, stick, and groundhog.
4. Cut out the ground hog and color it.
5. Glue the groundhog to the stick.
6. Place the stick in the cup and make the groundhog go up and down in "his hole."

Labels

> **Activity:** Groundhog Pop-Up
> **Skill:** making shadows
(Tab)

> **Theme:** Winter Holidays
> **Activity:** Groundhog Pop-Up
> **Skill:** making shadows

(Folder)

Groundhog Master

Dixie Cup

Cut a slit in the bottom of the cup.

Glue green construction paper around the cup for a grassy look if desired.

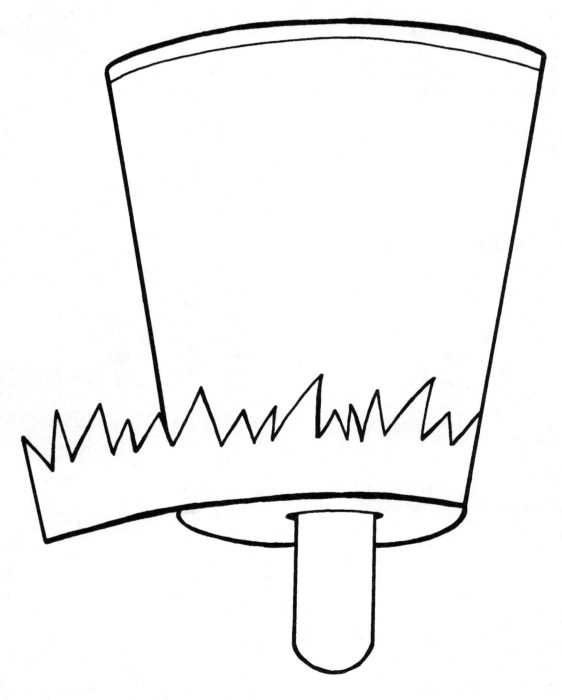

Shadow Ideas

Rabbit's Head

Duck's Head

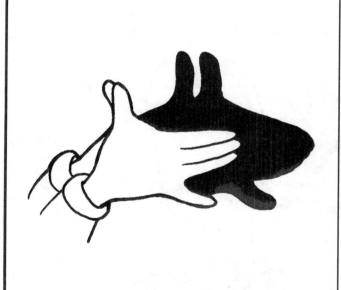

Dog's Head

Flying Bird

Groundhog Flannelboard Story

(Place Papa, Mama, and babies on the flannelboard.)

Mama and Papa Groundhog were standing deep in their underground home, talking and watching their two babies all curled up asleep.

"Oh, Papa," said Mama, "The children were so excited about your trip up, up, up into the outside world tomorrow that they finally fell asleep."

"Well, Mama, if I see my shadow tomorrow, we'll know we have six more weeks of winter. Then I'll come back down, and we'll curl up and sleep for six more weeks.

(Clear off the groundhogs. Put up the tunnel.)

(Papa Groundhog speaks.)

"Every year I have to crawl up this tunnel to see if it is cloudy or sunny. We groundhogs have been doing this for years and years and years just so people will know if spring is coming."

(Have Papa slip down the hole a little.)

"Oops, I'm out of climbing practice. Four months in hibernation and my muscles won't work."

(Let Papa get to the opening and peek over the edge. Place either the sun or the cloud on the flannelboard.)

If the cloud is put up, Papa says . . .

"Wow! Six more weeks of winter. I'll hurry back and tell Mama we can get back to sleep."

If the sun is put up, Papa sees his shadow and says . . .

"Oh good, we'll have spring now. I'll go back and get the family."

Flannelboard Master

Papa Groundhog

Baby Groundhogs

Mama Groundhog

Flannelboard Master (cont.)

Clouds

Shadow

Flannelboard Master *(cont.)*

Sun

Abraham Lincoln's Log Cabin

Activity: Abraham Lincoln's Log Cabin
Skills: art experience, small-muscle control, tasting

Materials Needed

- Abraham Lincoln books and posters (Check the school library.)
- small milk cartons—one per child (Check the school cafeteria.)
- large box of pretzel sticks (amount depends on size of the class.)
- containers to place the pretzels in—two
- glue or glue sticks
- ballpoint pen

How to Make This Activity

- Set the posters and books at a center.
- Place milk cartons, glue, and pretzels at the center.
- Place the folder with directions at the center.

Teacher's Directions

- Read stories and discuss Abraham Lincoln and his early life growing up in a log cabin.
- Demonstrate how to make a pretend log cabin:
  - ✓ Take one milk carton.
  - ✓ Place glue on the carton.
  - ✓ Glue on pretzel sticks (logs) around the entire milk carton. Glue them next to each other.
  - ✓ Put the child's name on the bottom of the carton with a ball point pen.
- Discuss eating a few pretzels and deciding how they taste: sweet, sour, or salty.

Children's Directions

1. Take one milk carton.
2. Put glue around the milk carton.
3. Place pretzel sticks around the carton and glue them close together.
4. Eat some pretzels. Are they sweet, sour, or salty?

Labels

> **Activity:** Abraham Lincoln's Log Cabin
> **Skills:** art experience, small-muscle control, tasting

(Tab)

> **Theme:** Winter Holidays
> **Activity:** Abraham Lincoln's Log Cabin
> **Skills:** art experience, small-muscle control, tasting

(Folder)

Sample for Folder

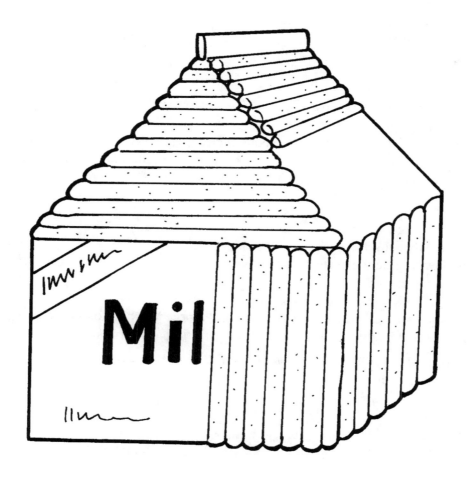

Glue on stick pretzels.

President Washington Flag

Activity: President Washington Flag
Skills: writing, art experience

Materials Needed

- 9" by 12" (23 cm by 30 cm) white construction paper
- duplicating master of George Washington
- duplicating master of flag
- books and posters about George Washington
- glue sticks
- crayons
- contact paper

How to Make This Activity

- Duplicate the master of George Washington—one picture of Washington per child, cut into a square to fit the flag square.
- Duplicate the master of the flag on white construction paper—one flag per child.
- Complete one flag with writing samples, glue in the folder, and place contact paper over the flag.
- Place all materials at a center, counter, or table.

Teacher's Directions

- Read stories of George Washington, show pictures, and discuss his life.
- Discuss the first flag with the stars and 13 stripes.
- Demonstrate how to glue the picture of George Washington in the square on the flag paper (where the stars would normally go).
- Demonstrate how to color seven red alternating stripes.
- Demonstrate how to write words or phrases about George Washington on the white stripes.
- Younger children may just make the flag without printing any words or phrases.

Self-Checking Feature: The children may look in the folder to see how the flag is completed and to see the writing samples on the flag.

Children's Directions

1. Take one flag paper and one George Washington square.
2. Glue the George Washington square to the small square on the flag.
3. Color seven red alternating stripes.
4. Print words about George Washington on the white stripes.

Labels

> **Activity:** President Washington Flag
> **Skills:** writing, art experience   (Tab)

> **Theme:** Winter Holidays
> **Activity:** President Washington Flag
> **Skills:** writing, art experience      (Folder)

Washington Master

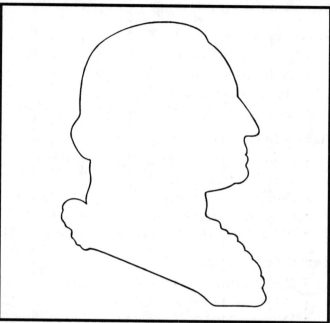

Theme: *Winter Holidays*   *Activity: President Washington Flag*

Flag Master

Sample for Folder

Sample Words and Phrases

- George Washington

- First president of the United States

- Father of our country

- Cherry tree

- Ax

- Valley Forge

- Soldier

- Surveyor

- Virginia

- Revolutionary War

- Mount Vernon

Valentine Heart Puzzle

Valentine's Day presents many options to discuss, such as friends, sharing, caring, cooperative learning activities, etc. Bring in posters and stories showing the many activities surrounding Valentine's Day. The children will love to be involved in art projects such as Valentine's bags, cards for their families and friends, special handprints, paintings of their friends, etc.

Activity: Valentine Heart Puzzle
Skills: matching capitals to small letters, matching numbers to sets

Materials Needed

- duplicating masters of A–Z heart puzzle
- laminate or contact paper
- duplicating masters of 0–10 number puzzle
- tagboard and resealable plastic bags
- 9" by 12" (23 cm by 30 cm) red, white, or pink construction paper
- glue and scissors

How to Make This Activity

- Duplicate masters of A–Z heart puzzle or 0–10 number puzzle on construction paper and glue each sheet to tagboard. Laminate or cover with contact paper.
- Cut apart and place each activity in a plastic bag; place the bag in a folder.
- Print the capital letter and small alphabets in the folder for the children to check their work.
- Print number and sets in a separate folder.
- Cover printing with contact paper to prevent smearing.

Teacher's Directions

- Demonstrate how to match capitals and small letters and how to match the numbers and sets.
- Other options for this activity of heart puzzles:
  - ✔ putting words together: friend • ship   sweet • heart
  - ✔ putting sentences together: *I like you. Friends are special.*

Self-Checking Feature: *Children may check the folder to match puzzle letters or numbers and sets.*

Children's Directions

1. Match the capital letter with the correct small letter.
2. Match the number to the correct set.

Labels

> **Activity:** Valentine Heart Puzzle
> **Skills:** matching capitals to small letters,
> matching numbers to sets

(Tab)

> **Theme:** Winter Holidays
> **Activity:** Valentine Heart Puzzle
> **Skills:** matching capitals to small letters,
> matching numbers to sets

(Folder)

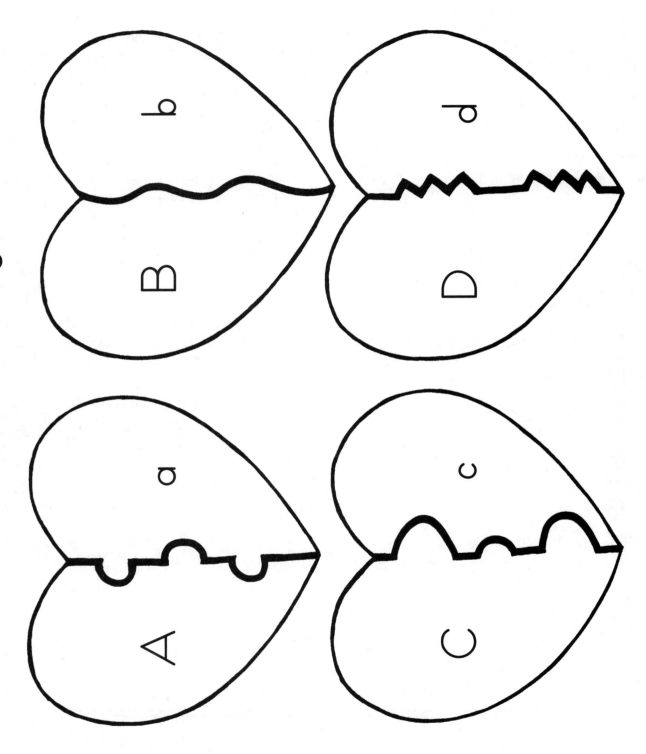

Letter Matching *(cont.)*

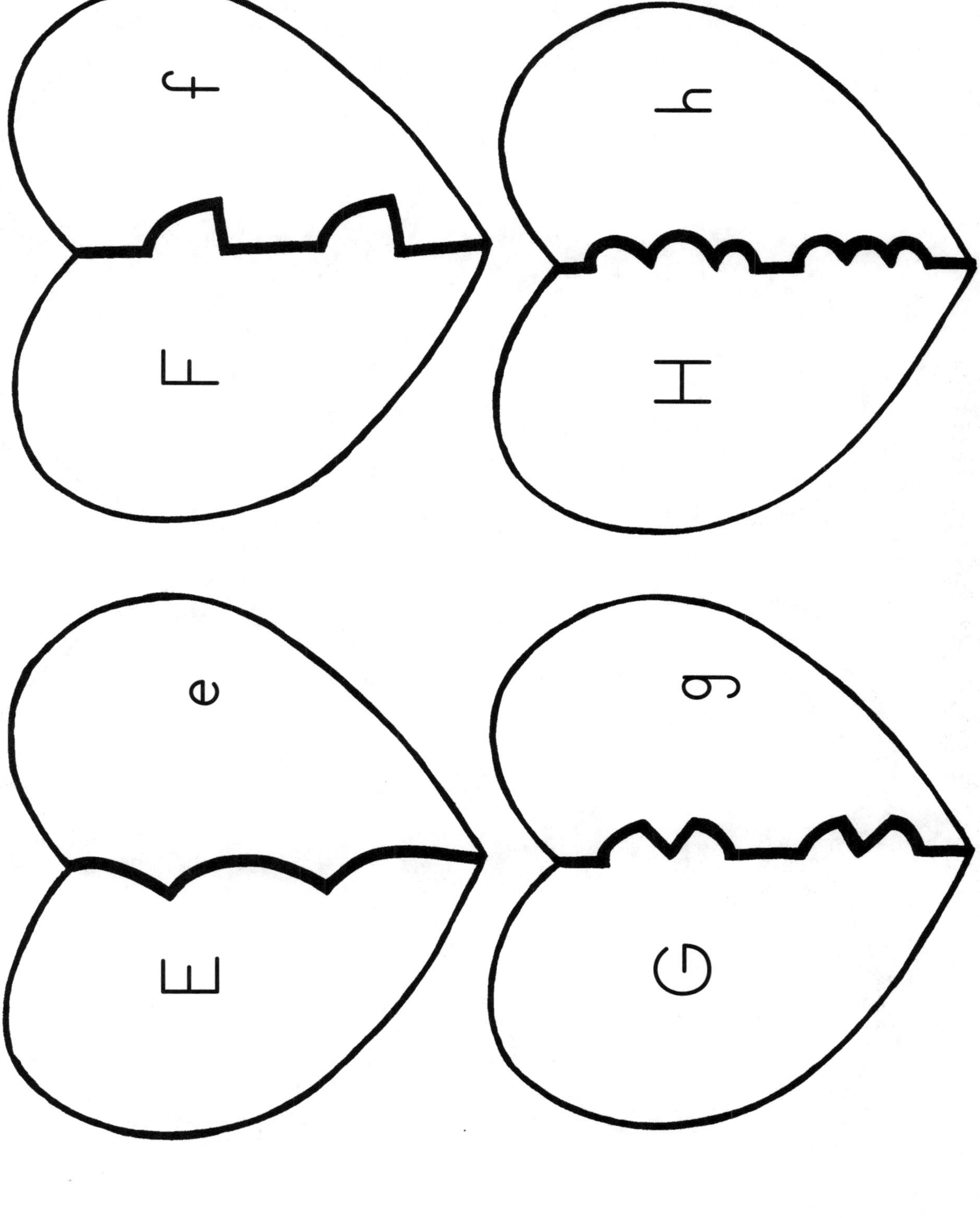

f

F

h

H

e

E

g

G

Letter Matching (cont.)

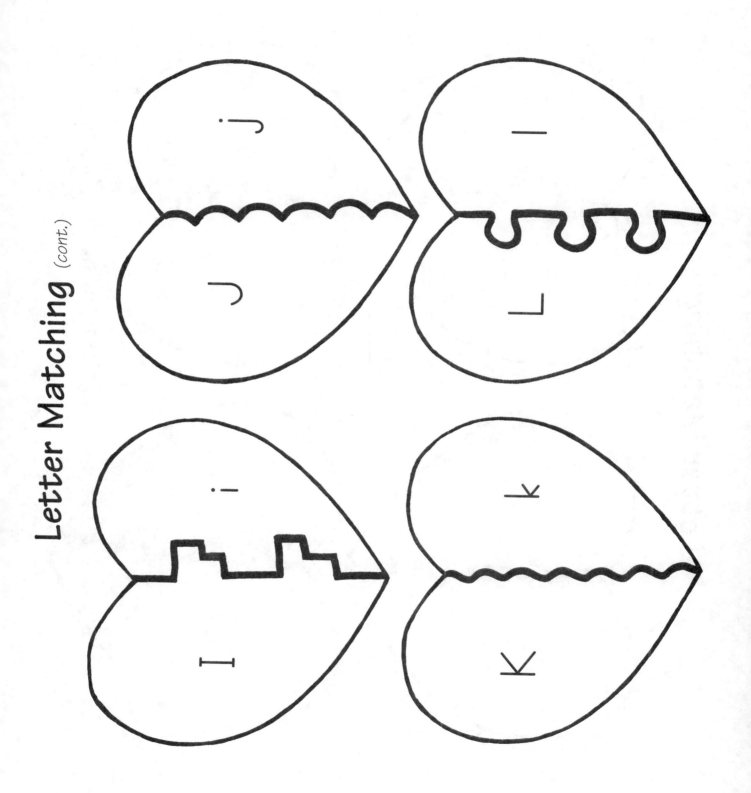

Letter Matching (cont.)

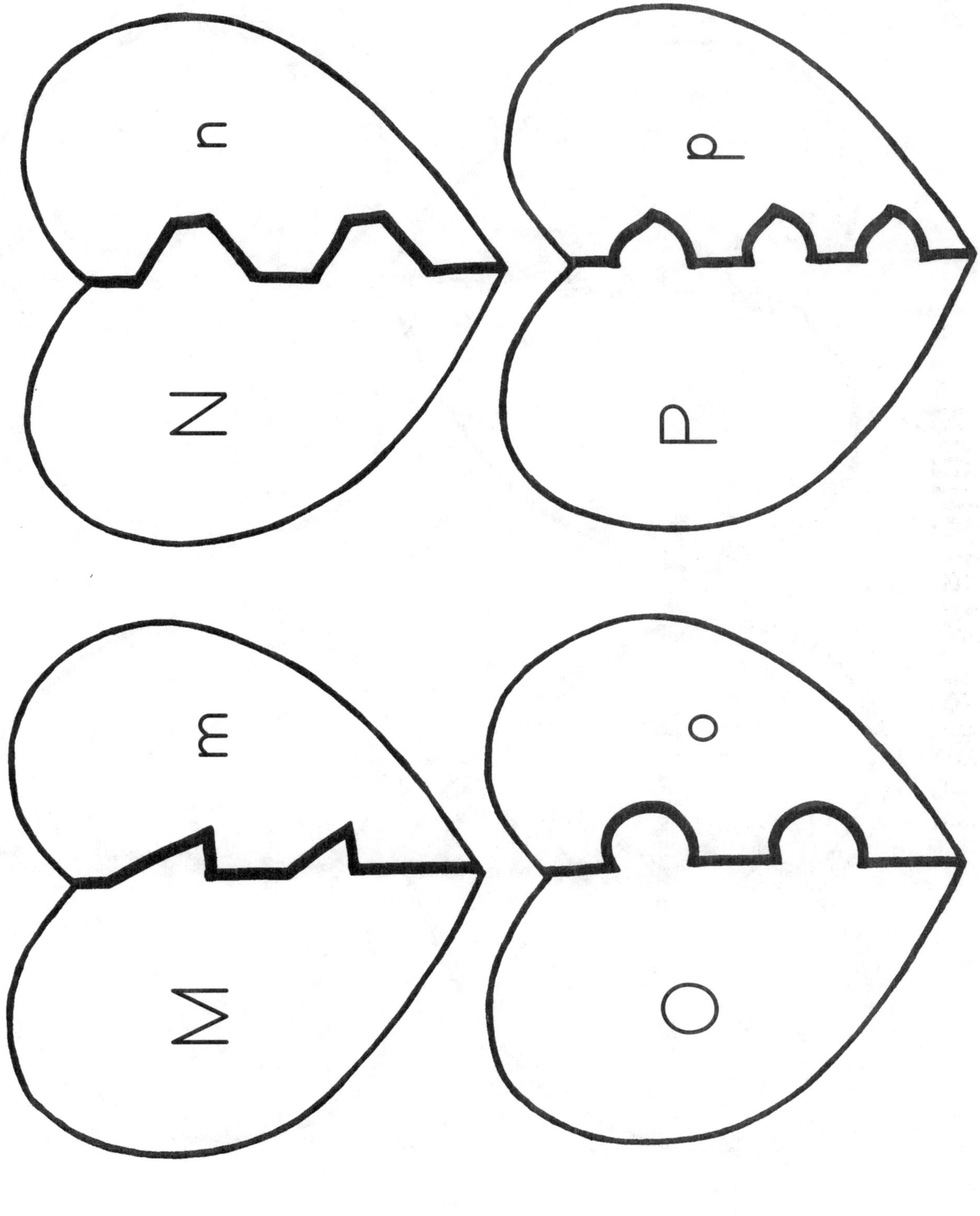

n

N

P

p

m

M

o

O

Letter Matching *(cont.)*

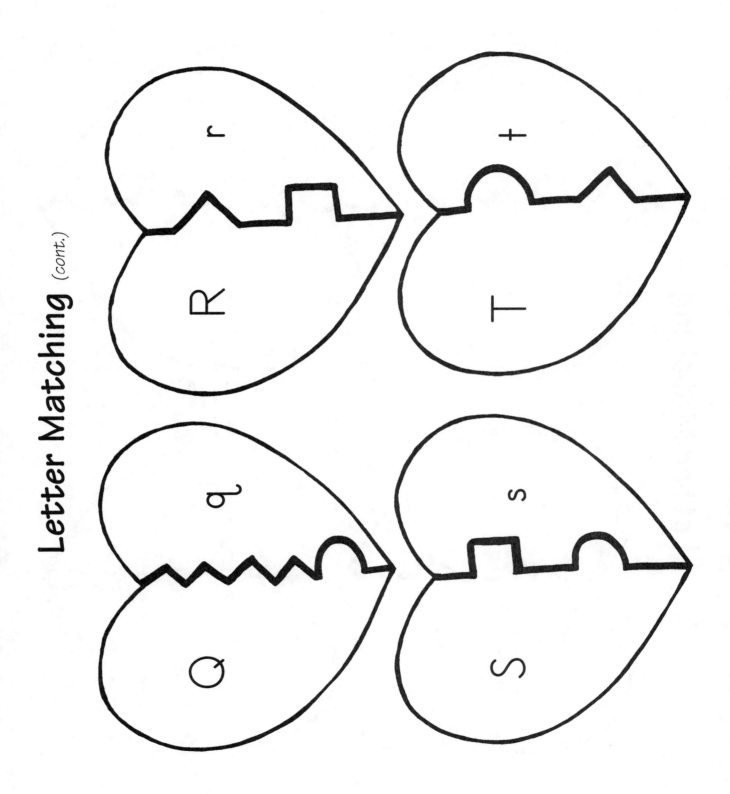

Letter Matching (cont.)

V

V

x

X

u

U

w

W

Letter Matching *(cont.)*

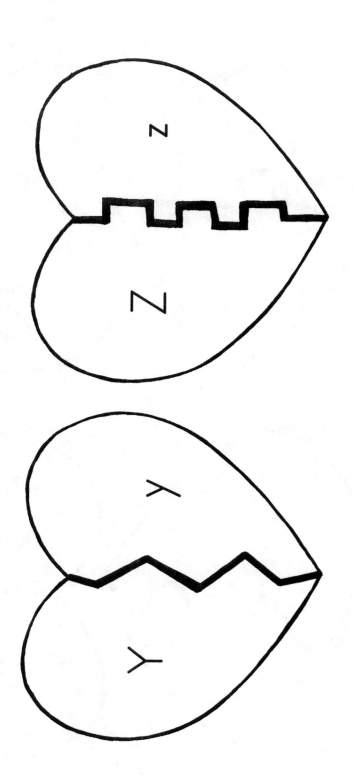

Numbers and Sets Matching

Numbers and Sets Matching (cont.)

Numbers and Sets Matching (cont.)

Numbers and Sets Matching (cont.)

Numbers and Sets Matching (cont.)

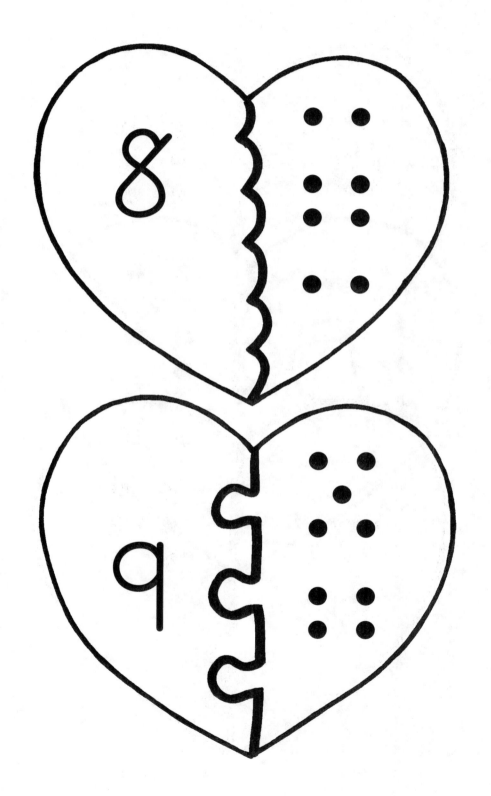

Numbers and Sets Matching (cont.)

Missing Valentine Heart Numbers

Activity: Missing Valentine Heart Numbers
Skill: number sequencing

Materials Needed

- 9" by 12" (23 cm by 30 cm) red, pink, and white construction paper
- tagboard
- duplicating master for the folder
- markers and crayons
- small rags
- duplicating masters of missing numbers
- laminate or contact paper
- resealable plastic bags
- glue

How to Make This Activity

- Duplicate masters—each one on a different color of construction paper.
- Glue each duplicated construction paper to tagboard.
- Laminate or cover with contact paper.
- Place each sheet in its own plastic bag with a crayon and rag for wiping off the numbers.
- Duplicate the master for the folder, glue to the folder, and cover with contact paper.

Teacher's Directions

- Show the children where the correct number order may be found in the folder.
- Demonstrate how to fill in the missing numbers with the crayon.
- Demonstrate how to wipe off the numbers with the rag.

Self-Checking Feature: The children may look in the folder for the correct number order.

Children's Directions

1. Take one plastic bag.
2. Fill in the missing numbers with the crayon.
3. Check your work.
4. Wipe off the numbers when you are finished.
5. Put everything back in the bag.

Labels

Activity: Missing Valentine Heart Numbers
Skill: number sequencing

(Tab)

Theme: Winter Holidays
Activity: Missing Valentine Heart Numbers
Skill: number sequencing

(Folder)

Valentine Heart Numbers Master

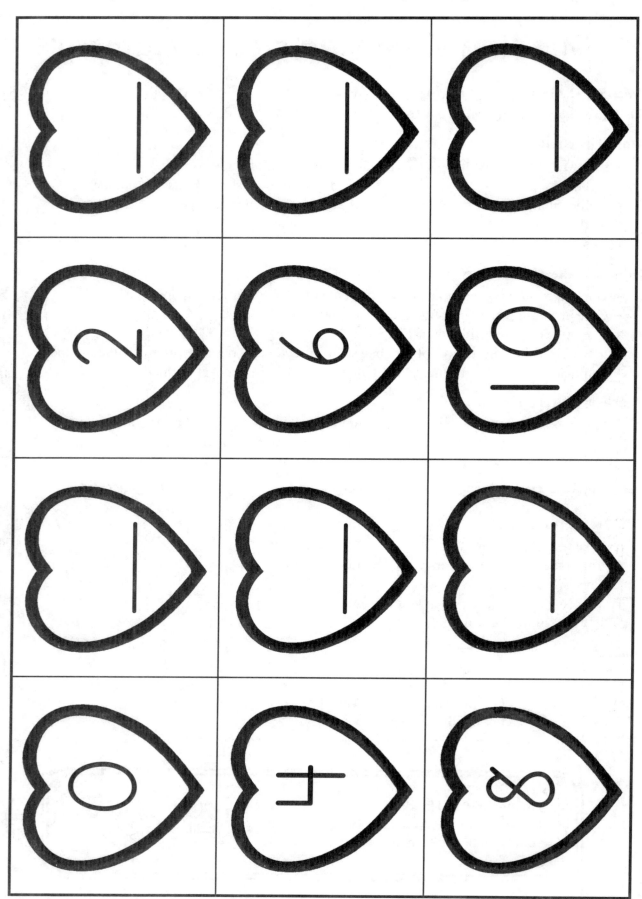

Valentine Heart Numbers Master (cont.)

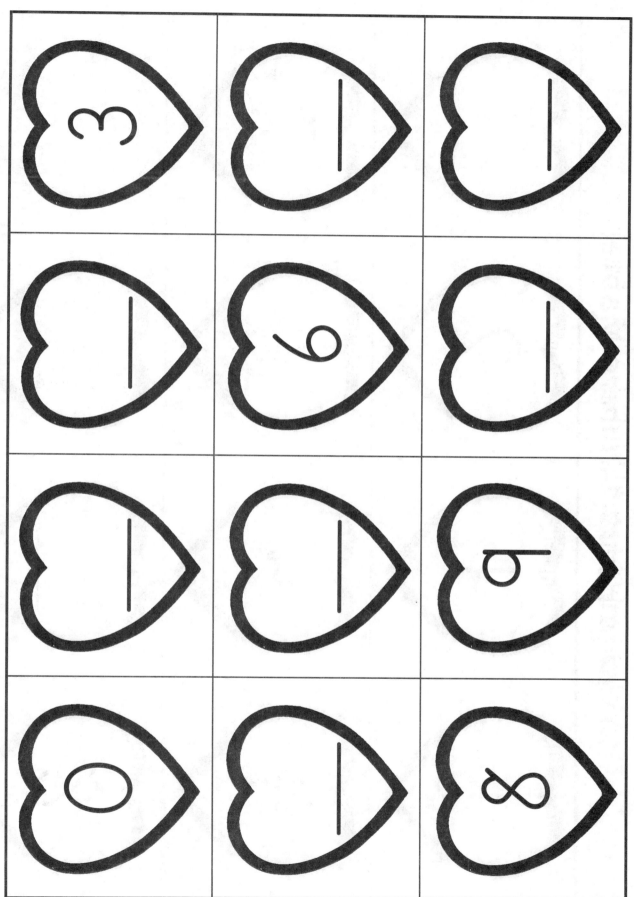

Valentine Heart Numbers Master (cont.)

Sample for Folder
(Glue on in order for self−checking.)

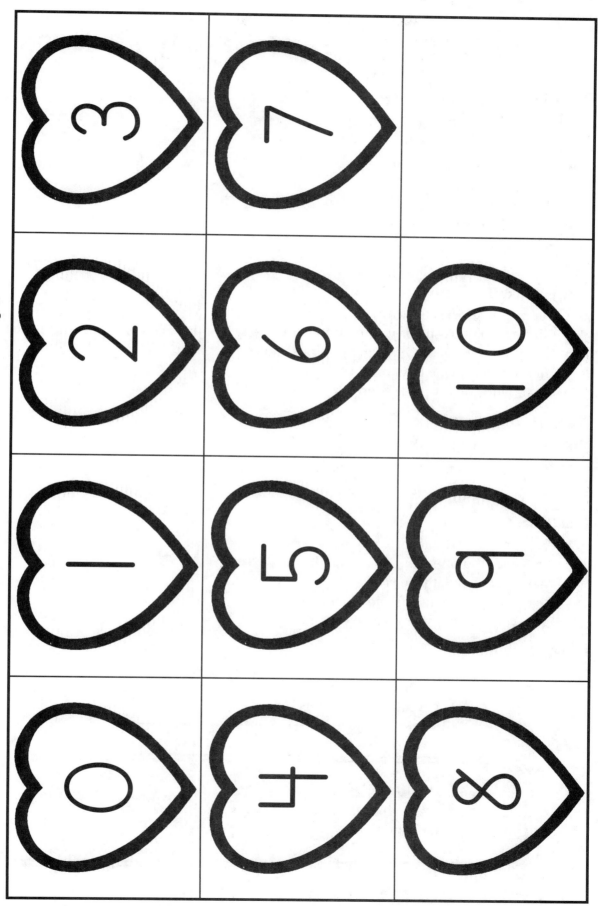

Valentine Heart Candy Patterns

Activity: Valentine Heart Candy Patterns
Skill: color patterns

Materials Needed

- heart candies (available at the grocery store)
- strips of manila paper
- glue sticks
- resealable plastic bags
- markers or crayons
- contact paper

How to Make This Activity

- Cut manila paper into strips.
- Fill four small plastic bags with heart candies—two or three colors of candies in each bag.
- Duplicate masters for the folder pattern samples.
- Glue samples in the folder and color the hearts.
- Cover with contact paper.

Teacher's Directions

Demonstrate many varieties of patterns.

Self-Checking Feature: *The children may look in the folder for pattern ideas if they are unable to think of a pattern.*

Children's Directions

1. Take one bag of candy.
2. Take one strip of paper.
3. Make a pattern with the candy.
4. Read your pattern to a friend to check it.
5. Glue your candy pattern on the paper.

Labels

> **Activity:** Valentine Heart Candy Patterns
> **Skill:** color patterns

(Tab)

> **Theme:** Winter Holidays
> **Activity:** Valentine Heart Candy Patterns
> **Skill:** color patterns

(Folder)

Samples for Folder
(Color the hearts.)

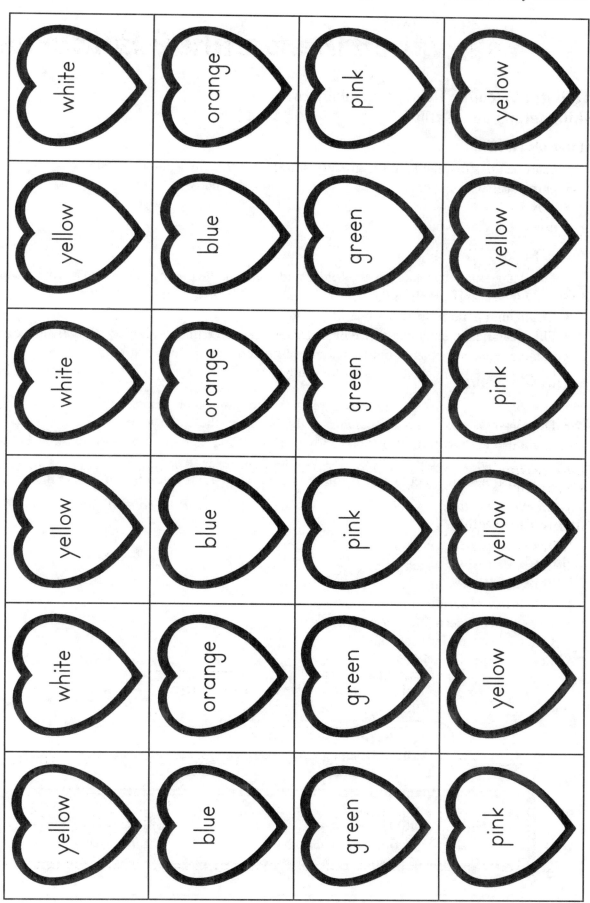

Valentine Candy Graph

Activity: Valentine Candy Graph
Skills: graphing, sorting, counting, color words

Materials Needed
- heart candies (available at the grocery store)
- graph masters
- crayons
- glue
- three resealable plastic bags
- pencils
- contact paper

How to Make This Activity
- Duplicate smaller master for the folder and color the hearts the correct color for self-checking.
- Glue the sample graph in the folder and cover with clear contact paper.
- Duplicate the larger graph—one per child.
- Place candies in each bag—five or six colors in each bag but not more than five of each color.
- Place graphs and bags in the folder and place at a center along with crayons and pencils.

Teacher's Directions
- Demonstrate how to sort the candies in a bag into the same colors.
- Demonstrate how to lay the candies in the boxes by the color words.
- Demonstrate how to lift up each candy (one at a time) and color a heart the same color as the candy. Put each candy back in the bag after a heart is colored.
- Demonstrate how to count each colored heart and write the number in the small boxes.

Self-Checking Feature: The children may look in the folder for the color if they are unable to read the color word.

Children's Directions
1. Take one bag.
2. Sort the candies into the same colors.
3. Lay the candies by the correct color word.
4. Color a heart under each candy.
5. Put the candy back in the bag.
6. Count each candy heart color and write the number in the box.

Labels

> **Activity:** Valentine Candy Graph
> **Skills:** graphing, sorting, counting, color words

(Tab)

> **Theme:** Winter Holidays
> **Activity:** Valentine Candy Graph
> **Skills:** graphing, sorting, counting, color words

(Folder)

Sample for Folder

(Color the hearts the correct color for self-checking folder.)

We graphed and counted candy hearts.

♡ Pink						
♡ Yellow						
♡ Green						
♡ Blue						
♡ Purple						
♡ Orange						

Valentine Candy Graph

We graphed and counted candy hearts.

♥ Pink						
♥ Yellow						
♥ Green						
♥ Blue						
♥ Purple						
♥ Orange						

Saint Patrick's Green Book

Activity: Saint Patrick's Green Book
Skill: creative writing

Materials Needed

- books and pictures about Saint Patrick's Day
- duplicating master of "Green is . . ." paper
- contact paper
- small Saint Patrick's Day pictures for the folder (Small stickers could be used.)
- light green copier paper
- pencils
- crayons
- marker

How to Make This Activity

- Duplicate the "Green is . . ." master—one per child.
- Write Saint Patrick's Day words in the folder and place a corresponding picture by each word.
- Cover with contact paper.
- Place all materials at the center with the Saint Patrick's books and posters.

Teacher's Directions

- Discuss Saint Patrick's Day—the legend and the country of Ireland.
- Discuss words such as *leprechaun, lucky, Irish, green, rainbow, gold, four-leaf clover,* etc.
- Demonstrate the "Green is . . ." paper:
    —Decide what is green.
    —Write the word or phrase you choose.
    —Color a picture about Saint Patrick's Day.
- Save the children's papers for a class book or to put in their journals or portfolios.

Self-Checking Feature: The children may look in the folder to find words and pictures about Saint Patrick's Day.

Children's Directions

1. Take one "Green is . . ." paper.
2. Decide what is green and write it on the paper.
3. Color a picture about what you wrote.

Labels

> **Activity:** Saint Patrick's Green Book
> **Skill:** creative writing

(Tab)

> **Theme:** Winter Holidays
> **Activity:** Saint Patrick's Green Book
> **Skill:** creative writing

(Folder)

Sample for Folder

- Saint Patrick's Day

- leprechaun

- rainbow

- shamrock

- Ireland

- pot of gold

- green

- Irish

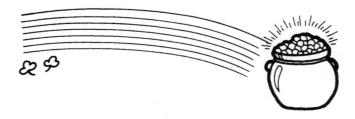

Saint Patrick's Green Book Master

Green is _____

_____

_____

Bunny Finds His Egg

Easter is a theme which is great fun for children. It may be extended to include spring, growing things, baby animals, eggs, the farm, etc., using a variety of songs, videos, posters, and books available.

Activity: Bunny Finds His Egg
Skills: matching capitals to lowercase, matching letters to beginning sounds, and matching numbers to sets

Materials Needed

- duplicating master of egg and bunnies for
  —capital to lowercase letters
  —letters to beginning sounds
  —numbers to sets
- markers and glue

- small stickers (available at grocery or teacher supply store)
- tagboard and laminate or contact paper
- resealable plastic bags—three
- 9" by 12" (23 cm by 30 cm) construction paper—three colors

How to Make This Activity

- Duplicate the masters on construction paper—each set different to color code the activities.
- Glue the duplicated paper on tagboard, laminate, and cut out the bunnies and eggs.
- Put each set in a plastic bag and label each bag.
- Print in the folder for self-checking:
  —capital to lowercase (A a, B b, etc.)
  —letters to beginning sounds (*a* apple, *b* basket, etc.)
  —numbers to sets (0, 1 *, 2 * *)
- Use stickers to represent sets or markers to draw the sets.

Teacher's Directions

- Demonstrate how to match the bunnies and eggs in each activity.
Self-Checking Feature: *The children may look in the folder to find the answers or to check their work.*

Children's Directions

1. Match the capital letter to the lowercase letter.
2. Match the letter to the correct beginning sound picture.
3. Match the number to the correct set.

Labels

> **Activity:** Bunny Finds His Egg
> **Skills:** matching capitals to lowercase letters, matching letters to beginning sounds, matching numbers to sets

(Tab)

> **Theme:** Easter
> **Activity:** Bunny Finds His Egg
> **Skills:** matching capitals to lowercase letters, matching letters to beginning sounds, matching numbers to sets

(Folder)

Matching Letters to Beginning Sounds

Matching Letters to Beginning Sounds *(cont.)*

Matching Letters to
Beginning Sounds (cont.)

Matching Letters to
Beginning Sounds *(cont.)*

Matching Letters to
Beginning Sounds (cont.)

Matching Letters to
Beginning Sounds *(cont.)*

Matching Letters to
Beginning Sounds *(cont.)*

Matching Letters to
Beginning Sounds *(cont.)*

Matching Letters to
Beginning Sounds *(cont.)*

Matching Letters to
Beginning Sounds (cont.)

Matching Letters to
Beginning Sounds *(cont.)*

Matching Letters to
Beginning Sounds *(cont.)*

310

Matching Letters to
Beginning Sounds *(cont.)*

Matching Capitals to Lowercase

Matching Capitals to Lowercase *(cont.)*

Matching Capitals to Lowercase (cont.)

Matching Capitals to Lowercase (cont.)

Matching Capitals to Lowercase (cont.)

Matching Capitals to Lowercase *(cont.)*

Matching Capitals to Lowercase *(cont.)*

Matching Capitals to Lowercase (cont.)

Matching Capitals to Lowercase *(cont.)*

Matching Capitals to Lowercase (cont.)

Matching Capitals to Lowercase *(cont.)*

Matching Capitals to Lowercase *(cont.)*

Matching Capitals to Lowercase *(cont.)*

Matching Numbers to Sets: 0-10

Matching Numbers to Sets: 0-10 (cont.)

Matching Numbers to Sets: 0-10 *(cont.)*

Matching Numbers to Sets: 0-10 (cont.)

Matching Numbers to Sets: 0-10 (cont.)

Matching Numbers to Sets: 0-10 (cont.)

Bunny Number Book

Activity: Bunny Number Book
Skills: tracing numbers, matching sets to numbers, learning number songs

Materials Needed

- duplicating masters of numbers 0–10
- markers
- stapler
- pencils
- crayons
- small resealable plastic bags
- small Easter stickers, animal stickers, spring stickers (available at a teacher supply store, variety store, grocery store)

How to Make This Activity

- Duplicate the masters from 0–10 (one per child).
- Staple each set together to make a 0–10 book for each child.
- For the folder sample: Print each number and place the correct number of stickers by the number. Cover with contact paper. Markers may be used to draw the sets instead of stickers.
- Place small stickers in plastic bags.
- Place number books, folder, stickers, and crayons at a center.

Teacher's Directions

- Review the number songs.
- Demonstrate how to trace the numbers and sing the song to the tune of "Jimmy Crack Corn."
- The children may use a pencil or crayon to trace the numbers.
- Demonstrate how to put on the correct number of stickers for the number (or to draw the set with a pencil).

Self-Checking Feature: The children may look in the folder to check the number and sets.

Children's Directions

1. Take one book.
2. Trace the number on each page.
3. Sing the number song as you trace the number.
4. Put on the correct number of stickers for each number

Labels

> **Activity:** Bunny Number Book
> **Skills:** tracing numbers, matching sets to numbers, learning number songs

(Tab)

> **Theme:** Easter
> **Activity:** Bunny Number Book
> **Skills:** tracing numbers, matching sets to numbers, learning number songs

(Folder)

The Number Song
(Sing to the tune of "Jimmy Crack Corn.")

Make a circle round and round,
Make a circle round and round,
Make a circle round and round,
To make the number O.

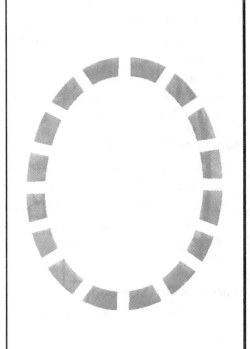

Start at the top and come straight down,
Start at the top and come straight down,
Start at the top and come straight down,
To make the number 1.

The Number Song *(cont.)*

Around and back on the railroad track,
Around and back on the railroad track,
Around and back on the railroad track,
To make the number 2.

Around we go and around again,
Around we go and around again,
Around we go and around again,
To make the number 3.

The Number Song (cont.)

Down and across and cut it in half,
Down and across and cut it in half,
Down and across and cut it in half,
To make the number 4.

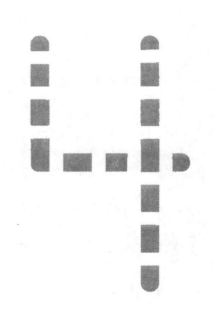

Down and around and give it a hat,
Down and around and give it a hat,
Down and around and give it a hat,
To make the number 5.

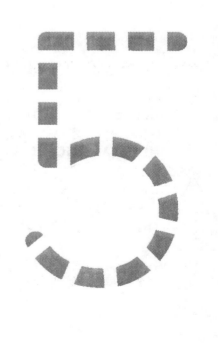

The Number Song *(cont.)*

Down we go and then around,
Down we go and then around,
Down we go and then around,
To make the number 6.

Across the top and down from
heaven,
Across the top and down from
heaven,
Across the top and down from
heaven,
To make the number 7.

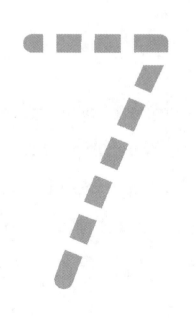

The Number Song *(cont.)*

Make an S and go straight home,
Make an S and go straight home,
Make an S and go straight home,
To make the number 8.

Make a balloon and give it a stick,
Make a balloon and give it a stick,
Make a balloon and give it a stick,
To make the number 9.

The Number Song *(cont.)*

Make a 1 and then a zero,

Make a 1 and then a zero,

Make a 1 and then a zero,

To make the number 10.

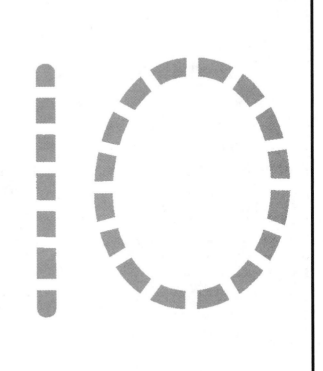

Bunny Number Book

Name _____

My Easter Handful Book

Activity: My Easter Handful Book
Skill: estimating

Materials Needed

- duplicating master of My Easter Handful Book and four resealable plastic bags
- pencils, stapler, and scissors
- four Easter items small enough to fit in a child's hand—for example, small ducks, small bunnies, small plastic eggs, jelly beans (available at a grocery or teacher supply store)

How to Make This Activity

- Duplicate Handful Book master—cover page and two copies of "I Guessed . . ." master per child.
- Cut on the lines and staple the books together. Each child will have a cover page and four pages in his or her book.
- Place several of the Easter items in the plastic bags, each type in a different bag.
- Place the books, plastic bags, and the folder with the directions at a center.

Teacher's Directions

- This activity may be adapted to any theme.
- A volunteer would be helpful for this activity.
- Demonstrate how to take a handful of the items in one bag.
- Demonstrate how to estimate how many there are without counting them.
- Show the children where to write their guesses on the paper.
- Demonstrate how to count how many items there are.
- Show the children where to write what they counted.
- Demonstrate returning everything to the plastic bag before taking a new bag.

Children's Directions

1. Take one Handful Book.
2. Take one bag.
3. Take one handful and guess how many there are.
4. Write your guess.
5. Count how many there are in your hand.
6. Write the number you counted.
7. Put everything back in the bag and take a new bag.
8. Color your book when you are finished.

Labels

> **Activity:** My Easter Handful Book
> **Skill:** estimating

(Tab)

> **Theme:** Easter
> **Activity:** My Easter Handful Book
> **Skill:** estimating

(Folder)

My Easter Handful Book

My

Easter Handful

Book

Name _____

My Easter Handful Book *(cont.)*

I guessed _____.

I counted _____.

I guessed _____.

I counted _____.

Easter Bunny, Easter Bunny

Activity: Easter Bunny, Easter Bunny
Skills: color word recognition, writing, reading words

Materials Needed

- duplicating masters of Easter Bunny book
- pencils
- contact paper
- markers
- color words printed in the folder
- stapler

How to Make This Activity

- Duplicate copies of Easter Bunny book—one set per child.
- Staple each book together.
- For the folder sample:
  —print the color words in their colors on one side of the folder.
  —print the color words in black on the other side of the folder.
  —cover the words with contact paper.
- Place children's books and the folder at a center.

Teacher's Directions

- Review other books the children know that are similar to this book—e.g., *Brown Bear, Brown Bear,* and *Teddy Bear, Teddy Bear.*
- Demonstrate how to trace over the color words.
- Demonstrate how to read the words and turn the page to see what color to use.
- Remind the children how to look in the folder for help with the color words.
- A volunteer at this center could help with reading the words.

Self-Checking Feature: The children may look in the folder to find the color words.

Children's Directions

1. Take one Easter Bunny book.
2. Color the Easter Bunny.
3. Read the words and turn the page.
4. Read the color word.
5. Trace over the color word with a pencil.
6. Color the picture that color.

Labels

Activity: Easter Bunny, Easter Bunny
Skills: color word recognition, writing, reading words

(Tab)

Theme: Easter
Activity: Easter Bunny, Easter Bunny
Skills: color word recognition, writing, reading words

(Folder)

Easter Bunny Book

Easter Bunny, Easter Bunny,

What do you see?

Easter Bunny Book *(cont.)*

I see a _____ red _____ egg looking at me.

Red Egg, Red Egg,

What do you see?

Easter Bunny Book *(cont.)*

I see a <u>brown</u> basket looking at me.

Brown Basket, Brown Basket,

What do you see?

Easter Bunny Book (cont.)

I see _____green_____ grass looking at me.

Green Grass, Green Grass,

What do you see?

Easter Bunny Book (cont.)

I see a ___yellow___ chick looking at me.

Yellow Chick, Yellow Chick,

What do you see?

Easter Bunny Book (cont.)

I see ____blue____ jellybeans looking at me.

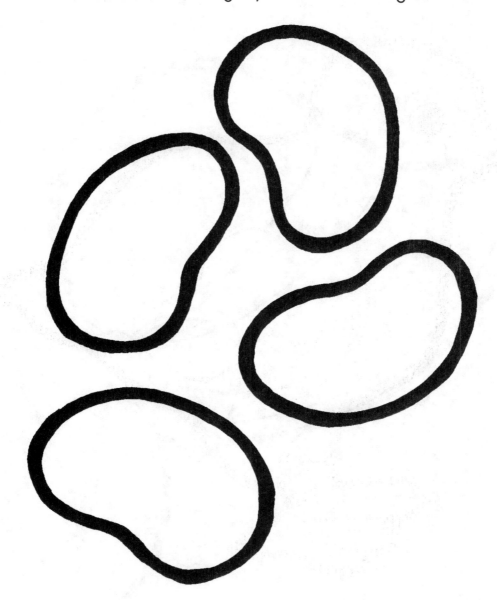

Blue Jellybeans, Blue Jellybeans,

What do you see?

Easter Bunny Book (cont.)

I see a _____purple_____ hat looking at me.

Purple Hat, Purple Hat

What do you see?

Easter Bunny Book (cont.)

I see a ______ butterfly looking at me.

Pink Butterfly, Pink Butterfly,

What do you see?

Easter Bunny Book *(cont.)*

I see an _orange_ flower looking at me.

Oh, how pretty all colors can be!

Activities Listed by Skills

Alphabet Recognition Skills
- ABC Feel and Guess 181
- ABC Follow Directions 182
- Alphabet Hopscotch 177
- Flannelboard Alphabet 179
- "Jack Be Nimble" 104

Alphabet Sequencing Skills
- Flannelboard Alphabet 179

Art Activities Skills
- Abraham Lincoln's Log Cabin 264
- Caterpillar Art 217
- Crystal Painting 139
- Groundhog Pop-Up 256
- President Washington Flag 266
- Turkey Fingerprint 248
- Word Caterpillar 219

Classification Skills
- How We Travel 106

Color Recognition Skills
- Apple Sorting 57
- Color Bead Patterns 29
- Lily Pads 18

Color Word Recognition Skills
- Apple Book 74
- Valentine Candy Graph 292
- Dinosaur Sorting 193
- Easter Bunny, Easter Bunny 341
- Lily Pads 18
- Teddy Bear, Teddy Bear 8

Cooperative Learning Skills
- ABC Feel and Guess 181
- Frog Count 156
- Hungry Caterpillar Sock Book 206
- Lily Pads 18
- Martin Luther King, Jr., Award 253
- The Worm and the Apple 80

Counting Skills
- Valentine Candy Graph 292
- Chocolate Chip Numbers 171
- Dinosaur Sorting 193
- Family Sizes 84
- Frog Count 156
- Number Beans 143
- Wrapping Paper Count 145

Creative Writing Skills
- Christmas Surprise 250
- Fossil Search 190
- Pilgrim or Indian? 232
- Saint Patrick's Green Book 295

Critical Thinking Skills
- Dinosaur Food 195
- Fossil Search 190
- Martin Luther King, Jr., Award 253

Estimation Skills
- Chocolate Chip Numbers 171
- My Easter Handful Book 338
- Snowman Guess 141
- Wrapping Paper Count 145

Eye-Hand Coordination Skills
- Going Places 116
- Shape Puzzles 35

Fine Motor Control Skills
- Abraham Lincoln's Log Cabin 264
- Caterpillar Art 217
- Frozen Pumpkin Squares 228
- Going Places 116
- Hidden Shapes 41
- M & M® Shapes 33
- Snowman Buttons 120
- Turkey Fingerprint 248

Following Directions Skills
- ABC Follow Directions 182
- Snowman Book 133

Graphing Skills
- Valentine Candy Graph 292
- Family Fun 86
- Indian or Pilgrim Graph 245
- Our Travel Graph 111
- Pumpkin Faces 226
- Shape Bus 38

Large Motor Control Skills
- Alphabet Hopscotch 177
- Lily Pads 18

Matching Skills
- ABC Feel and Guess (letters to beginning sounds) 181
- Bunny Finds His Egg (numbers to sets, letters to beginning sounds) 298
- Bunny Number Book (numbers to sets) 331

Activities Listed by Skills *(cont.)*

Matching Skills *(cont.)*
- Caterpillar Number Puzzle (numbers to numbers) 203
- Gingerbread Boys (colors) 24
- Valentine Heart Puzzle (numbers to sets, capitals to lowercase) 271
- "Jack Be Nimble" (letters to beginning sounds). 104
- Number Convoy (numbers to sets) 114
- "One, Two, Buckle My Shoe" (pictures to rhymes) 94
- Shape Puzzles (matching shapes) 35
- Snowman Buttons (numbers to sets). . . 120

Measurement Skills
- Crystal Painting 139
- Frozen Pumpkin Squares 228

Number Recognition Skills
- Caterpillar Number Puzzle 203
- Frog Count. 156
- Number Beans 143
- Number Clay 173
- "One, Two, Buckle My Shoe" 94

Number Sequencing Skills
- Apple Trees 61
- Caterpillar Number Puzzle 203
- "Jack and Jill" 98
- Missing Valentine Heart Numbers 285

Number Writing Skills
- Bunny Number Book (number songs). . 331
- Chocolate Chip Numbers 171
- Family Sizes 84
- Number Beans 143
- Number Clay 173
- "One, Two, Buckle My Shoe" 94
- Wrapping Paper Count 145

Oral Language and Vocabulary Development Skills
- "Hey Diddle, Diddle" 100
- "Humpty Dumpty" 96
- Hungry Caterpillar Sock Book 206
- "Jack and Jill" 98
- "Jack Be Nimble" 104
- "One, Two, Buckle My Shoe" 94
- "Pease Porridge" (opposites) 102
- Word Caterpillar 219
- Where Is the Turkey? (position words). 236
- Worm and the Apple (position words) . . 80

Patterns Skills
- Color Bead Patterns 29
- Valentine Heart Candy Patterns 290

Reading Words and Sentences Skills
- Easter Bunny, Easter Bunny 341
- Snowman Book 133

Science Activities Skills
- Abraham Lincoln's Log Cabin (tasting—sense perception) 264
- Butterfly Life Cycle 215
- Crystal Painting 139
- Groundhog Pop-Up 256
- Pumpkin Float 230

Sequencing Skills—Language Arts
- Families Do Things Together 89
- "Hey Diddle, Diddle" 100
- Pumpkin Sequencing 224
- Snowman Book 133
- Wormy Apples 46

Shape Recognition Skills
- Going Places 116
- Hidden Shapes 41
- M & M® Shapes 33
- Shape Bus 38

Size Recognition Skills
- Apple Sorting. 57
- "Humpty Dumpty" 96

Social Studies Activities Skills
- Family Sizes 84
- Martin Luther King, Jr., Award. 253

Sorting Skills
- Valentine Candy Graph 292
- Dinosaur Sorting 193
- Hidden Shapes 41

Visual Discrimination Skills
- Dinosaur Puzzles 200
- Gingerbread Boys 24
- Pumpkin Sequencing 224

Writing Skills
- Apple Book 74
- Easter Bunny, Easter Bunny 341
- Pilgrim or Indian? 232
- President Washington Flag 266
- Teddy Bear, Teddy Bear 8
- Word Caterpillar. 219

GOING OUT

GOING OUT

Veronica Zundel

HODDER AND STOUGHTON
LONDON SYDNEY AUCKLAND TORONTO

Ashleigh Brilliant Epigrams, Pot-Shots, and Brilliant Thoughts are
copyrighted and used by permission of the author, Ashleigh Brilliant, 117
West Valerio St, Santa Barbara, Cal. 93101 USA.

Bible quotations are from the New International Version unless otherwise
stated.

British Library Cataloguing in Publication Data

Zundel, Veronica
   Going Out.
   1. Relationships between men and women – Christian viewpoints
   I. Title
   261.8'35

   ISBN 0-340-42661-6

For Mum and Dad

who gave me a good example

Almost all the personal stories in this book are true, though names have been changed. To all those who agreed to be interviewed, many thanks for your frankness and insights; and apologies to any who recognise themselves and feel I have misrepresented them.

CONTENTS

Introduction   ix
1 Flushed and Blundering?   1
2 In the Beginning   14
3 O Brave New World   30
4 Take Your Partners   45
5 You and Me Babe—How About It?   59
6 Getting Somewhere   75
7 Love and War   89
8 Worlds Apart   105
9 You Do Things to Me   120
10 Handle with Care   134
11 Is This It?   149
12 Over and Out   165
Notes   173

INTRODUCTION

'What's going out got to do with Christianity?'

I got used to people asking that question when I told them I was writing this book. We hear endless sermons on marriage, and see shelves full of Christian books on it. It sometimes seems that every well known Christian is keen to tell us how to avoid becoming part of the divorce statistics. But when it comes to how we actually choose someone with whom to spend our life, or what we get up to while we're still looking — there's a deafening silence.

This worries me. For if the simplest statement of belief, 'Jesus is Lord', means anything at all, it means that faith in Christ must affect *everything* we do, and that God must have at least something to say to every question we ask.

And 'going out', as anyone knows who's ever done it or wished to, poses an awful lot of questions! Here's a sample of the sort of questions I'm thinking of:

'My parents say I'm too young for a boyfriend — am I?'

'I'm interested in him but I'm not sure if he's interested in me. Should I make the first move, or just keep waiting?'

'If I ask her out, will she take it as practically a proposal?'

'Why will he never show me any affection in public?'

'She's furious because I forgot to ring. Why is it so important?'

'We're really serious. Should we sleep together?'

'I want to end it, but I don't want to hurt him. What can I do?'

I'm sure you can think of lots more of your own!

I used to hunt in vain for a book that dealt with problems of this sort from a Christian viewpoint. Eventually I realised that I would have to write it myself!

In the process I've been constantly reminded that very few questions have simple answers. Maybe some don't have answers at all. But I don't think that makes them any less worth asking. Getting the question right may be as useful as finding an answer. And even if the answer isn't easily found, we may learn a great deal from looking.

Relationships are risky, and we all get in a mess over them. A book can't stop anyone getting in a mess. But it can tell them that someone else knows what it's like to be in that particular sort of mess.

Most important, a book can reassure someone that God is there in the mess with them — and that he knows the way out, even if they don't. I hope this book can do that for someone.

1

FLUSHED AND BLUNDERING?

*The way in which the young people of this
generation pair off determines the fate of the nation
. . . and we leave it to flushed and blundering youth
to stumble on its own significance, with nothing to
guide it but shocked looks and sentimental twaddle
and base whisperings and cant-smeared examples.*
H. G. Wells, *Tono Bungay*

During a brief spell as a teacher, one of the few good things
I salvaged was a small collection of delightful mistakes from
my pupils' homework. Still among my favourites is a
description of a man 'standing in a shop doorway taking
[sic] to a lady'. What appeals to me about this is that 'taking
to a lady' is such a recognisable activity − one we can all
immediately identify, even if we've never heard it given that
particular label before.

Perhaps because I'm not very good at them myself, I've
long been fascinated by relationships between men and
women. I'm intrigued by how a romance begins, grows,
succeeds or fails, and how the people involved make
decisions about the relationship at every stage. I watch
people make such a mess of it, and I make such a mess of
it myself. I can't help feeling, like Winnie-the-Pooh being

bumped down the stairs on his head, that there must be a better way of doing it if only one could stop bumping long enough to find out.

Roses and thorns

Books, plays, films and songs all conspire to tell me that falling in love is easy — it's staying in love that's the hard part. The traditional picture looks something like this: boy meets girl, all is sweetness and light, roses in bloom and moon in June and all that. Only later do thorns appear on the roses, and craters on the moon, and things start to get difficult. Then is the time for some hard work if they want to keep the relationship going.

According to conventional wisdom, the crunch usually comes at the moment when the last wedding present is unpacked and reality strikes. So all the books of good advice concentrate on telling the young honeymooners (they're always young — what about *old* honeymooners?) how to overcome the unexpected difficulties and build a successful marriage. Even better, some go so far as to tell engaged couples what difficulties to expect, so they won't be surprised when they happen.

I'm afraid, however, that in my experience the thorns and craters have a nasty habit of making their presence felt long before any thought of a visit to the jeweller's shop. In fact they may well be obvious before we've got as far as putting the label 'going out' on the relationship. My problem isn't making romance face up to painful reality, but turning painful reality into something a bit more like romance!

Am I doing this whole thing wrong? Or just choosing the wrong people? (Well, they have to be the opposite sex —

so that's bound to create difficulties for a start!) It's never like this in the movies . . .

A good temporary friend

And another thing. I guess we can safely assume that nowadays most people will have anything from one or two to a large number of boy- or girlfriends, before deciding to 'settle down' (or giving up the search!). Some of those relationships will be entered into with little thought of the future, just because going out with someone is the thing to do, or out of loneliness, or in the hope of some romantic excitement.

I saw a Charlie Brown cartoon once in which Charlie met another boy at summer camp and wrote of him in his letter home, 'He's the sort that makes a good temporary friend'. It may sound callous but I rather like that idea. I think many 'going out' relationships could well be classed as 'temporary friendships'. But how can we ensure that they are *good* temporary friendships? For while popular opinion may say 'all's fair in love and war', I happen to believe every relationship puts us under an obligation to treat each other fairly, with care and consideration.

So there's the problem I've set myself. How, in this weird and wonderful modern social institution called 'going out', can I act in a just and loving way — and without getting my head bumped all the way down the stairs? How can I enrich and be enriched by the other person, instead of, as so often, just hurting and being hurt?

I don't know the answers — if I did, I'd probably be enjoying myself too much to have the time to write this book. But I hope in the course of asking the questions, I might just learn a bit more.

Portrait gallery

But maybe you are one of those lucky people in the middle
of an idyllic, roses-in-bloom-and-moon-in-June romance
and can't understand what all the fuss is about (if so, please
tell me how you did it). So let me introduce you to a few
people. This is what reality looks like from where I, they,
and probably most of the people reading this book, are
standing.

First in the portrait gallery is Rachel. She's fifteen, rather
shy, and hasn't yet had a boyfriend. This summer, at a
camp, something unexpected happened: an older boy made
it clear he liked her. One evening he actually held her hand.
She felt she'd taken a big step forward in growing up.

Since then they've kept in touch by letter, and he's been
to her home a few times. He's never said in so many words
that they're going out but he's obviously 'keen'. Last time
he arrived with his friend — who was clearly rather taken
with Rachel too. Rachel, however, thought the friend was
horrible!

This Saturday, they turned up again. Peeping out through
the curtains, Rachel managed to see who was at the door
before they spotted her. Without stopping to think, she beat
a hasty retreat out of the back window, leaving her mother
to make the excuses and entertain the two boys.

I won't say what I think of Rachel's solution to unwanted
admirers — only that I've done similar things myself! Let's
meet one or two slightly older 'young lovers', and see how
they get on.

Aren't we wonderful?

Susie is seventeen, and has been going out with Jim (on and
off) since she was fifteen. When she met him she thought

he was 'the ant's pants' (she's Australian, so translate as you will): tall, good looking, wealthy, good at sport. Susie really likes his parents too — she'd love to be part of a family like that. I'm going to march him up to the altar if it's the last thing I do, she told herself when they first got together.

Lately, however, Susie's been getting less and less happy about Jim. All they ever seem to talk about is how many runs he's made at cricket, or how many people he's reported as a football umpire, or else what a wonderful couple they are and how this romance is going to last for ever. He never bothers with things she cares about, like religion or politics, or with her family and friends. Sometimes she just listens to him on the phone for forty-five minutes at a stretch, thinking all the time, Soon he'll notice how he's treating me — but he never does. 'If this is you having a good time,' a friend remarked recently, 'I'd hate to see you having a bad one!'

Unlike Susie and Jim, nineteen year olds Jan and Nigel share a lot of ideas and interests. They really enjoy each other's company, never have rows, and have been together for three years now. Their families are assuming they'll get married — in fact Nigel's mum has offered to buy them a house. But now they're at different colleges, with new circles of friends. Jan has started thinking about her future, too. She loves travelling, and meeting people from other cultures, and wouldn't mind a career that takes her around the world.

When she tries to picture a life with Nigel, all she can see before her is a vacuum cleaner and a line full of nappies. She's not convinced she ever wants the kind of home-centred lifestyle that he seems to be looking for. Yet she's been so happy with him — how can she ever bear to end it?

Last chance

Then there's Paul, in his final term at college, and about
to go on to further training. He's a bit wary of women at
the moment, having just 'escaped' from a relationship with
a foreign student living in the same house. All he thought
he wanted to do was tell her about his faith, but somehow
their discussion and prayer sessions kept turning into
passionate grapplings on the sofa! Paul felt very guilty about
this.

During the last two years he's been quite good friends with
Nicky and her boyfriend Mark. Mark and Nicky got on well;
in fact they sometimes seemed like an old married couple.
But all the time Paul had a suspicion that Nicky was rather
attracted to *him*. Now, just before finals, Nicky has finished
with Mark — and she's been making it quite clear that she's
set her sights on Paul.

Paul's not sure he really wants to get involved with Nicky.
However he's getting a little worried about his lack of a
girlfriend. After all, a great number of people meet their
life partner at college and he's only got a few weeks left to
do so! What chances will he get when he goes to his new
college, where nearly all the students are male?

Last weekend he decided to ask Nicky out to the theatre;
though he pointed out carefully that he'd asked several other
people first, none of whom were free. He didn't want her
to take his invitation as too significant . . . In spite of all
his caution, however, he now finds that somehow he's
landed himself in an intense relationship, with lots of reading
poetry to each other and gazing up at the stars. He's even
broached the subject of marriage. But still there's a nagging
doubt at the back of his mind — is this really the right thing?

Getting nowhere fast

A little further up the age scale we meet twenty-five-year-old Amanda. She's enjoyed being single so far, but wouldn't at all object to giving it up. At the moment she spends a lot of time with Phil, in fact she regards him as her 'best friend'. Amanda feels increasingly that she could share her life with this man. She's been infatuated before, but now she thinks she is genuinely in love — she cares for Phil, respects him and is attracted to him.

But Phil never openly acknowledges that they are going out. He gives her presents, which makes her think that she is in some way 'special' to him; he's even said to other people that he would like to marry her. But he won't commit himself explicitly to her. On her part, she fears confronting him; what if he rejects her? Will she lose his friendship? What if she has misinterpreted the situation? She's beginning to despair of this relationship ever 'getting anywhere'.

Michael, aged twenty-seven, knows what Phil feels like. He often develops very close friendships with women, which go on for many months, even years, without 'getting any further'. He dreads taking that step which signals something other than 'just good friends'. None of the standard ways of doing so feel right. 'It's so pathetic to say, "Will you go out with me?'' he complains.

Meanwhile at a Christian conference somewhere, a famous preacher is telling his audience that 'you should not be doing anything to look for a marriage partner — God will provide if he wants you to marry'. Some of the audience lap up this spiritual-sounding advice, others groan inwardly, and Amanda and Michael are both left exactly where they were before.

Stop it, I like it!

Let's meet some more 'flushed and blundering' youth and
not-quite-youth. Harry, now in his late twenties, had a
painful adolescence, and he'd really like to have a close
relationship with a woman. But because of his insecurity
he's always asking out women who don't really interest him
much, and then quickly finishing with them. He has rather
a reputation amongst his friends for being a flirt . . .

When he goes out with a woman he usually gets quite
physical, quite soon. It makes him feel closer to her (and
besides, he likes it!). But he does happen to believe that sex
is meant for marriage only, and so far has avoided 'going
all the way'.

So it gave him a shock when he went out with Brenda
the other night. She was rather more responsive to his
advances than he'd expected − in fact she made it quite clear
that she didn't really care how far they went! The fact that
they'd shared a whole bottle of wine on an empty stomach
didn't help. Harry managed (just) to stick to his principles,
but he felt he'd had a narrow escape. 'I always thought it
was the woman's role to keep things under control. It was
quite a challenge when it was *me* who had to say "No".'
And part of him still wishes he'd said Yes − he might just
have ended up feeling less lonely . . .

Maggie had a difficult family, with an unstable and
unpredictable father. She threw over her childhood
Christianity, and the rules that went with it, when she was
a teenager. At sixteen she slept with her first boyfriend. In
her mid-twenties, under various pressures, she had a
breakdown, and at twenty-nine is still recovering. She's
regained, if somewhat shakily, her faith in God, and now
feels her earlier sexual experiences were wrong.

However, recently she got involved with a very attractive, but very immature man. Against her better judgment, she ended up in bed with him on more than one occasion. She knows in her heart of hearts that, like previous boyfriends, he didn't really care for her welfare. But he was *so* sexy, and she wanted so much to be loved . . . 'It's awfully hard to stop when you've started,' she says.

Thirty-five-year-old Alan, on the other hand, wishes someone *had* 'led him astray' when he was younger! At school he concentrated on work rather than social life, mainly out of shyness. He didn't have friends of his own sex, let alone go out with girls. Christine, whom he met at university, was his first real girlfriend. It worried him a bit, while they were engaged, that she wasn't very responsive to him physically. But he thought it was just because she shared his high principles about sex. They seemed to get on well in every other area.

He soon knew better. Sexually, the marriage was a failure, and before long the strain showed in other aspects of the relationship. Within a short time they were divorced. Now, over ten years later, he still feels he hasn't even started in the dating stakes, let alone the mating stakes. 'I just wish someone would regard me as a sex object!'

Left-overs

Of course, once Alan gets to forty he'll be past it anyway, and it won't matter. Or will it? Valerie is forty and her husband died a year ago, leaving her with three teenage children. She's had a tough year, but now she's recovering. She really misses David: his company, the mutual support, and not least their sex life. She's attractive, intelligent and lively and she's beginning to feel she would like to marry again — or, at the very least, to have some male company and affection.

As she looks around, however, the available men of the right age aren't a very inspiring bunch. If they haven't been married, it's often easy to see why; if they are divorced, it may be even easier! As for those who do look fairly eligible, they seem to be more interested in women under thirty . . .

Besides, even if she finds someone, she's not sure what it would be like going out at forty. It's such a long time since she last did any courting, and things were so different then. And how can you conduct a relationship freely with three teenage children looking on?

Forty-five-year-old Barry is one of the 'left-over' men who don't greatly impress Valerie. He was divorced some years ago as a result of his wife's desertion. He finds it lonely living alone, and never gives up looking for someone new.

The women Barry takes out are generally independent professional women in their late twenties or early thirties, with strong views of their own. Barry has what some would call an 'old-fashioned' way of treating women. He feels happiest taking the lead in the relationship, and believes strongly in a set of rules roughly covered by the term 'gentlemanliness'.

He finds it very hard to see why so few of his girlfriends respond to his approach. He always seems to end up clashing with them over some issue or other. It's very discouraging — he thinks feminism has a lot to answer for . . .

Stranger than fiction

All these stories are true, though names have been changed, as they say, to protect the innocent. So there's a small

selection of real people trying to make sense of their own
and other people's feelings and behaviour, with little more
to guide them than scraps of 'folk wisdom': 'Never run after
a boy or a bus,' 'There's plenty more fish in the sea,' 'Faint
heart never won fair lady' . . .

Apart from demonstrating that truth is stranger than
fiction, all these people have another thing in common. You
may have guessed it from some of their attitudes. At least
one person in each mini-saga is a Christian. And so am I.
Is this what causes all our problems? Possibly. But it could
also be a key to some better solutions . . . couldn't it? Well,
that's the major question I *do* hope to answer in these pages.

Before I start on that ambitious task, I want to pick out
some key truths I think the stories in this chapter illustrate.

First of all, *relationships between men and women, boys
and girls, are frightening*. Throwing in our lot, to whatever
degree, with another person quite properly makes us feel
rather as though we're just about to take an exam for which
we haven't prepared. And no one is exempt: the forty-year-
old widow is probably just as nervous on the first date as
the fourteen-year-old schoolboy — if not more so!

Second, *relationships are complex*. Listen to pop radio
for half an hour and it's all there — the extraordinary
mixture of joy and pain, hopes and fears, which make up
this thing called, often inappropriately, love. Being asked
out can send us into an ecstasy of joy greater even than being
selected for the school hockey team or the star part in the
dramatic society production. Or it can plunge us into a
desperate panic of, Oh no, how can I get out of *this* one?
Going out can give us the most blissful moments and
memories we get in a month of Saturday nights. Or it can
fill us with the greatest depression, self-hatred, guilt and
hopelessness we ever experience. Relationships which start
in an idyllic glow can, for quite obscure reasons, suddenly

become a dead weight of conflict and misunderstanding. Those which start with all sorts of difficulties can
unexpectedly mature into strong and rewarding commitments.

Third, *relationships involve our whole selves*. Going out
with someone doesn't occur in isolation from the rest of life,
a kind of recreation in which we shut off from our work,
our ambitions, our ideals and our other friendships. As soon
as we get close to another person, spend more time with
them, share our thoughts and feelings, weigh up the
relationship's 'prospects', we also have to ask how this fits
in with everything else. We are forced to think about what
kind of lifestyle we want, where we are going, what our
priorities are. Friends and family are involved too, and their
opinions and insights matter.

Last, *relationships have a moral and spiritual dimension*.
As a Christian, I have to consider everything I do in the light
of the command to love God and neighbour. As a result,
I may have to reject certain ways of behaving. And that
surely involves a lot more than just whether I sleep with
someone or not. It's to do with how I treat people who, like
myself, are made in God's image. I have to ask myself what
course of action will best express honesty, respect and
sensitivity to the other person. And that's not simple when
my own self-respect and my most sensitive feelings are
involved, and in an area of life where it's all too easy to
deceive yourself!

Learn as you burn?

There are two ways of learning, whatever the subject. We
can learn by doing — generally the favoured way amongst
educationalists today. But when it's human lives we're

handling, there are also dangers involved. Although mistakes are a great way of learning, some mistakes ought never to be made. *Finger-burning for beginners* is a do-it-yourself manual I'd rather be without!

The other way of learning is by getting the theory straight, as far as possible, before we get too deeply involved in the practice. Practice is still essential, of course (what else makes perfect?); and without it, we won't make much sense of the theory. Ideally, perhaps, theory and practice ought to run alongside each other; that way the theory prepares us for the practice, helps us avoid the worst pitfalls, and gives us tools for reflecting on what we're doing. Meanwhile the practice puts flesh on the bones of the theory — and the practice is, after all, the very thing we're learning *for*!

With all this in mind, I'm going to approach my subject in two ways. The first is to hunt out some foundations and pointers to guide us in 'going out' relationships — that's the theory part. At the same time I'll look frequently at the kind of situations people actually get themselves into in practice, and see what can be learned from them.

We've already seen a fair bit of 'what actually goes on' in chapter one. So in chapter two I'll start with foundations. And since I've already admitted I believe that the truth about all of life is to be found in God, I'll look first in what may seem an unlikely place to find help with going out, but a good place to find God's truth: the Bible.

2

IN THE BEGINNING

The truth that in the sight of God male and female are equal gave a new meaning and potential, not only to marriage, but to every relationship between man and woman.
D. S. Bailey, *The Man-Woman Relation in Christian Thought*[1]

There is one fact of life that I have never heard discussed in any seminar
And that is that all women think men are funny and all men think weminar

Ogden Nash

Going out. Dating. Seeing each other. Involved. My bloke. My fellow. My girl. My bird.

Look in a Bible dictionary for any of the above and you won't find them! Nor will you get any further with old-fashioned terms: walking out, courting, keeping company; sweetheart, suitor, swain. And you'll search in vain for a story on the lines of, 'So Isaac asked Rebecca what she was doing on Saturday night', or a verse which begins, 'When your boyfriend stands you up . . .'

The fact is, men and women simply didn't get together

in that way in Bible times — or throughout most of history.
'God invented sex, but dating is an American creation,' says
Tim Stafford.² The modern Western pattern of pairing up
freely and splitting up freely is less than a century old, and
even today it doesn't always apply in more 'traditional'
societies.

So is God's only statement on the strange, enjoyable and
painful effects men and women have on each other, the
peculiar way they treat each other, the muddles they get into
— 'No comment'? Or perhaps, since the Bible doesn't
recognise going out, we can assume God disapproves of it
and we should all go back to strict separation of the sexes
and arranged marriages?

I think the answer to both questions is No. But we have
to look a little deeper, beyond the Bible's apparent silence
on romance, to see why. I'll tackle the first question first:
what if anything does the Bible say which *might* have a
bearing on what you're doing next Saturday night?

Someone like me

It seems like a good idea to start with the first blind date
in history: the introduction of Adam to Eve.

Genesis offers two angles on the story of creation. Chapter
one gives a God's eye view of the earth's development, from
its beginning in the birth of light, to its climax in the arrival
of human beings. Chapter two homes in on a particular
geographical area and a particular pair of people.

In chapter one, each stage ends with the words, 'And God
saw that it was good'; indeed after making men and women
he pronounces it 'very good'. But in chapter two there's
some added detail on that final stage. First God creates the
male sex. And then something very striking happens: God

declares this situation *not good*. There's something
incomplete about humanity. So God takes immediate steps
to remedy this. And, according to your point of view, that's
either where human life really gets interesting, or where all
the trouble starts.

Why introduce this time gap between the two sexes? Some
interpreters (mostly men!) take it to imply that, in the Bible's
teaching, men are the real 'rulers of creation' and women
are added only to make men's task easier and more pleasant
(oh, and to have babies). But I prefer another way of seeing
it.

Before making the woman, God presents the man with
all the animals, and gives him time to conduct a census
of them. Not surprisingly, this inventory reveals that none
of the animals qualify as a fitting companion. This
amazing discovery isn't made for the benefit of God, who
already knows it, but for the man. The story is illus-
trating, in dramatic form, a fundamental truth about the
world:

Humanity is only complete when it is male and female.

The time gap highlights this. Neither sex on its own does
full justice to 'the image of God'. Woman is not an extra
or a slightly improved animal, but the other half of the
picture.

In order to complete the picture, God first puts the man
to sleep. I don't think this is just a general anaesthetic for
a painful operation! It could be to stress that this new
companion comes from and belongs to God, and isn't
Adam's own creation or possession. God then makes the
woman out of the man's own body; and finally wakes the
man up so they can take a look at each other.

Now comes the bit I find really exciting, Adam's reaction:

> 'This is now bone of my bones
>   and flesh of my flesh;
> she shall be called "woman",
>   for she was taken out of man.'

The *Good News* translation brings the point out even better: 'At last, here is one of my own kind'. In other words, what Adam sees is not an alien creature, something totally other and incomprehensible. It is *a person like himself*. So here's a fundamental truth:

> *Men and women are equally human*.

The focus in this symbolic story is not on the difference between the sexes, but on their likeness. At the deepest level, men and women have the same human characteristics. How could it be otherwise when they are both in the image of one God?

You may think that so far I'm stating the obvious. But it isn't so obvious if we look at how men and women often behave. We regard each other as mysterious and incomprehensible. We ask aggrieved questions like, Why can't a woman be more like a man? At times we see the other sex as an irritating intrusion on what would otherwise be a nice quiet planet. Our very language betrays our attitudes: the *opposite* sex, the *battle* of the sexes. Something must have gone wrong . . . but I'll come to that in a minute.

United we stand

First, a bit more about the original design.

'It is not good for the man to be alone,' says God to himself (I'm glad God talks to himself . . .), 'I will make a helper suitable for him' (Gen. 2:18). The English word 'helper' usually means an assistant or 'second-in-command'. But the original Hebrew is the same word as that in Psalm 118:7 — 'The Lord is with me; he is my helper'. This word is *always* used of an equal or a superior, *never* a subordinate. Like it or not, women and men are colleagues, joint caretakers of creation. 'Let them rule . . . over all the earth' (Gen. 1:26) means just that: let *them* rule. That's why none of the animals will do. It has to be someone on the same intellectual and spiritual level.

As my biological clock ticks away, I'm also glad to notice no mention of children when the woman is created. She is a partner, not a childbearing machine. Nothing suggests that her job is to be a domestic servant, a pleasure object, a substitute mother. Nor is the man shown as a meal ticket for life, a live-in handyman, a social status symbol or a substitute father! They are *both* told to take responsibility for raising children, *both* given dominion over the physical world (Gen. 1:28).

It doesn't sound a lot of fun so far; until the next bit: 'For this reason a man will leave his father and mother and be united to his wife, and they will become one flesh.

'The man and his wife were both naked, and they felt no shame' (Gen. 2:24–5).

Here are two people with a lot in common emotionally, intellectually and spiritually. But as soon as they look at their bodies they notice they are also quite different (gosh — how intriguing . . .). Being different, however, doesn't mean they go their own separate ways. They are created to relate with the greatest possible intimacy: emotional, intellectual, spiritual and physical. Being naked is a powerful symbol of their potential unity: there is no need to hide in any way.

So here's a third fundamental truth:

Men and women are made to share with each other.

I can find nothing in Genesis one and two about different roles; nothing about who leads and who follows; nothing about playing elaborate games to 'catch' a man or a woman, or to get your way when you've got one. The values which shine from this story are total equality, total commitment, total honesty, and total trust.

I think we've now got some good general principles for relationships between the sexes. Adam and Eve aren't, of course, really on a blind date; they are the subjects of an arranged marriage. But these two characters also stand for the whole of male and female humankind, married or not. So what we learn from them can also give us insights on going out and courtship, as well as a host of other kinds of relationship.

Not a love story

All right, I admit it, I've painted a rather idealistic picture of the relationship between men and women. Not a lot like you and me. So now I'll also admit that I *do* believe in the doctrine of the Fall: that, because human beings have deliberately disobeyed God, the world for which they are responsible has got severely distorted. In fact I suspect one major evidence for this is the way things go persistently and perversely wrong in the relationship of the sexes.

To see just how distorted things are, I'll look again at those basic principles and see what's happened to them.

Instead of recognising both sexes as essential, most human cultures now see the male as the 'normal human being' and the female as a sub-group. Women are reduced to limited roles, seen as a service industry to men rather than as equal partners, even regarded as less than human; theologians in more than one religion have had heated debates about whether women have souls! (Of course, sometimes women look at men in this way too — it's not just one sex that can be seen as a sex object or simply 'handy to have around the house'.)

Instead of seeing each other as equally human, men and women act as if they belonged to different species. Social patterns keep male and female activities and friendships largely separate from each other, so the differences get exaggerated. It really does look sometimes as if men and women live in two distinct cultures, even within the same nation. And, as always when two cultures try to co-exist, hostility and fear arises. Love and equality are replaced by possessiveness and power: woman's impulse to cling to man, his impulse to dominate her:

> 'Your desire will be for your husband,
> and he will rule over you' (Gen. 3:16).

It's interesting that in Genesis, it's only *after* the Fall that Adam names his wife as he has previously named all the animals. She has become just another creature to be defined and controlled by him. No longer are they joint rulers of the earth; her contribution is reduced to populating it (Gen. 3:20).

Instead of sharing, men and women start to hide from each other. Adam and Eve become ashamed of their nakedness, and cover themselves. This isn't about modesty, it's about the destruction of intimacy. It's a picture of a world where communication between the sexes is blocked and confused by deceit, misunderstanding, conflict of wills, contempt mixed with lust, fear mixed with longing. In the bittersweet game called the sex war, men and women devise all kinds of stratagems to get the better of each other. And when all else fails, they can always make jokes at each other's expense.

Divided we fall

All of this is bound to have its effect on how women and men make friendships, discover their own sexuality, and search for a partner. The Fall opens up a whole new range of ways in which men and women can damage, deceive and exploit each other. 'He done me wrong' or 'She broke my heart' are the basic plots, not only for popular music throughout the ages, but for a large proportion of poetry, novels, plays, opera, film and TV drama. Behind a lot of this pain is the fact that sexual desire has somehow cut loose from love and commitment.

Now desire on its own is a dangerous thing. It can make us treat people as just there for our own gratification; or it can lead to literally murderous reactions: envy, hate, possessiveness, vengeance. Recognising this, societies have tried all sorts of safeguards to keep individual emotions under social control — from the chastity belt to the chaperone . . . From earliest times, the favourite policy was to keep young women and men socially separate (must have been very boring) and to have marriages arranged by parents, priests or other figures of authority. (Fourth-century Christians carried this separation of the sexes so far that a male corpse was not buried next to a female corpse until the latter had decomposed!)

However, as unnumbered 'eternal triangle' novels and plays testify, being denied the freedom to choose your own partner can also have its problems. 'Love' may be a deceptive guide to suitability, but banning love is no solution — it will probably break out in a more destructive form. So from matchmakers to computer dating, all kinds of attempts have been made to find a balance between giving free rein to possibly immature and headstrong individuals, or exercising such severe control that no room at all is given

to personal feelings. And no one's found the perfect answer
yet.

   And that brings me to my next question: what about the
way we do it now? Is 'going out' itself a product of what's
gone wrong with male—female relationships? Or is it just
another way of trying to deal with the problem? A brief look
at history (and herstory) may help.

A 'suitable' match

Before 'going out' came along, the official purpose of a man
and a woman getting together was always marriage. And
in choosing a marriage partner, other factors were more
important than love. In early societies, after all, marriage
was as much a contract between families as a union between
individuals; and it helped if the families had similar ways
of life and beliefs, and if both gained in practical terms.
In particular, it helped if the price was right! (and we
mustn't forget that many social groups still function this
way . . .)

   However there have always been a variety of methods of
finding a marriage partner, and some of them have been
more like 'going out'. The Bible records quite a few ways.
Isaac (Gen. 24:1—4) happily accepts his parents' choice of
a bride, as many Asian young men still do today. But when
Samson fancies a Philistine girl (Judg. 14) he asks his parents
to get her for him, and persists in his request against their
advice (with disastrous results). Even women(!) sometimes
had at least the right of refusal. Rebecca, though handed
over bodily by her family to Isaac whom she hasn't even
met ('Here is Rebecca; take her and go', Gen. 24:51) is also
given some choice: 'Will you go with this man?' (Gen.
24:58). Other biblical women, like Ruth, even take the

initiative in courtship, with resounding success (is that why
I like Ruth so much?).

I'm particularly heartened by the daughters of Zelophehad
(Num. 36) who, very unusually, inherit their father's
property. They are thus free to marry whoever they choose.
But, advised by Moses, they agree to marry only within their
own tribe, to keep the land from leaving the tribe. An
intriguing example of personal freedom balanced with social
responsibility!

Nor is the Bible totally lacking in 'love stories'. Isaac's
was an arranged marriage, Jacob chose his own bride, but
both stories provide us with perhaps the most touching verses
in the Bible: 'So she (Rebecca) became his wife, and he loved
her; and Isaac was comforted after his mother's death' (Gen.
24:67); 'Jacob served seven years to get Rachel, but they
seemed like only a few days to him because of his love for
her' (Gen. 29:20).

'Arranged' courting, then, might still leave room for
personal preference. And it seems the 'working classes' have
always given more choice to the individual. Among peasant
farmers and in the early industrial period, women shared
the workload, and the sexes couldn't be kept strictly apart.
You might have a chance to find out quite a bit about each
other before committing yourselves. But if you were sensible
you wouldn't choose someone just because you fancied them
or enjoyed their company. Where life was a struggle for
survival, you needed a reliable hard worker who would
contribute to the household economy. A man 'taking a wife'
would also like to know she was fertile; and many peasant
societies waited for the wedding ceremony until the first child
was born. In nineteenth-century Scotland, for instance, nine
out of ten brides were pregnant or already had children by
the groom.

Overall, it looks as if even when restrictions on the sexes

mixing were greatest, the poor always had something not unlike our dating — 'walking out' for country lads and lasses, or a 'follower' if you were a Victorian domestic servant. But the more respectable you were, the fewer followers you got through before making up your mind.

The game of love

However, alongside the search for a marriage partner, there's always been another motive that brought men and women together: a yen for excitement plus, sometimes, an education in social graces. Where unmarried girls have been kept secluded, this kind of 'affair of the heart' has usually involved the already-married or the 'not quite respectable': the ancient Greek and his high-class, cultured mistress; or the medieval lady whose husband was away at the Crusades, and who inspired her ardent but chaste young admirer to noble deeds, and reams of passionate poetry.

In more liberal times, something very like 'going out' operated: in the Elizabethan age for instance, unmarried youth could dally while dancing or get 'accidentally' lost in mazes, and young men could call their sweethearts pet-names like bird, mouse, lamb, puss, pigeon, dove, chicken, kid, pigsney (or 'love' or 'honey' if you wanted to get away from animals). The philosopher Burton complains in his *Anatomy of Melancholy* that: '. . . it is almost impossible for two young folks equal in years to live together and not be in love, especially in great houses, prince's courts, where they are idle, fare well, live at ease, and cannot tell otherwise to spend their time.'[3]

After a brief seventeenth-century clampdown, the eighteenth century sighed on sofas or picked up admirers in pleasure gardens, and newspapers carried adverts on the

lines of 'I saw you at the theatre last week — smile at me
next week if interested.' The eighteenth-century American
Puritans had a fascinating arrangement called 'bundling',
in which a boy and girl shared a bed overnight with the girl's
ankles tied together, clothes sewn up or a board down the
bed to guard against hanky-panky! Even the virtuous
Victorians invented the Valentine card. The Edwardian 'new
woman' went on mixed boating trips or out motoring; the
twenties flapper could recline in bed like a movie star and
talk for hours on the phone to her boyfriend.

By the 'never-had-it-so-good' fifties America had a regular
magazine called *Datebook* giving advice to girls on how to
deal with over-ardent young men, how to behave when
meeting the boyfriend's parents, etc. Its guidelines for first
dates, double dates, blind dates, stay-at-home dates, car
dates, study dates and even church dates are mind-boggling!
A modern girl might have several boyfriends between the
ages of fifteen and twenty-five, and end up not marrying
any of them — and she wouldn't be regarded as 'loose'
(unless she had 'gone too far' and 'got caught'). Going out
was still seen as a preparation for marriage, but not every
relationship had to be seen as 'serious'. And with the
permissive sixties even the rules on sexual behaviour were
thrown out, and you could sleep together and live together
with never a thought of 'for ever and ever'.

Ask the elders?

While all this was going on, where were the Christians?
Whether they were ruling or in the minority, Christians have
always had views on courting and how it should be
conducted. For instance the Catholic Church of the late
Middle Ages, unhappy at marriages made purely for

financial gain, declared that only full consent on both sides
made a marriage, and any private commitment between a
boy over fifteen and a girl over twelve was legally binding
(that'd scare them at the high school!). Later, fearing
immorality, the Puritans made courting without parental
permission a punishable offence.

But perhaps because our form of 'going out' is so new,
or because there's no obvious teaching on it in the Bible,
or because they couldn't think of a sensible alternative,
modern Christians have largely accepted it by default. So
is it time to put up a 'No Smooching' notice?

In the last few years, some of the more extreme authority-
based charismatic communities have taught that a man
shouldn't ask a woman out unless he believes God may be
calling them to marry (a woman asking a man out isn't even
considered!). Even then, he should ask advice or permission
from a church leader first. This is basically going back to
a modified 'arranged marriage', and I can see some point
in it. It by-passes a lot of potential hurt, and makes people
think twice before arousing one another's emotions and
expectations. It involves others in the relationship from its
beginning — a very valuable asset.

However, it also puts a lot of pressure on that fragile
thing, a newly emerging relationship. Lifelong commitment
has to be on the agenda right from the start — and it's hardly
surprising if many men feel too scared ever to make a move
at all! Besides, it's only really appropriate to people over
a certain age — can you imagine, at fourteen, asking the
elders if you can take a schoolfriend to the pictures?

To ban 'casual dates' may work for a community-living
situation, where people have a daily chance to form
friendships through working, playing and worshipping
together. But for the rest of us, some form of dating, in
groups or pairs, may be the only chance we get to meet and

communicate at a deeper level than the classroom, the office or the Sunday service allows.

Janet and John grow up

Let's be realistic. Nowadays friendships with some romantic element — whether you call them 'just good friends' or 'puppy love' — happen to most adolescents and young adults. They may be building up heartbreak, bitterness or cynicism. On the other hand they may be providing immensely valuable lessons in finding one's own identity and relating to the 'opposite' sex.

To enter into a serious commitment, without ever having 'practised' on less serious ones, is a major risk. I think of Pete and Janie, who met at seventeen and married at nineteen. They shared their faith, got on well together, and were glad to have found each other so soon. But now, ten years later, Pete flirts outrageously, in Janie's presence, with other women. He can't help wondering what life might have been like if he hadn't married his first girlfriend. Janie takes it very well — but what tensions are going on underneath?

In contrast, I knew as soon as I started going out with James that this wasn't going to be for ever. Yet I felt it was worth staying together for two precious, never-to-be-repeated years of our time at university. It was a very maturing time. Who knows if he would have been ready for his subsequent marriage (or I, indeed, ready for singleness!) had we not gone out for those two years?

Going out is not just about searching for Mr or Ms Right. It's about finding out how to communicate, learning to be close, discovering who you are through encountering others, growing into an adult. Even if I never make it up the aisle, I shall be glad I've made it to the back row of the pictures, the disco and a few romantic summer afternoons in a punt.

I think the Bible does say something relevant to this. When Gentiles first joined the Church, the apostles had to decide whether they were going to ask these converts to adopt Jewish customs in joining what was still a Jewish sect. They concluded (Acts 15) that beyond a few basic rules, Gentiles should be free to serve Christ through their own culture.

What I learn from this is that each 'people-group' must obey Christ in terms of its own way of doing things (unless that way actually contradicts any rules of Christian living). 'Going out' is the normal custom in Western culture. We may want to make ground rules about physical involvement, or give advice about how to court courteously; but we can hardly say the whole system has to be abandoned – unless we have something really workable to replace it!

Allowed but not compulsory

One final word in this chapter. If going out is normal and I've never done it, am I abnormal? I don't think so. There are loads of people who are happily married to their first-ever boy/girlfriend, or happily single without ever having got romantically involved. I think Genesis 1:26–8 tells us that to understand and experience our humanness properly, we need to relate across the sex barrier. But it *doesn't* imply that everyone has to have loved and won, or even loved and lost.

If you happen to know any well-adjusted nun, monk or anyone else publicly committed to singleness, you'll know what I mean. Being able to relate freely and fruitfully to people of both sexes doesn't depend on the number of relationships you've had, or the label, married or single, you wear (after all, many married people can't relate!). It depends on what you have learnt from your experience.

So if you do count yourself as a non-starter in the race to romance, I hope you will still think it worth reading on.

3

O BRAVE NEW WORLD

O brave new world, that has such people in't!
Shakespeare, *The Tempest*

It had happened at last. What seemed like years of waiting
(though it was probably only months) was over. At just
thirteen, I had finally reached my goal. Now life was really
beginning.

What occasioned all this excitement? I had my first real
'date'. All right, it was only Lawrence, whom I'd known
(and with whom I'd regularly played 'weddings') since I was
seven. And we were only going to the fair. But something
about the way he asked, 'Would you and your friend like
to come to the fair with me and my friend?' made it clear
this wasn't kids' stuff. A foursome, after all, could also be
two twosomes. And going to the fair was quite different
from building shelters in his back garden. This was definitely
a date.

A year of secondary school (single-sex) had made its mark.
Only a year ago Lawrence was just another friend who
happened to be a boy. Now he was transformed into a figure
of fantasy, a potential conquest. What might happen at the
fair? Would the foursome 'pair off'? Would I get a kiss at
the end of the evening? (I'd done a lot of imagining kisses,

soft and dreamy. . .) Would my padded bra develop one of those embarrassing dents?

None of the above happened. We didn't pair off. I didn't get the kiss till over a year later, from Percy in the park (and it wasn't at all soft and dreamy, but sloppy and rather unpleasant). The padded bra behaved itself for once. But the most important thing was that I had had a date, and I was now officially and certifiably a teenager.

Virgin territory

Shakespeare knew a thing or two about 'love's young dream'. His character Miranda, whom I quote at the start of this chapter, lives her early years on a remote island with her father, his magical servant Ariel and a sub-human monster, Caliban. When she meets the shipwrecked young Ferdinand — her first sight of a young man — he seems to her 'a thing divine'. Confronted by his father and friends, her first sight of men in the plural, she cries out in wonder: 'How many goodly creatures are there here! How beauteous mankind is!'

For me, becoming a teenager was rather like discovering Miranda's 'brave new world'. I'd had crushes before: on film stars, or on my parents' friends who were mostly old enough to be the film stars' fathers, let alone mine. But boys had been simply ill-mannered, boring kids, few of whom one would want to be friends with.

Now boys were suddenly interesting. They had the potential to be romantic heroes and make you into a romantic heroine. Acquiring a boyfriend, or at least finding a name to write on your school bag, was the major goal in life.

It didn't really matter much what the boyfriend was like.

Of course, if you could ensnare Dave the Rave whom all
your friends fancied, rather than Spotty Muldoon the local
bore or Wandering Hans the octopus-like German exchange
student, then your date had more status value (and you also
had a better chance of an evening to remember, rather than
one you'd try hard to forget). But even if you *did* secure
a reasonably decent specimen, there was no guarantee that
the result would be a 'deep and meaningful interpersonal
encounter'. In my case, I was much more likely to get bored
after a week and wonder what I had ever seen in the bloke.

Conquest of the unknown

I suspect that for many young teenagers like the one I once
was, the pursuit of the other sex is undertaken not in order
to share one's thoughts and life with someone, but more
in the spirit of mountain climbing: 'because they are there'.
Get to the summit and there's not much to do except plant
a flag and come down again.

Like mountain climbing too, there's the challenge of the
unknown. Before adolescence sets in, you know all about
the other sex — they're just kids like you but with some
apparently pointless differences, who get given different toys
at Christmas and like playing different games. You might
get a kick out of pushing one into the swimming pool or
having your friends say, 'He's your boyfriend, inne?' but
it doesn't mean much.

But when your body starts changing shape and developing
weird habits, and the differences get more obvious, the other
sex mysteriously changes into the 'opposite' sex: creatures
from another world, whose bodies do strange and oddly
pleasurable things to you (and to whose bodies you might
do strange and oddly pleasurable things . . .). What are the

tricks for catching one? How can you interpret what they do or say, or how they look at you? How do their minds work? And, more interestingly, how do their bodies work? What would happen if I . . . well, it would be a shame not to try.

At the same time almost everyone and everything around you conspires to tell you that this is what growing into a real man or a real woman is all about. Girls' magazines (and they start younger and younger now) instruct you on how to dress, how to make up, how to act, how to get round parental prohibitions, all in the cause of catching that fella. They even have titles like *My Guy* (presumably a successor to *My Little Pony* — the girl up the road's got one, can I have one too?). Meanwhile the boys are passing round 'adult' magazines (translation: those which encourage men to be most childishly self-centred) and speculating on whether they could get Tarty Tina from the third year to show hers, and if they would be as good as the ones in the centrefold. Randy Andy from the fourth year claims he's already seen Tarty Tina's, and done a lot more than that, but no one believes him.

Pass or fail?

Pressures on adolescents come not only from their maturing bodies and their growing awareness of sexual powers, but from the psychological processes they are going through: beginning to separate from parents, developing into an adult with personal views and commitments, learning what it means to be of a particular gender in a society where gender can be all-important.

The typical questions of adolescence are all about identity and belonging: Who am I? Am I normal? Am I attractive?

Will I be accepted? Sometimes it seems that alongside the
school exams there's another and much more crucial test,
where the examiners are more merciless, the pass marks
constantly changing, and our whole lives depend on success
or failure!

Negotiating relations with the other sex is a major part
of this whole process of testing out one's identity and place
in society. It's no accident that popular slang talks of
'scoring' or 'making it' with someone: competition and
conquest are the stuff of which relationships at this stage
are often made. 'Playing the field' is another revealing
expression. It implies trying out different ways of being,
different styles of relationship with different kinds of people,
as well as trying to keep one's 'batting average' high.
'Playing' also has the sense of play-acting, adopting different
roles and façades, whether it's being the hero or heroine of
some dramatic or sensational film or novel (I'll be Cathy
if you'll be Heathcliff), or 'playing Mummies and Daddies'
in a mock-up of cosy domestic bliss.

Playing around?

All this talk of play and scores sounds rather callous and
flippant, doesn't it? It sounds a lot like using other people
for your own enjoyment and self-advancement. So isn't
playing the field rather irresponsible? Shouldn't we be
encouraging the young to take things more seriously?

This is where I go back to Shakespeare. (I wouldn't like,
à la *Desert Island Discs,* to put him on a level with the Bible;
but as I said he did know a thing or two worth knowing.)

In his comedies, there's quite a bit of courting, and it often
takes the form of playing apparently frivolous games.
Rosalind and Orlando, in *As You Like It,* are my particular

favourites. They've met once and made an instant impression on each other (Orlando rather dashingly won a wrestling contest against the Giant Haystacks of his day, and Rosalind gave him her necklace as a prize). Since then, she has been forced to flee to the forest dressed as a boy, Ganymede (I hope you're still following this). There she keeps coming across soppy poems hung up on trees, in praise of Rosalind — who is, of course, herself. As Ganymede, she meets up again with Orlando, who's been writing them. 'I know how to help you get over this Rosalind,' s/he says (somewhat more poetically), 'I'll pretend to be her and you can woo me. I'll be as uncooperative as I can, and you'll soon go off her.'

So Orlando and Ganymede-pretending-to-be-Rosalind go through a whole mock-courtship, mock-quarrel, mock-wedding, while all the time she really is Rosalind and he doesn't know it. By the time he finds out the truth, they've negotiated all the potential rough passages of their relationship and are set fair to get on well. The game has paid off.

Play, I think this demonstrates, is a serious activity. Playing games of all sorts is a vital way of learning about ourselves and others, especially for those in the process of growing up. Children's play enables us to discover our mental and physical abilities, and how the world around us works. Adolescent play enables us to discover our social abilities, and how the world within us and within other people works. Whether it's Rosalind and Orlando, with marriage prominently in mind, or window-climbing Rachel and her unwanted admirer with nothing in mind but a bit of admiration, the dating game gives a chance to imitate 'what the grown-ups do' and see what it's like.

Playing fair

So where does consideration for others come into this particular game? Let's face it: people who are going through all the physical and emotional upheavals of adolescence are bound to be somewhat self-centred, and don't need encouraging to be more so. Teenagers are also young enough to retain the impulsiveness of children: a quality which is endearing enough when seen as spontaneity, but which can be risky in those whose bodies and emotions are developing! Can mere teenagers be trusted to play fair? I think we can only sort out this one by a case study.

Steve was still at school when he noticed a fellow-pupil he really fancied. Like him, Kay was interested in books and theatre, and she was also very attractive and always stunningly dressed. She was also very young! When Steve asked her out, she consulted her mother. 'Wait two years', was Mother's answer — which was dutifully passed on to Steve.

Steve was prepared to wait — but he didn't see why he shouldn't enjoy himself in the meantime. So he asked Julie out instead. They got on quite well and went out for a whole two years. But the minute the 'trial period' ended, Steve decided to claim his share of the bargain, and finished with Julie.

Assessing this kind of behaviour is difficult. Was Steve 'using' Julie? Or was their relationship, even as a 'stopgap', still a valuable stage in their growing up? Was Kay's mother over-protective? Or was she wise to protect her daughter against someone who could pick up and drop people in as carefree a manner as Steve appeared to do to Julie?

I've tried looking up 'finishing with', 'throwing over', and even 'chucking' in my concordance, but the Bible doesn't appear to have anything. So I'm going to try using my own judgment (well, Paul tells us more than once in 1 Corinthians to do exactly that — see 1 Cor. 10:15 and 1 Cor. 11:13). Let's look at what effect 'taking things more seriously' might have in the case of Steve, Julie and Kay.

Suppose we ask Steve to take his commitment to Julie more seriously. After all, he's occupied two years of her life, which is a long time when you're young; she's got used to having him around and is pretty attached to him. Doesn't he have a responsibility to her?

Of course he does. But that responsibility isn't the same as it would be if they were twenty-five and engaged. We've all, I'm sure, seen enough bad marriages made through people taking a relationship too seriously too young, and not having the courage to break it off simply because they've gone through all their teenage years together.

But perhaps Steve's responsibility began when he first asked Julie out? If he had taken her feelings more seriously, would he have not asked her out at all? Again, I have problems with this. At that age, waiting a whole two years for Kay, forgoing all other relationships in the meantime, would have been to take his relationship with *Kay* too seriously. How could she feel free in a friendship with a boy who had been that dogged in his pursuit of her? The pressure would be much too great — almost emotional blackmail!

Rules of the game

Hang on, though — I'm not letting Steve off entirely from the serious charge of 'playing with people's emotions'. I've said that playing at grown-up games has some use. But anyone who plays games knows they have rules. In Steve's case, I think the rules look something like this: Julie is a person. She cannot be treated just as a useful companion or an acquisition to show off to friends. So Steve does have a responsibility to her: not because they are committed to each other for life, but just because they are two people involved in an emotional relationship — and, what's more, at an age when emotions get very intense. He had a responsibility when he first asked her out: to tell her straight that he was still keen on Kay. He had a responsibility all the time they were going out: to be aware of her feelings and his own, and to judge whether it was better to continue the relationship or end it. And now he has decided to end it, he has a responsibility to do so as kindly and honestly as he can; and to allow her to express all her feelings about it (even if it makes him the target of some home truths he doesn't like!).

Kay is a person too, and a unique one. Maybe, being 'old for her age', she *is* ready for a boyfriend. Or maybe Steve needs to look closer and see the vulnerable child under the apparently assured façade — and not exploit that child. And Kay's mum has a hard task too: working out when you can entrust your 'baby' to the dangerous world is a tricky task and there's no set age.

Perhaps the fairest thing of all would have been for Steve to be 'just friends' with both Kay and Julie, and not take either relationship very seriously. If Kay's mum is worried, she can insist they go out in a group, or meet at her home. I suspect more problems arise nowadays from teenagers being under pressure to go straight for a 'committed' relationship, than from too much casual dating!

But, naturally, as Steve is still only in his mid-teens, he is only capable of applying the rules in a mid-teen sort of way: not very maturely, not very reflectively, and with quite a few mistakes. Adult games have adult rules, and it takes adults to apply them. Teenage games have teenage rules, and we can expect the inexperienced not to be very good at keeping them.

Danger – inflammable material

That, of course, brings me to the weak point in my defence of playing the field. I'm sure you've spotted it long ago. Play may be necessary and educational and all that, but what about 'playing with fire'? We don't let small children find the matches: might it not be equally dangerous to let slightly larger children open that box labelled 'sexual emotions – not to be used as a toy'? Not only can it hurt a lot to be a teenager in love, but games of 'mummies and daddies' have a habit of turning into games of 'doctors and patients', at which point the game usually requires some shedding of clothes!

After all it was quite safe for Orlando and 'Ganymede', since he didn't know that this really was Rosalind with whom he was doing a spot of wooing. They could be all alone in the forest and nothing untoward would happen. But in the real world, in the age of AIDS, who would dare put a potentially lethal 'freedom' into the hands of the most impulsive and unreflective section of society?

I don't want at this stage to go into the rights and wrongs of sexual experimentation or sex outside marriage – I'll come to that later. I'll simply say that in my observation and experience, adolescents are easily influenced, easily deceived and, most important, easily damaged creatures. They need and deserve some protection. Not being old and wise enough to handle, all by themselves, adult games with adult rules, they can do with having some of those rules imposed from outside.

I'm thinking of Maggie, whom we met in the first chapter.

At sixteen she was confused, looking for affection, probably full of dreamy ideas about affairs gleaned from novels and films. She was old enough to be sexually aware, desperate enough to fall into bed with the first boy who showed her some tenderness, and too young and reckless to think about the implications.

A month later, when she thought she was pregnant, the whole thing didn't seem quite so romantic. Years later, it was obvious that that first affair hadn't made her any happier; it just made her more open to subsequent ones, and pushed her further into the habit of being unable to stand up for herself with men. Maybe a 'No' at the start would have made her more able to say 'No' later — not just to sex, but to others' uncaring and exploiting behaviour.

Maggie's story highlights the risks of playing with that inflammable material, human lives. This particular game is one I wouldn't personally recommend. It's not that I think sex outside marriage is the worst possible sin and virginity must be preserved at all costs. It's not even because of the possible physical consequences short- and long-term, though they too are important (in spite of sex education and freely available contraception, unwanted teenage pregnancies continue to rise, and so do venereal diseases and cervical cancer). The reason I wouldn't recommend it, is what it does to young emotions and developing personality.

Where's this heading?

We started this chapter in the realm of short-term experiments, since that's what being an adolescent is largely about. But we've now moved to long-term effects; and this is where the whole subject becomes more relevant to you, who are most probably *not* a teenager any more (sad, isn't it?). It's also where I finally want to abandon Shakespeare and get into the Bible (what a relief, the woman's a Christian after all).

All through my reflections on those glorious and awful teenage years, one question has been battering at my mind. It's asked by the apostle Peter in his second letter to the churches (2 Pet. 3:11): 'What kind of people ought you to be?'

When Peter asks the question, he has just been reminding his readers that the physical world is not the whole of reality. Spiritual battles of good and evil are being fought out in the arena of human lives. If this is true, then everything we do in our human lives has a positive or negative value in that war. No wonder Peter asks such a searching question.

It gets answered, too. Peter answers it briefly: 'You ought to live godly and holy lives'. But that's a bit general. Paul answers it in greater detail in his letters. His recommendation to the Ephesians, for instance, is to ' . . . become mature, attaining to the whole measure of the fullness of Christ'. The result: 'We will no longer be infants, tossed back and forth by the waves, and blown here and there by every wind of teaching and by the cunning and craftiness of men' (that last bit appeals to me!); 'instead, speaking the truth in love, we will in all things grow up into . . . Christ' (Eph. 4:13−15).

What's the relevance of this to going out? I've already said that adolescence is a time of discovering who we are in relation to others − building, as it were, a social self. It's the right time to ask, 'What sort of person do I intend to be?' because so much of the answer is still up for grabs. We may try out and discard different styles of being and relating, but all the time we are laying foundations and establishing patterns for how we'll be in the future.

So which is it to be? Will we choose patterns which push

us towards true maturity — to be measured, as Paul tells us, against the character of Jesus? Or will we get stuck into patterns which simply reinforce immaturity, and leave us as grown-up kids, even middle-aged teenagers, who have a whole load of stuff to unlearn before we can learn anything better?

Perhaps the most important question to ask of ourselves in any dilemma is not, 'Is this a sin?' or 'Is this hurting anyone?' or even, 'How dangerous is this particular game?' — though these could all be useful, if difficult, questions. Perhaps an even better question would be: 'What sort of person is this turning me into?' A person who takes all she can and gives as little as she can get away with? A person who is more interested in ego-boosts than love? A person who avoids commitment at all costs? A person who, when things don't go exactly as he wants, turns his back and runs away? A person for whom another's body is just a set of sensations, not the awe-inspiring dwelling-place of God's image, of individuality and intimacy?

I think these are the kinds of questions adults in charge of teenagers ought to ask too. Too often 'discipline' is based on worry about external consequences: will my daughter get pregnant? will my son get VD? will parents think this school is irresponsible? If I had a teenage son or daughter, I hope I'd look more at internal consequences: Is this helping my child to grow up mature and responsible? One day, I won't be there to make their decisions for them — so I'd better make sure they get some reasonably supervised practice in making them for themselves.

When we were very young

Try looking back at your own teenage years in the light of Peter's question. What style of dealing with people did you adopt? What were your favourite 'strategies for success'?

Maybe like me, you established a habit of flinging ycurself into relationships very quickly, assessing them very quickly, and getting out of them again very quickly, without much thought for the other person. Maybe on the other hand you were always very cautious, analytical, holding back and terrified of doing the wrong thing. Maybe you tended to make very deep commitments, always believing that this was the real thing and was going to last for ever. Maybe you did that once, got hurt and resolved never to give anything of yourself again.

Maybe you spent your whole time fighting off admirers you considered unworthy, and wondering why you never managed to attract anyone with a bit more class. Maybe you were the compassionate type and could never manage to shake off any unwanted admirer who called on your sympathy. Maybe you always went for people a lot older or younger, but never quite asked yourself why. Maybe you felt you'd missed your timing at the starting gun and never succeeded in launching yourself into the field at all. Maybe you were even very sensible, and avoided all the pitfalls. I doubt it, though, since if you'd achieved that you'd be so perfectly together that you wouldn't bother reading this book!

My guess is that you will begin to see a pattern, and that it will tell you a lot about any problems you face now. That's why I've bothered to spend a whole chapter taking a look at the 'awkward age' — because what happens during those years has so much lasting influence.

Leaving it all behind

I don't want to imply that whatever our teenage years land us with is irredeemable. God forbid that anything or anyone

should be irredeemable! Unlearning what we would prefer
not to have learnt is possible at any age — and later
relationships can help us unlearn what we regret having
learnt in earlier ones.

Some of what people have to deal with as teenagers can
be a very heavy burden: family conflicts, bereavement,
sexual abuse. Some problems may go back to earlier
childhood roots; and they will have a major effect on
relationships and will take a lot of healing. Whatever we
have been burdened with or burdened ourselves with when
young — whether it's as serious as incest or perversion, or
only a tendency to injudicious flirtation — it *is* possible by
the grace of God to leave destructive feelings and habits and
acquire new ones. Getting off on the wrong foot in
relationships doesn't mean we have to hobble along for ever.

However, looking more closely at our own and others'
experiences may help us avoid making some of the worst
mistakes in the first place. Let's now begin to do that by
exploring how people choose the relationships they do.

4

TAKE YOUR PARTNERS

Most couples can cite cogent reasons for selecting a new car, house, item of clothing, or household furniture, but can give few, if any, for selecting each other.
David Klimek, *Beneath Mate Selection and Marriage*[1]

Brian arrived on my doorstep at eight o'clock on a Sunday morning, having travelled down from the North on an all-night coach. 'I'm looking for somewhere to have a kip,' he announced (people do this sort of thing when you live near a station). My parents, who had had the same idea the night before, took this unexpected awakening in their stride. 'Yes,' remarked my mother philosophically as we went off to church and left Brian sleeping it off on the sofa, 'I can see he's your type.'

What led her to that inspired conclusion? And what did she mean by it? I think what she had spotted was a combination of several things. The first and most basic was physical. He was tall, lean, a little ungainly and oddly vulnerable-looking, and he had a *gorgeous* regional accent. Not the only characteristics which attract me, but certainly a good selection of them.

But the physical thrill alone wouldn't have been enough. At what I'll call the social level, he was also very funny. I loved the quick repartee we automatically set up. I warmed to his sense of style, too — the first time I met him he knelt at my feet (ah, I thought, this is the kind of man I like). And he *could* be serious when he wanted to, even if it wasn't often.

And then there was what I'll call the emotional level. All the foolery was a clue that, underneath, Brian was actually very mixed up. He was a fantasist — very inventive but quite unwilling to face reality. All this added up to a good reason why going out with each other would have been a disaster. But at the same time it was precisely why I was drawn to him. Anyone more stable and mature, I would have dismissed at the time as 'boring'.

All this my mother, knowing me rather better than anyone else, instinctively spotted. We both knew he was the sort I went for. It was also obvious he was not at all suitable for me. The result: I flirted with him, lent him my sofa, made (usually unsuccessful) physical advances to him. But I never thought of him as a potential 'boyfriend'. I'd got him categorised: for amusement only.

Type casting

The story of Brian illustrates many of the hidden factors beneath the choices we make about relationships. From the moment we launch ourselves into this curious social system called 'going out', we are constantly asking questions and making judgments about who to say 'Yes' or 'No' to, what status any current relationship has, whether to start a new relationship.

Is so-and-so really the sort I'm looking for? Are they too

much like the last one, with whom I had such a bad time? Is this 'just' a friendship or is it developing into something else? Even if we're 'permanently on the sidelines' we'll speculate about what adventures we'd engage in, and with whom, if only we dared.

Not only do we ourselves ponder and wonder, but others love to give us the benefit of their advice. And we, in our turn, pronounce on others' relationships and give them the thumbs-up or the thumbs-down. 'What does she see in him?' 'She's no good for you.' 'You two could really get on'. 'We'll only be bad for each other.' It's all much more intriguing than the TV soap operas.

Most of us, however, don't really know ourselves very well. Our judgments about ourselves, and hence about our relationships, are only semi-conscious, and tend to run on pre-set patterns determined by our personality. And some of the unconscious forces that drive us on can be very destructive. So it can be very revealing to look at the phenomenon of 'my type': how we unconsciously sift through all the members of the other sex displayed on the social supermarket shelves and pick out the one we wouldn't mind taking to the check-out, given half a chance.

Like and unlike

'Opposites attract' is a piece of folk wisdom often trundled out to explain why, for instance, quiet shy analytical chemist Howard is obsessed by flamboyant actress Consuela, who yawns at all his tales from the laboratory, rather than that nice Susan who never seems tired of them. Yet sometimes 'birds of a feather flock together' seems more appropriate, as people with problems always seem to go out with people with equally big problems. So which saying is right?

A little psychology may make this clearer. Psychologist David Klimek, in the book I quote at the head of this chapter, suggests that people are attracted to someone of opposite character type, but similar emotional maturity and ability to relate.

According to this theory the outgoing, 'over-the-top' type will seek out a 'steady' person to fulfil his need to be controlled, while the depressive introvert chooses someone 'wild' to help her lose control. It's a way of looking to another person to supply the psychological experiences and expressions we lack. Hence Howard and Consuela.

At the same time people almost unerringly gravitate to a partner whose emotional health and stability is roughly similar to their own. The mature will tend to choose the mature, the unhappy to choose the unhappy and the confused to choose the confused. I'll quote Klimek's comment because I find it rather amusing. 'Only an emotionally ill person has the pathological conflicts and destructive impulses necessary to satisfy the other'.

I can just hear the lovelorn neurotic saying 'Darling, I adore your pathological conflicts and destructive impulses!'

Seriously, though, observation does seem to confirm this. Social workers will tell you how often the daughter of a home with a violent father will marry a violent husband. The positive equivalent is that the daughter of the manse will often marry a minister! Robin Skynner, in *Families and How to Survive Them,* [2] finds that even complete strangers, put together in a room and asked to get into pairs, will find someone whose pattern of family relationships mirrors their own to a remarkable degree.

Psychologists see in these 're-run' relationships an unconscious attempt to act out the problems of home again but 'get them right this time'. We may feel a buried guilt, thinking that difficulties in the family were all our fault, and we have to make reparation; or that to be put in a particular emotional position — such as that of 'victim' — is our destiny, which it is our obligation to fulfil. At its simplest, it's just a matter of what we're used to: when we put ourselves in a similar situation to one we already know, it just 'feels right'.

Love me do

Now this way of pairing up may be positive or negative. Klimek suggests that where two individuals are relatively emotionally healthy, opposite character types can complement each other. Their relationship can be the arena in which any conflicts and unmet needs of the past can be healed and a new maturity reached.

But where the underlying conflicts and needs are too deep, the partners expect so much from each other that neither can fulfil the other's hopes. Then the differences in their styles will become a source of further conflict: the tight-fisted depressive, for instance, finds his manic partner's impulsive spending intolerable, while she can't bear his 'carefulness'. Couples like this can be incredibly destructive to each other — as Brian and I certainly would have been.

The less we have been emotionally satisfied by our relationships with parents, family and any other romantic partners, the more we are likely to seek from this new opportunity. And the more disappointed we will be when it doesn't materialise, because the other person is only fallible like us. Or indeed because, though we long for emotional involvement, we may also be terrified of it and defend ourselves from it by every means we can find.

For the emotionally needy, then, finding a partner can lead to a double bind: the needy person feels too threatened and insecure to cope with a fairly 'together' partner; but choosing another needy person just multiplies the problems.

Take the example of Helen. She's a classic case of the child who felt it her job to keep her family together. In effect, she had to be 'Mum' to her brothers and sisters and even her parents. Helen now seems to feel most at home with immature ungiving men who put her in the same position she had in her family — expecting a lot from her but not giving her the nurture she needs. In fact she shows a very common pattern of relationship: getting involved with people who she knows will eventually reject her, because being rejected confirms her own self-image, her feeling of 'I'm worth nothing in myself, people only want me for what they can get out of me'. Until she finds a way to believe in her own value, she won't be able to cope with a more mature relationship.

Probably all of us are a little like Helen. Very few of us are utterly convinced that we are loved unconditionally, for ourselves — even though it's a central doctrine of Christian faith! So when we enter into what's supposed to be a love relationship, we may quite sincerely declare, 'I love you,' but much of our behaviour and body language may be crying out, 'Please love me'. Meanwhile our partner is giving out the very same message! This isn't necessarily self-centredness, just basic human need.

Chemistry lessons

Well, there's a few ideas as to why people pair up as they do.

You can't hang too much on a neat theory, of course, and there are a lot of other factors. Most of us tend (conveniently) to be attracted to people who live not too far away and who move in roughly the same social circles —

'Cupid's arrow does not travel very far,' say one pair of researchers.[3] (We prefer our familiarity spiced with a little novelty, however, like the Finnish schoolboy who preferred 'real girls' from other schools to the girls at his own!) Common interests are also a well-tried 'starter factor' — after all, a keen birdwatcher is most likely to socialise with other birdwatchers, so it's not surprising if the man who catches her eye happens to be one too . . .

And then there's good old 'chemistry' (I don't mean the sort Howard does). But even that generally works in tandem with other motives. Our eyes and other bits may long to feast on someone's body, but what we do about it will depend on how we feel about them as a person. Even 'pure lust' is usually tied up with other sorts of attraction — you may consciously despise the person you 'fancy', but those strong feelings are a response to something in their personality which links in disturbingly with something in yours. Most people, too, fancy those who are not 'out of their league'. However much we may fantasise about film stars, we would probably turn down more than a single date with one; we feel happier and safer with someone whose level of physical allure is about on a level with our own.

When you look at all the levels, then — the physical, the social, the emotional — I suspect it's always going to be the emotional that's the decisive one. That's just because of the kind of relationship a romance is: a relationship which opens up the totality of our emotional life, which makes total demands on our emotions and offers tempting vistas of total emotional satisfaction.

That's why I think it's important to know yourself if you are planning to get to know someone else. 'Try to have a sane estimate of your capabilities,' is how Paul puts it in Romans 12:3 (J.B. Phillips translation). That, of course, includes the worst you're capable of as well as the best! In

the interest of doing this, let me suggest a few of the
commonest self-deceptions that can lead to breaking your
heart over someone you probably shouldn't have touched
with a bargepole — or rejecting someone who might have
been a really good thing!

Cinderella's slipper

Remember the Ugly Sisters trying on Cinderella's glass
slipper and doing everything they could to pretend that it
really fitted them? One, finding the slipper too big, cut off
her toes to get into it; the other, finding it too small,
desperately tried to stretch her foot to fill it. We often
perform equivalent mental contortions to persuade ourselves
that a relationship 'fits'. Here are some of the ways we do it:

My saviour. If you're uncertain about your identity,
unhappy about your life or maybe just plain lazy, you may
look for the perfect Mummy or Daddy, who'll take all
decision-making out of your hands, put up with all your
faults and give you constant affirmation. It's only too easy
to project this fantasy onto someone and believe that they
can be the one to transform your entire life: best friend,
priest and therapist all rolled into one. Unfortunately, no
human being can actually live up to this! If you see someone
who appears to, better look twice — especially if they show
an inclination to believe the same about themselves.

Rescue job. The problem is, quite a lot of us do think
we can be someone else's salvation, for this world if not for
the next. So you may find yourself on the other side of the
equation, thinking you can redeem an emotional wreck
whom everyone else has given up on. What a triumph it
would be if you made it! However, it's extremely unlikely,
I'm afraid. The problem with this kind of relationship is

that it's playing at being a parent and a child, rather than meeting each other as two equal adults. It may work for a while, but what happens if the child begins to grow up and the parent feels threatened, or if the parent gets tired of the responsibility and the child no longer gets 'fed'?

It ought to hurt. This is another pattern that can arise out of insecurity or emotional immaturity. Somehow your circumstances have made you feel you don't deserve happiness, in fact it's quite right for you to be unhappy. So when you find a partner who makes you feel miserable, you conclude they must be the right person for you. You may fiercely defend their behaviour against criticism and tell everyone what a kind person they really are. They, of course, have a vested interest in keeping you under this illusion, since it means they get someone who will tolerate their misconduct!

Against the odds. Another popular game is to cling to someone who clearly doesn't fit the bill by common-sense standards, and tell yourself that 'love conquers all'. Never mind if the person doesn't share any of your ideas or goals in life, is a notorious heartbreaker, or has a spouse they never quite get around to leaving; never mind if all your friends hate them and the feeling is mutual; they are still the person for you because . . . well, because of the way you feel.

Showpiece. Being able to parade our 'ideal relationship' in front of the world is a very strong motivation for ignoring the realities of it! Laura and Guy, when they met, had both just ended other long-term relationships. Both were at similar stages in their education, both doing arts degrees, both had very similar dramatic spiritual experiences at the same summer camp. 'We felt God had brought us together.' But in fact the relationship had so many expectations loaded on to it that it started by being overwhelmingly intense, and ended with Guy abandoning his new-found faith and Laura at the same time. Were they really God's gift to each other — or were they just acting out a fantasy, projecting themselves as the perfect couple?

Desperation. Of course you may also accept a relationship you don't really want, just for the sake of having someone around. This is one to watch particularly if you haven't been involved with anyone for years and are desperate to know that you're still wanted! Christians can encourage this sort of thing with the teaching that 'with God's grace you can make it work with anyone'. This is nonsense, and merely a sanctified version of 'any relationship is better than none' — definitely *not* a biblical doctrine.

Walking shoes and old boots

If there are many ways of persuading yourself that a particular relationship will work, it's also possible to delude yourself into rejecting one that would actually do quite well. Determined to have that crystal slipper, you may refuse to try a perfectly comfortable walking shoe.

Life, however, has a way of jolting us out of over-fixed or inappropriate ideas of what we're looking for. I'm always heartened by my friend William who, at thirty-four, was still saying that he wanted an eighteen-year-old girl whom he could 'mould'. He never found one! At thirty-five he met a thirty-seven-year-old widow with two children. He took the risk of going out with her, and they're now happily married.

Perhaps, however, you're making the opposite mistake: thinking that it's you who aren't up to scratch. It's a self-fulfilling prophecy: for if everything about you — your posture, your clothes, your conversation — loudly proclaims 'nobody wants me' then no one will dare to contradict you. A shoe thrown on the junk pile will look like junk, even though all it really needs is re-heeling and a good polish!

Occasionally people in this position have their self-esteem restored by an unexpected relationship. More usually, they have to seek other ways of building their confidence (through counselling, or a new departure in their working life). Then 'miraculously' they will suddenly become more desirable. Confidence (not big-headedness!) is attractive.

True romance

How then, with all this potential self-deception, can you work out what to do about X who's pursuing you or Y whom you fancy like mad?

I'll start with a biblical guideline. In Philippians 4:8, Paul suggests what should go into a spiritual health diet. Fill your minds, he says, with 'whatever is true, whatever is noble, whatever is right, whatever is pure, whatever is lovely, whatever is admirable . . .' Is this just about not reading porn magazines? I doubt it. I'm always struck by the fact that 'true' is the first adjective in the list. And that puts Mills and Boon as well as *Playboy* on the suspicious list! The former may be more pure and lovely but neither has much to do with truth.

Now in the area of men—women relationships, there are plenty of people (including ourselves) trying to fill our minds with things that aren't true, however much we'd like them to be. We are stuffed with ideas about what's appropriate to 'romance' (red roses?), even what names are more romantic (why are novels full of characters called Darcy or Max de Winter?). Everyone has their opinion on how love's course ought to run, at what age people ought to be 'settled down' (and woe betide them if they're not), and who may pair up with whom (just see how an older woman and a younger man, or a taller woman and a shorter man are regarded, compared to the other way round).

As well as the junk that society feeds us with ('boys don't make passes at girls who wear glasses') we collect mental lumber peculiar to ourselves — 'never trust a man with a small nose' was what one woman's mother saddled her with. Christians add their own pennyworth, sometimes made up of what everyone else thinks thinly disguised in spiritual language ('it's the man's job to do the asking because he's the head'. . .).

All this makes it all the more vital that we look for what is true in relationships, and act accordingly.

We can learn a great deal from observing others' relationships. Being friends with a couple who are unafraid to be open about their relationship is a rare privilege. (If nothing else it can rapidly teach you that nothing on this earth is perfect!) Married, engaged and even 'going steady' couples could do a lot more to involve friends in their joys and sorrows, not in an unhealthy way by making them 'piggy-in-the-middle' in conflicts, but in a healthy way by sharing the ways in which they have grown through knowing each other.

Good literature, too, can be surprisingly educational. Though 'happy ever after' novels, or the steamier sort, give you totally false expectations of relationships, more searching works are full of insights about human personality and relationships. I've found some of the women's writing published by Virago has moved me deeply and made me think hard — particularly novels by Rosamund Lehmann and Antonia White, often sad but strangely hopeful too. And I think they could teach men a few things about how women see them. Or, for a male viewpoint, Arnold Bennett's

Clayhanger trilogy is a most revealing — and entertaining — study of love and conflict. Maybe the most fascinating of all, though it's a long read, is George Eliot's *Middlemarch,* described by Virginia Woolf as 'the only novel written for grown-up people'.

But I don't think you can get it all worked out by seeing what someone else does, or by sitting in your room reading this or any other book. The most frequent way of getting to know ourselves, after all, is to relate to others. We can learn a lot about ourselves from ordinary friends, if they are not too kind to us to point out our faults. But it's amazing how much more you discover in the emotional hothouse of a romantic relationship! So sometimes you just have to be brave, get involved, and be ready to clear up the mess afterwards if it doesn't work.

That may mean having the odd relationship which is not too good in itself. I've already stressed that a relationship, good or bad, which eventually ends isn't necessarily a failure — if you've learned from it. The trick is to learn from *one* mistake!

If your observation and experience have filled your mind with enough truth, then you won't need a set of instructions on what to do about X, Y, or Z. With the help of friends, prayer and common sense, you'll be able to work it out for yourself. Guidance, after all, is not a matter of shutting your eyes tightly and hoping God will tell you what you want to hear, any more than love is shutting your eyes tightly and hoping it will work out. It involves your brain as well as your heart.

Finally, getting a true perspective on things is not a technique but a habit of mind. It may take quite a few years and quite a few emotional bruises to be honest about yourself. I do believe it can be done. I might even be getting a little better at it myself. I met another 'Brian' the other day, who displayed a very sudden and disproportionate keenness on me. It took me a while to recognise his Brianishness and realise what a very poor prospect he was. I acted first and thought later, and then had to rethink fast. But at least I *did* notice in time to get out quick. I wouldn't have done a few years ago.

In the interest of thinking *before* acting, I'm going to look next at how, having decided we want or don't want a particular relationship, we then go about communicating our intentions to the other person — and discovering theirs.

5

YOU AND ME BABE — HOW ABOUT IT?

Are we having a relationship — or just doing research on each other?

Ashleigh Brilliant
Pot-Shots No. 626
© Brilliant Enterprises 1974

So here you are, knowing yourself a bit, hoping you've learned from a few past mistakes, and still looking for that elusive good-enough romance. You're a little more sure of your own identity now, and a little more sure of the kind of person you can get on with (or at least the kind you *can't* get on with — you're never going for a madcap like Chas again, or anyone as dull as Robert . . .).

Here you are, and there's that interesting Neal Garth from the evening class who's been looking your way a lot recently. He bought you a drink after class last week and you had that fascinating discussion. Neal with an 'a' . . . distinguished name . . . and he has an aristocratic look . . . Should you offer him that spare theatre ticket you've got for Friday?

On the other hand there's John from church, who's a very good friend, and has given you so much support over the years. Your relationship has always been brother-andsisterish, but on Saturday after the barn dance he actually kissed you good night. Only a quick peck, but it was certainly a surprise — so much so that you're not even sure if you liked it or not. What did it mean? You've often wondered if he wanted a different kind of relationship. Where do you go from here?

Meanwhile John is agonising over whether he was reckless on Saturday night. He's wanted a girlfriend for ages but it's only recently that his best friend put it into his mind that you might be a candidate. He feels it's his responsibility, as a man, to make the first move, but he's loth to risk 'spoiling a good friendship'. Besides, he's rather scared that you may just laugh at him. You've always rather intimidated him, and he was looking for a quieter, less demanding girl . . .

As for Neal, he doesn't really want to get tied down, and though he quite fancies you, he thinks you could be a bit too serious. And there's that remark you made about only wanting to go out with other Christians — he's not sure he'd qualify. So he's keeping you at arms' length while he thinks about it. Tune in for next week's exciting episode!

Question time

If discovering the truth is your aim, step one is obviously to ask yourself a few questions. Such as:

Why am I interested in this person? How much reality and how much fantasy is there in my attraction to them? Is Neal really someone with whom I can form a close friendship, or just a good-looking man with an interesting name?

What do I want from this person? I may be looking for a marriage partner, or moral support in my first year at college, or someone to go dancing with, or just reassurance that I'm still in the running. Any of these may be appropriate or inappropriate in the circumstances.

What does this person want from me? If all I'm after at present is a little gentle flirtation, and I look for it from someone who's got a desperate crush on me, I might well end up doing them a lot of damage. John, for instance, looks like the kind of person one shouldn't play around with.

Are we good for each other? Even if you do get on well, that doesn't necessarily mean you should be together. I can remember a number of uncommitted, quite enjoyable relationships which were really mutual 'stopgaps' until 'something better' came along. They didn't do any obvious harm. But I don't think they did much for our maturity. We were encouraging each other in a 'pick them up and drop them again' attitude to other people.

Is the timing right? How would a new relationship fit in with the rest of my life? An American I knew started going out with a girl at his college, just before he was due to come to England for a year. While he was in England, he got involved with an English girl. The relationship was never really defined or made public, and it was complicated by his guilt about 'two-timing'. When he went back, the American relationship soon petered out. Tempting as it was to have a girl in both ports, I don't think it was the best time for him to go out with either!

Am I prepared to pay the price? In a cupboard I have what I call the 'had-a-bash-ery department': relics of all the hobbies I once started but didn't keep up. That's all very well with sports and craft equipment, but people can't be tried out and discarded like that. Every close relationship means taking some responsibility for the other person — the hopes you may arouse in them, the fact that you may be keeping them from meeting someone else. The same applies to yourself, of course! Is there enough potential to make it worth risking pain?

Have I let God in on this? This is a difficult one. Many of us keep the 'romance' part of our life in a locked room marked 'No entry'. Others get so spiritual about it they do nothing *except* pray, for fear of making a mistake! I think the ideal is to talk to God about everything, but not expect a blinding flash from Heaven with detailed instructions on what to do next. God gave us brains to think things out for ourselves! Pray, then act, then pray again about the outcome, is a good policy.

Making moves

Let's assume you've thought, prayed and observed enough to decide it's worth moving closer. Is there a good or bad way of doing so?

There are certainly a lot of *different* ways of doing so. Remember Michael, who complained that 'It sounds so pathetic to say "Will you go out with me?" '? I do sympathise. It is a bit like a line out of a teenage magazine photostory. Not much better are some offers I've had: 'Shall we give it a whirl?' for instance (sounds like back to the fairground again!) or 'Let's see how it goes – no strings attached . . .' (before the first date he gives me the small print already?). Then there's my favourite line from an American cartoon: 'Hang it all, I'm stuck on you'!

I suppose any of these are better than the story I heard from Amanda, who worked with overseas students. One day a student came to her office and asked, 'Would you mind marrying a Korean?' 'Not if he was the right man for me,' she answered. 'Well,' came the reply, 'there's a young Korean man downstairs and he's looking for a wife.' There's nothing like laying your cards on the table, but I don't think somehow that he'd quite got his cultural differences sorted out!

We all have our own way of making that terrifying first move, and they're not all verbal. Harry was on a coach tour round Europe, and really liked one of the group. 'Somewhere between Brussels and Salzburg, on the coach, I dragged her into my arms and she stayed there.' His non-verbal signal was received, understood and replied to in the affirmative, all without saying a word. It worked! However it would be a mistake to think that every time Harry drags someone into his arms, he's after a long-term relationship. He's just a habitual hugger. When they got back to Britain they still had to sort out whether this was just a holiday romance or had potential for going on — and that needed words as well as hugs.

Beg pardon?

Amongst this variety of opening gambits, I'd hesitate to pick out a right and wrong way. We can't exactly go straight to the Bible for examples: the best we'd come up with is sending your father's servant and asking a girl to water your camels! (you've got to admit that 'Will you water my camels?' beats 'Come and see my etchings' . . .) What I would stress is the importance of *making sure the other person understands the language you're using*.

I'll explain that. Everyone has a different style of communicating. Some of us, like Harry, tend to get physical before we get verbal. Some are the other way around. Some will do neither, but wave a spare theatre ticket a few times and hope the message gets through. Some will come out with classic lines like 'Can I see you again?' or 'What are you doing next Saturday?'. I'm told that in America the unmistakable way of asking someone to 'go steady' used to be to offer her your class ring; in the UK we don't have class rings, so we have to be more inventive.

Any of these styles is fine, provided both people understand what they mean. But with the less explicit ways, there's a lot of scope for failing to get the hint, or reading rather more into it than is actually there. Sooner or later most of us will have to find a way to make quite sure of the answer to that question: 'Are we having a relationship?' (And if so, what kind of relationship?)

Truth or forfeit

'Speak up, girl, you've got feet!' said my German teacher once to my great amusement. But maybe she spoke more sense than she knew. In the end speaking out is often the only way of stepping closer to someone.

To find out what John meant by that kiss, the only way is to ask him! If your friendship is real it will survive the answer, and probably be deepened, even if it isn't turned into a romance. And the only way Neal will know what he's letting himself in for is to make his views heard — maybe not the minute you offer him that ticket, but as soon as he senses that things need clarifying.

All this is frightening, of course. Anyone but a megalomaniac will be afraid of rejection when they lay their heart on the line. Being accepted over-enthusiastically, or taken more seriously than you intended, can be equally unnerving — when Bob asked Judith out, her first response was, 'I'm not sure I want to get married', which must have been a shock for Bob, who hadn't actually asked her to marry him (yet)!

Owning up to your hopes, fears and doubts demands courage and a certain level of self-confidence. Young teenagers often delegate a friend to do it for them: 'Hey, my mate fancies you – do you fancy him?'. Something's wrong, however, in my opinion, when a thirty-year-old can't be a bit more direct.

Christians, in my experience, can be very wary of speaking out about relationships. There seems to be a general feeling that it's not quite nice to discuss such things, and the really spiritual person will just open up the Bible and get a verse telling them what to do. Sitting in your room with a photograph of the beloved in one hand and your Bible-reading notes in the other, feels a lot safer than facing possible rejection, misunderstanding or heartbreak! Hence the number of earnest young men who pre-empt any discussion by announcing to a young woman they hardly know: 'The Lord has told me I'm going to marry you' (to which the only sensible answer is, 'I'll let you know when he tells *me*'!).

No kidding

I think the Bible is on my side here. We've looked at Paul's advice in Philippians 4:8 to give our minds a full tank of truth. But he also recommends in Ephesians 4:25 that we *speak* the truth: 'Therefore each of you must put off falsehood and speak truthfully to his neighbour, for we are all members of one body'.

Now whenever there's a 'therefore' in Paul's letters, it usually means something important comes before it. In this case, the bit before is along these lines: now you belong to Jesus you are no longer dominated by your own instincts and impulses, which used to lead you so astray, but you are being transformed into a new kind of person with God's own truthfulness and justice. *Therefore* there is no excuse for messing each other about. Remember that in Christ you are also part of each other in a new way.

This is clearly a million miles away from the attitude typified by a 1920s advice book: 'Do you know how to put obstacles in a man's way and make him want you all the more?'. That kind of playing with people has no place among Christians. There is *no way* a follower of Christ can indulge in behaviour which is deceptive, irresponsible or manipulative towards a neighbour. And 'neighbour' does, believe it or not, include the person you fancy or who fancies you.

I want to stress this point because one of the main things which drove me to write this book is the fact that so few Christians seem to practise it. I've heard Christians give advice like, 'Don't let him know you're interested; play hard to get'. I've seen Christians suddenly and inexplicably 'dropping' a friendship because they didn't want it to go further but hadn't the guts to say so. All too often when it's a matter of dealing with the opposite sex 'love your neighbour as yourself' seems to go out of the window. This simply won't do.

The better part of valour

Of course truthfulness isn't tactlessness. 'There is a time', as my favourite cynic Ecclesiastes says, 'to be silent and a time to speak' (Ecc. 3:7). Paul follows up his command to speak the truth with an immediate qualification: 'Do not let any unwholesome talk come out of your mouths, *but only what is helpful for building others up according to their needs*' (Eph. 4:29).

As one who tends to analyse every relationship to death almost before it's begun, I've had to learn that sometimes it isn't a good idea to launch straight into a string of questions about my intentions, the other person's and the general prospects for the whole enterprise. You can overwater a houseplant cutting, and you can overload a new, hesitant and vulnerable relationship (which in many ways resembles a delicate plant!). It takes a fine judgment to know when to take the risk, and past experience will affect how you decide. If the last time you declared your feelings to someone, it cleared the air wonderfully, you may try the same tactic again. If however they laughed their head off, you probably won't!

I reckon Paul gets it right when he talks a little earlier in Ephesians about 'speaking the truth in love'. Keep both terms – truth and love – in balance and you can't go far wrong.

What about praying together about a potential relationship? It sounds like a good way of tuning in to God's guidance from the start, but I have some reservations about it. First of all, it's hard to pray naturally with someone you don't know well, and it could increase rather than decrease your shyness with each other. Second, it can make things a lot more 'heavy' than they need to be at this stage. And third, praying can create a warm 'spiritual' glow which gives you an illusion of greater closeness than you really have, and distort your view of the relationship. So here again, it's a matter of using your judgment as to what's appropriate.

Now you mention it . . .

One of my favourite (true) love stories which illustrates the effects of speaking up, is that of Chrissy and Tom, who were in the same house group. One day he said he wanted to talk to her about something. She'd had her eye on him for some time, and inwardly jumped with excitement, thinking he was about to confess to the same feelings. As he was rather shy and tongue-tied, she decided to help him out by saying that she was interested in him too. As soon as she'd come out with it, she realised that he was looking rather confused. In fact the possibility of their going out had been the last thing on his mind — he'd wanted to discuss something quite different!

It could have ended there, with embarrassment all round. But now that Chrissy had put the idea in Tom's mind, he discovered he didn't altogether dislike it. They're now happily married. Some misunderstandings turn out rather well . . .

It would be foolish to build too much on this apparently 'happy ever after' ending (in any case, marriage is more like 'and they worked very hard ever after . . .'). In many other cases, the answer to 'You and me babe, how about it?' will be 'Sorry, forget it'. Personally I'd still rather be told the truth, however painful, than have to guess it.

A woman's right to ask

Chrissy and Tom's story raises another question. There may be no standard way of making the first move, but a lot of people think they know who ought to make it. It's a man's job to do the hunting, they say; a woman can try every trick in the book to make him run after her, but she mustn't run after him. This usually goes with lots of pseudo-anthropological stuff about 'man the hunter', Victorian views about female reticence and modesty, twee humour like, 'A man chases a woman until she catches him', even theories about how the sex act shows us that it's 'natural' for men to take the initiative and women to be 'receptive' (what boring sex lives these people must have).

Let me say right out that I think this is a load of balderdash. Queen Victoria proposed to Prince Albert (she had to). Ruth made the first move towards Boaz (creeping under his blanket in the middle of the night — not an approach I'd recommend today!); and much of that beautiful biblical erotic poem the Song of Songs is an account of a woman running all around the town looking for her man. Nothing in the way God made men and women makes it inevitable that it's always got to be the man who asks for the date.

All the same, any woman who believes this and wants to act on it will need a lot of courage. I've asked quite a few men how they'd react if asked out by a woman, and without exception they said, 'Great, I'd love it'. The idea of being relieved of the burden of responsibility and the risk of rejection, freed from the 'go-getter' image and allowed to be their sensitive and shrinking selves — all that sounds very attractive in theory. But in practice, as many brave women find to their cost, being asked out tends to send a man into a blind panic, scuttling away from you as fast as he can go.

I wonder if what men really mean by 'I'd love to be asked out' is 'I'd love to be asked out by a stunningly attractive woman who isn't so assertive that I find her threatening'. But of course that's just the kind of person who *won't* ask them out: if she's that attractive she won't need to, and if she's not very assertive she won't dare to. If they're honest they might put it another way: 'I only want to be asked out by someone I actually want to go out with'. Sorry boys — we all want that, but it doesn't work that way. If we girls have got to kiss a lot of frogs before we find a prince, you might have to put up with a lot of Ugly Sisters before you meet Cinderella. Fair's fair.

Scrape him off, Jane?

But what then are we to do about the frogs and the Ugly Sisters when they appear?

At the time I started writing this book, a group reached number one in the charts with 'StarTrekking', a catchy little number including the memorable words: 'There's Klingons on the starboard bow, Scrape 'em off, Jim'. Not being a 'Trekkie' I'd never met Klingons before, but it seemed like an ideal title for the creature I want to talk about now: the unwanted suitor. Nothing clings on like a rejected candidate in the dating stakes.

In my experience, there are two favoured styles for dealing with clinging Ivy or creeping Ivor. Method one, more often adopted by males, is simply to avoid the lovesick maiden, ignore all her efforts to engage you in conversation, and generally treat her as if she's got a highly infectious plague.

Method two, usually preferred by females, is to tell the poor chap as often as possible, and in words of one syllable, that you're not interested, and hope that he'll eventually get the message. According to the soft-heartedness of the female victim, this may or may not be accompanied by reassuring assertions that he's a very nice person, but not for her.

You'll no doubt gather that I personally go for method two. Simply turning your back on someone, especially if you've previously seemed to be friends, can be very hurtful. Richard spent quite a bit of time talking to Geraldine, who went to his church. Geraldine valued the friendship; but suddenly, she found that Richard wouldn't talk to her any more. All she could think was that he must suspect her of amorous intentions — which she really didn't have. She was deeply upset, and it took a few months before she had the courage to confront him and sort it all out. It would have been far better if Richard had confessed his fears at the start, rather than apparently 'dropping' her.

Richard and Geraldine's story shows the importance of not jumping to conclusions too soon. In the church, where there's often a shortage of single men, lots of us women would love to spend time with men as friends; but find our approaches are constantly rebuffed because men seem to think we're desperate to 'get our claws into them'. Dear brother: when that sister keeps talking to you after service every Sunday, please don't assume she's got a handy combination engagement ring and lasso ready to fling at you. And even if she *does* turn out to be dying of unrequited love, do treat her as a fellow human being and not as a kind of garden pest.

A word of warning, too, about dismissing a potential relationship too hastily. This is a difficult one for women. There's a general opinion that 'When a woman says "No," she really means "Yes".' I couldn't disagree more. This lie is used not only as an excuse for the vicious crime of rape, but more widely to push women into relationships they really don't want. However, precisely *because* men can be so 'pushy', a woman may back off out of self-protection, from something which may turn out better than expected. So for women and men, it's worth asking: is this offer really unwelcome, or do I just need time to get used to the idea?

Kind to be cruel?

In my experience, relationships don't come in nice tidy 'all-or-nothing' packages. Every one is different, just as every person is different, and they tend to find their own level and make their own rules. Occasionally, having cleared the air on the romance front, you can carry on as the best of friends. When it's acknowledged that one fancies the other something rotten and the other doesn't, a friendship can be healthier than when it's only suspected and never confirmed.

But there's a very fine balance between trying to stay friends and stringing a person along. It can be very nice to have someone who thinks you're the best thing since sliced bread. It's tempting to push them just far away enough not to lose them completely, and keep them available by tossing them the occasional morsel of encouragement. I've done it myself!

This is *not* friendship. In friendship, both people have equal power. In an exploiting relationship, all the power is on one side, while the other waits like a dog under the table for the next crumb to fall. It may look generous — but it's a cruel way of being kind. However much you want admiration, you may have to be more cruel to yourself to be kinder to the other person.

None of this is easy. As Jackie complained, 'I hate having to say, "No," because if they've plucked up the courage to ask it's really hard on them . . . I'd hate to be a boy.' Rejected suitors can sometimes be as thick-skinned as a rhinoceros. They can seem not to understand your declaration of lack of love; refuse to accept it; even respond to it with abuse ('Oh, you're just neurotic, you'll never make a relationship with anyone . . .'). All this can try your patience. But remember, however hard it is, you're dealing with a vulnerable person who will take your response as a measure of their personal worth — not with a door-to-door encyclopedia salesman who's called at an inconvenient time. And remember, too, we're called to pray for those who persecute us!

When truth hurts

Finally, a word to the other half of the equation. What if *you* are the rejected swain or constant nymph?

Love hurts, whether it's real, imaginary, one-sided or even returned. And if someone is hurting us, however unintentionally, we want to do something with the hurt. We can turn it in on ourselves, turn it back on the other person, or maybe just write a poem with it. On the whole, I think the poem is the healthiest, so long as you don't imagine it's publishable. If you're not into poems, may I make a few other suggestions?

Try to keep in touch with reality. Dreams are exciting and necessary, but they're *your* dreams, not the other person's. Don't impose them on him/her. He's probably not the person you dream he is, anyway — if you did go out with him you'd soon know that. She doesn't feel about you what you feel about her; she can't manufacture those feelings, and you have no right to expect her to.

Focus on real hope, not false hope. Christian friends are fond of bucking up the lovelorn with verses like Jeremiah 29:11: 'I know the plans I have for you . . . plans to give you hope and a future.' Apart from the fact that this was addressed to a nation in political turmoil, not to a heartsick single, the Bible repeatedly stresses that our hope is to be *in God* — not in what we've decided God ought to do for us. God promises us good things, but not always what we think we'd like.

Be open to other relationships. Carrying a candle indefinitely for your great love is dramatic, but destructive. OK, you don't feel for Henry the Second what you felt for the unavailable Harry the First. And you're sure there'll never be a Hal the Third. Nevertheless, you might have some really good times and do a lot of learning, with Henry the

Second; and it might even prepare you for a more lasting relationship with Hal the Third, when you meet him.

See it in proportion. I used to wait for the one relationship which would satisfy me on every level. It doesn't exist — not with another human being. Even if that fascinating man I long for also longed for me, I'd still need rewarding work, other friends, hobbies. Well, I can have all those things now, without him. In other words, that unattainable love is not the centre of life. God is, and he has a whole load of other satisfactions — and opportunities for service — in store for us.

Accept help. 'Hope deferred makes the heart sick,' says Proverbs 13:12. It's hard enough living with an unfulfilled longing, but twice as hard if you keep it to yourself. Don't be self-indulgent in dwelling on the unique charms of the beloved, but do share it all with one or two sensible friends. A lot of the why not and the what now will become clearer as you do.

Enough of this sad story. This book is mainly about relationships which *do* happen, so let's carry on looking at the hazards to be negotiated when they do.

6

GETTING SOMEWHERE

No relationship grows without pain . . .
                                                    'Harry'

Jane and Sarah met at the youth club barbecue. They liked
the look of each other. They met a few more times, and one
thrilling day Jane invited Sarah to go ice skating. At the end
of the evening, Jane took a deep breath and said, "Will you
be my friend?' 'Well, we can give it a go,' answered Sarah,
'but let's not get too involved.'

In the last few weeks they have been getting closer — but
they keep falling out. Jane wants to meet more often, but
Sarah wants to keep her other friends. Sarah's parents don't
approve of Jane, and think she should concentrate on her
exams. Sarah got really jealous when Jane spent the whole
evening with Tracy. Jane gets bored by Sarah's passion for
archaeology. They're both wondering whether it's all worth
it — but when they agreed to spend a fortnight apart, they
really missed each other.

No, this isn't a tale of lesbian love. It's an attempt to
shock you into realising how odd the institution called 'going
out' is. If Jane and Sarah really behaved this way, we'd
think there was something wrong. If Jane and Simon do,
it's normal. True, some of the problems above do arise in

same-sex friendships. But in 'going out' they seem to arise in a unique form. That's why I'm always wary of referring to going out as a 'friendship'. It is and it isn't.

So what is it that makes going out such an explosive mixture of joy, sorrow, love and hate? In the next few chapters I'm going to explore a few of the landmarks and obstacles that appear as a relationship develops, the difficulties that threaten to send a relationship onto the rocks, and how we negotiate our way among them.

Laying down the law

'Is she really going out with him?' sang Joe Jackson several years back. The first thing we do in a new relationship is to discover just what set of rules is operating.

We do this implicitly in any friendship. But in 'going out', we're more likely to do it explicitly, asking just what kind of commitment we're both making. Who decides how often we see each other? Who else we see? What kind of activities we share? Are we both allowed to get in touch whenever we like, or is that 'pestering'? Are we *obliged* to keep in touch frequently?

How you handle such questions at the beginning is a measure of how strong the relationship will be. If one partner, for instance, evades all the issues and the other feels afraid to bring them up, this suggests a lack of real 'investment' in the relationship on one side. At the other extreme, if you want to set up watertight rules from the first date, this shows excessive insecurity!

Many issues will be worked out unconsciously, as each tests the other to discover where they stand. It's a bit like the way two dogs meet and decide whether to fight or play (except that the human way of 'sniffing around' is more discreet!).

At this early stage we may play all sorts of games; flirting, changing our mood rapidly, acting out behaviour we've learned from films or books, introducing the person to a new environment to see how they react. One of my own favourite 'set-ups' (for men with cars only) is to go on a day out and discover whether he is willing to stop for tea at a nice olde-worlde tea-shoppe. A man who'll only stop at the Wimpy, or refuses to stop at all, has failed. I wonder what tests men have put *me* through without my realising it!

Power play

What am I actually doing with my 'tea-shoppe test'? I'm checking whether his tastes are similar to mine. I'm finding out how willing he is to fall in with my wishes. Most importantly, I'm asking where the power is; in his hands or in mine. Can I make him fit my picture of how I want things to be, or will he dominate me?

It isn't a very admirable way of approaching things. But in the real world relationships inevitably involve struggles for power, because we are frail human beings who need to feel secure and strong. The moral issue is not whether or not there will be a power game, but how we play it. We can play it competitively, fighting for control. This way only one person wins; indeed if it destroys the quality of the relationship, no one wins. We can capitulate and let the other person walk all over us, which is good neither for their maturity nor our own. Or we can play the game co-operatively, seeking to sort things out together. This way, if it works, both win.

David Klimek helps us to look at this negotiating process

more closely, by outlining several stages a relationship has to go through in establishing itself.[1] At each stage there are positive or negative choices to make, which decide whether the relationship grows healthily. Each stage builds on the success of earlier ones, but at each stage the relationship can get 'stuck' and stop developing. I'll explain the stages briefly.

Where do I stand?

Stage one is the 'testing out' stage, where you're finding out what the other person is really after, whether they have, as the Victorians used to say, 'honourable intentions' towards you. Is he serious about this relationship, or am I just a bit of fun? Is it really me she wants, or just someone to be seen with?

One danger of this stage is that you might feel compelled to give in to all the other person's wishes, or appear to agree with them more than you actually do, for fear that any conflict will break the relationship. Or, if you're a more dominant person, you might aim for the same end by trying to mould the other person to fit in with all *your* ideas! Something like this happened with Ruth and Paddy – Ruth found that Paddy had 'funny ideas about what should happen, and didn't tell me anything about it – I was unconsciously acting in his own private drama.'

Of course, this means that there isn't any genuine relationship there to break, since you're relating with a 'front', not your true selves! Most people can't keep up this pretence for long, since sooner or later they'll feel the urge to say what they *really* want or think, and then the strength or weakness of the relationship will begin to show.

Shyness can also be a factor in hindering this early stage. Shy people, especially if they've never had a 'romantic' relationship before, may feel they haven't got anything interesting to share with the other person. Why should he/she want to know about my grandparents or where I went to school? And, even in these days of mixed education, you find less socially confident young people complaining, 'I don't know how to talk to boys/girls'. (The answer is: the same way you talk to human beings. Yes, that's what they are. If you still haven't discovered this by your twenties, take a deep breath, be brave, and find out.)

Well, since this person takes enough interest in you to spend at least one evening with you, they probably do want to know a bit more about you. And if you do run out of conversation, don't assume you've failed to be scintillating enough – it may just be that this particular relationship hasn't got so much going for it after all. Which is in itself worth knowing.

A different tendency of the early stage, with more outgoing people, is to be very 'open' on the surface, leading the other person to think you're sharing a lot of yourself – whereas in fact you're keeping a lot more hidden and not even acknowledging that it's there. I know I've done this a lot! It can take quite a long time to get past this mask, and needs a perceptive person to see it's happening; but if the couple reach a certain degree of emotional intimacy, the amount that's been kept 'in reserve' will be apparent.

The important thing at this stage, if you do find the relationship continuing, is to make a genuine commitment to each other, however limited that is. If you're unsure about how 'serious' you want to be, it's OK to say so. But if you're not prepared to let it *grow* into something deeper, but want to keep it perpetually at the 'no strings' level, then that's highly unfair to the other person and you probably ought not to be starting at all. If you're not open to future development, you can't be open to relating in the present.

Don't mess me about

Stage two is to do with trust, and how much responsibility each partner is ready to take on. Does he care enough about me to put other things and other people second? If she promises to do something, can I rely on her to do it?

This is a stage at which faithfulness becomes an issue, because obviously trust can't develop unless you're sure you're special to the other person and not just one of many. And faithfulness is not just about whether your partner kisses or flirts with someone else. It includes the loyalty which stops them from passing on your secrets or talking negatively about you behind your back.

A major danger here is the temptation to keep one's partner 'under surveillance', never giving them a chance to go astray. It's almost inevitable that they'll eventually feel oppressed by the relationship and want to withdraw from it! The corresponding temptation on the other side is to expect your partner's trust while doing absolutely nothing to earn it!

If you're the one under suspicion, it's important to *demonstrate* to your partner that you can be depended on — what you do communicates far more than what you say. Especially if the lack of trust takes the form of jealousy or 'clinging', it's useless for the 'offender' to protest that their partner is just 'too possessive'. No amount of assurances that 'I do really care for you' will patch things up. What the jealous partner needs is to *see* that care. 'I care for you but I'm not willing to change behaviour that upsets you' is a nonsense.

But the less trusting partner has a responsibility too: to make reasonable and not ever-increasing demands. No one can live happily under constant testing! (Of course, if your partner really *is* totally unreliable, the time has come to give them a straight talk . . .)

Most of all, trust has got to be mutual; it's not a question of gritting your teeth and forcing yourself to trust the other person, or them to trust you. Trust is the ability to depend on each other and share with each other, and it's a *product* of closeness as well as a *pre-condition*. We need basic trust to be close, but growing closer makes us trust more.

You, me and us

Stage three is about dependence and independence, allowing both partners to have space to be themselves. If I have interests or views my partner doesn't share, will he/she find this too threatening? Can I disagree without bringing emotional 'punishment' down on my head?

Two obstacles can make this stage impossible to handle. One is insecurity: one partner may be afraid to be alone and demand non-stop attention, or else they may fear making any demands of their own and want to be 'taken over' and absorbed in the other person's life. The other obstacle is unwillingness to give: one person may guard their own activities fiercely and have to be begged or threatened in order to give any attention to their partner. In either of these cases the couple cannot achieve the right balance between being together and being separate — one constantly tries to hold on to the other, the other constantly pulls away.

Again, building each other's confidence is a key to growing in this area. If your partner is afraid to let you go for fear you won't come back, you need to do something to allay those fears. Trying to push them away and force them to 'stand on their own feet' won't work, because they will just feel more insecure and hold on tighter. The more affection and encouragement you give, the less clinging they will need to be. This isn't easy, if you feel 'smothered'! But if they're feeling unloved, love is the only thing that will help.

On the other hand if you're the possessive one, you need to understand why you're being like that. Are you letting too much of your happiness depend on this relationship, instead of keeping your life more balanced? Do you need to tackle deeper problems to do with your own feelings of worth? Or is it that the other person genuinely hasn't given you enough demonstration that they care?

All of us have what psychologists call 'dependency needs' — the need to be reassured that we are valued and important to someone. We also have a need to be independent, to act in our own right — and we can't do that until our needs for dependency are met to some extent. But the goal is to be *interdependent* — to relate at a deep level, neither keeping ourselves rigidly distant, nor being swallowed up by the other person.

I care because I care . . .

Finally there is the stage when we are ready to change our behaviour for the other person's good, without needing a complicated set of rules to force us into it. The choice here is whether we will care spontaneously, or have to be frog-marched into caring — which isn't, of course, caring at all. It's rather like the difference between law and grace — will we do God's will because the Bible or the church says we must, or because we love God?

Obviously getting to this stage depends on having got through the others at least moderately successfully. A relationship that gets this far is a very mature one; and that probably means it's a relationship between two very mature people! As one young person said, 'As you get older you work at it more — when you're younger, if problems come up, you just ditch the person.' A mature relationship takes years rather than months to get to, and probably means we've been through some immature relationships first. Fortunately, relationships are a good way of maturing!

In practice the stages overlap, and under stress we may find ourselves going back to 'revise' an earlier one. In fact most 'going out' couples never get much beyond the early stages, and indeed few marriages make it to stage four. But the stages provide a map of where we might get to, and a way of seeing how far we've got.

In a 'successful' relationship, there's openness to positive change, constant adjustment to each other and to circumstances, and frequent communication, which is the way we find out what needs adjusting and begin to adjust it. A 'blocked' relationship can be caused by reluctance to face problems, by pressure to have problems solved 'instantly', or by anger which makes us explode at the other person, or 'close off' from them. If there's this much anger, it's probably left over from past experience, and it may need expert counselling.

I think Christian faith can be a help or a hindrance in developing a mature relationship. A rigid, guilt-laden view of Christianity can be used as a stick to beat the other person or oneself into submission, and thus be a block to real sharing of feelings and growing in understanding. A person with this distorted view of their faith may feel that expressing emotional needs to their partner is 'weakness' and that they should depend only on God. Or else they may think the opposite, that a relationship between Christians should be so close that they need no other friends or independent activities. Both of these ideas prevent people exposing their real selves, with their varying needs for closeness and for space.

But for those who understand the real freedom Jesus gives, faith can promote maturity in relationships. When he started to go out with Judith, Bob found his new-found faith in Jesus made a significant difference in the process of building up trust and allowing her space. Bob's father had deserted the family when Bob was a baby, and his mother and grandmother, who brought him up, had been very dominant. But because he now felt more secure in the fact that Jesus loved him enough to die for him, he was not so desperate to get affirmation from Judith as he had been with previous girlfriends.

And at a practical level of course, Christian faith implies being an active part of the church, which should put us in contact with many more sources of help in our relationships than we might otherwise have access to: ministers, pastoral workers, Christian counsellors and just ordinary Christian friends.

Who knows about this?

Mentioning outside helps brings us to an important question: when and how far should you make your relationship public?

Some couples, particularly where one or both is in a public position, feel they need to keep their relationship secret. One curate I know and his girlfriend (now his wife) arranged to leave parties separately! This may be necessary occasionally, since eager friends and relations can put on a lot of pressure for the relationship to be more significant than it is. Even less public figures feel this weight of other people's expectations at times: Harry says he's experienced 'pressure from people in my church to be further on in a relationship than I really am', while Laura felt her fellow Christians were seeing her relationship with Guy 'in terms of our potential ministry as a couple' and as for Jan, she had to contend with her boyfriend's mother wanting to buy them a house!

Nowadays it's not only the older generation who want to get in on the act, either. A single parent may well want to keep her new relationship from the curious eyes of children for a while — not to mention the eyes of concerned friends who are keen to get her 're-settled'. In the words of Judith, a new relationship sometimes needs 'protecting from other people, like a young flower'.

The trouble with going on keeping things secret, however, is that after a while it calls into question how committed you really are to the relationship. Why don't you want others to know? Are you ashamed of your partner, or do you want to avoid being called to account for your treatment of them? Personally I would always favour making things public as soon as appropriate (obviously not till you both agree that you *are* going out!). To know that your partner acknowledges you in public is an essential part of that early stage of creating trust. It's fairer to other hopeful admirers; it's a duty to others (such as children) who may be involved; it makes the commitment more secure.

It also means, as I've suggested, that you can get help if problems arise. People around you may see things more clearly than you can when you're in the midst of it. It's all very well to say, 'But you don't know how great she really is'; what they do know is that to all appearances she is treating you appallingly. Maybe if you listen to them you'll realise too, and confront her.

Whenever possible, getting advice and support from others should always be something you do together as a couple, not independently. Then the third party can get the full picture, not just the grouses of one side or the other.

It's only right and proper . . .

If other people can be pressurising, one of the biggest
pressures on a developing relationship is the sheer weight
of what we ourselves hope from each other. Our
expectations may be very specific and concrete: I call them
concrete because, in the words of the old joke, they're
usually all mixed up and permanently set! Here's a selection:

'He ought to treat me like a lady' (i.e. order my food for
me, pay for it, open the door for me, and so on and so
on . . .).

'She ought to knit me jumpers, like my mum does.'

'He ought to ring me when we haven't spoken for a week.'

'She ought to introduce me to her friends/parents/
church.'

'He shouldn't expect me to sit around while he spends
hours under his car.'

'She shouldn't flirt with her cousin like that, even if he
is her cousin.'

'He ought to tell me why he's feeling down, and not make
me guess.'

'She ought to have a life of her own and not depend on
me so much.'

You could probably add to the list yourself . . .

Some of these arise from our experience of family life.
We may want our partner to reproduce everything our
parents did ('My father always buys the drinks — why don't
you?') or hope they'll make up for everything our parents
didn't do ('My father wasn't around — you be my daddy').

Some expectations are picked up from romantic stories:
'Heathcliff was in Cathy's arms in one bound — why are
you so undemonstrative?'. A lot of them concern what we
think makes a *real* man or a *real* woman, which often has
little to do with reality.

Pessimists aren't disappointed . . .

Is the answer, then, to expect nothing, so you can only be pleasantly surprised? I don't think so! If you didn't hope for something from the relationship, you wouldn't have started it.

I think the answer is to sort out what you realistically *can* expect from what you can't.

You can expect the person to give time to you. I had one (very short-lived) boyfriend who was so busy he would say things like, 'I can see you on Thursday week between nine and nine-thirty pm.' I don't think he really wanted to go out with me, and he soon demonstrated it by disappearing unceremoniously. However:

You can't expect them to live for you alone. They've still got other friends, work, church, hobbies, commitments. If you disagree about the balance between these and your relationship, you'll have to work it out between you.

You can expect them to consider your feelings. It's you they've chosen to relate to, and they can't have your company, care and cuddles without taking your emotions on board too. If they seem reluctant to do so, you have a right to object. However:

You can't expect them to guess your feelings. Marriage counsellor Jack Dominian says, 'What most couples long for is that look of instant understanding which comes without a word being said'.[2] I agree, but behind that 'instant' understanding there's usually a long process of far-from-instant explanation!

You can expect them to adapt to you. Attraction at first sight is commonplace. Love takes more effort. A person who thinks they can love without changing in the process is an immature person. You could be the one to help them mature . . . but not by giving in to their every whim. However:

<u>You can also expect to have to adapt to them!</u> Their lifestyle, habits, thoughts, feelings, friends and family are different from yours. Some differences are exciting; some will be inconvenient, puzzling, annoying. You've then got to decide what you'll do about it: insist your way is best, or reconsider.

To sum it up briefly if negatively, *you can expect conflict.* That's not necessarily a bad thing, or a sign of having made the wrong choice. Many Christians (and others) see conflict as a threat, to be avoided at all costs. But in fact conflict is how we learn. If we never had difficulties, we'd never learn anything — as with new skills, so with new relationships (and older ones!). When you encounter a clash, that shows you how much you still need to learn about relating. And knowing how much there is to learn is the first step in learning.

So there should be a lot of learning in going out, because there are a lot of sources of conflict! In the next chapter, I'll go into more detail about some common conflicts that arise.

7

LOVE AND WAR

Dear Charlie, I hate you, Love Martha
Quoted in Alan Loy McGinnis, *The Friendship
Factor*[1]

My boss claims never to have rows with his wife. I have to
believe this, since he's a truthful person, but I think he's
either very exceptional or has a different definition of 'row'
than mine. Perhaps he'd admit to the occasional
'disagreement'?

For the rest of us, 'differences of opinion', to put it
politely, are an inevitable part of any close relationship.
Indeed, your first row may be the point when you really start
to get closer, though the second row may be the point when
you break up! It all depends on how well you can handle
the clashes.

Let's look, then, at some of the commonest causes of
disagreement, and at ways of handling them.

What we gonna do then?

I laughed at *Datebook* magazine's encyclopedia of
everything from arts dates to zoo dates; but maybe they had

something. Just how you actually spend your time together is one of the first hurdles when you start to go out.

Is 'out' literally where you're going? How will you agree what play or film or group to see, how much money to spend, who pays? Or will you simplify the matter by sitting in Mum and Dad's front room for the evening — or if you're older, in your own front room?

If you're the shyer sort going to a show might be a good way of side-stepping the long silences as you wonder what to talk about (though you won't get far if you don't talk at all!). Besides, spending all your dates 'getting to know each other' in the front room, presents a great temptation to concentrate on non-verbal communication to the exclusion of the verbal kind. It's amazing how many people who are too shy to talk deeply aren't too shy to kiss deeply! Indeed, much physical involvement goes on because one partner is afraid to say they'd rather cool it and get back to talking. This is silly — if you don't know each other well enough to discuss your physical relationship, you don't know each other well enough to have one.

However you decide to spend your time, the very process of deciding is part of making a relationship. So it's important to aim for mutual agreement, and to major on activities that give you space to discover each other's personalities, likes, dislikes and feelings. In the words of an Irish teenage girl, 'a long walk and a long talk are better than anything else' — certainly better than 'snogging in the movies or shouting in the disco'.[2]

Your world or mine?

Remember Jim in chapter one, who was full of his own cricket scores, but showed no interest at all in Susie's concerns? The furthest he ever got in exploring her world was to ask her once what her father did.

'Common interests' are the first thing computer dating agencies seek out. I'm not sure how vital they are. For some people they are a priority, for others they aren't. What *is* vital is that both partners should care enough to gain some insight into the things that matter to the other.

Emma reads, and writes, a lot of poetry. Andy delighted in declaring to her, 'Poetry is rubbish'. She in turn took no interest in his pursuits. Frank on the other hand came to a poetry festival with her, and confessed, 'I was useless at this stuff at school but I'm beginning to understand it'. She went with him to see historical astronomical instruments. She was totally bemused, but tried hard to see what he saw in them.

Andy couldn't be bothered to enter Emma's world — maybe he was embarrassed by not being competent in it. Frank made the effort, and she responded. I know which relationship is healthier.

How deep is your love?

I once went out in a large group with Winston and Shelley, who were going out with each other. For the whole evening, Winston talked and joked with everyone — except Shelley. If I was told they were complete strangers, I'd have believed it! Shelley was a very insecure person, and he could hardly have chosen a worse way to treat her. Anyone would have been jealous.

Jealousy is not always about 'unfaithfulness', real or suspected; we can be jealous of our partner's friends, their interests, their work, even their faith.

Of course, jealousy may be inappropriate. That's where

defining boundaries comes in. Not long ago, Joe and Erica
were officially 'just friends' and so were Erica and Doug.
Both friendships had some kissing and cuddling in them.
Now Erica and Joe are closer, and she no longer feels right
kissing Doug.

If Joe feels sure of Erica's commitment to him, he won't
stop her seeing Doug altogether. But if he feels threatened,
either she will have to (perhaps temporarily) sacrifice her
friendship with Doug, or find other ways to show Joe that
she puts him first. I think the latter would be better.

Part of the furniture

'I feel I'm taken for granted' is probably a commoner
complaint of women against men, though it can happen the
other way round too. What does it actually mean when you
take it apart?

I've talked of 'going out' as different from other kinds
of friendship; more important to us than other friendships,
more scary, with more emotional ups and downs. Naturally,
if you feel this way about it, you want to know your
boyfriend or girlfriend feels that way too. And short of a
marriage proposal (which you may want, but perhaps not
yet), you want evidence that they do. Evidence that would
be accepted in court, or at least by your friends. At the very
least, for them to arrive on time, looking suitably
enthusiastic and dressed in their best (or if it's a house-
painting date, their worst?). Preferably, you'd like the extras
too: little presents, letters with smudged writing, zany
surprises. So if they never think of things like this, you're
understandably a bit irate. Do they really give a brass
farthing?

Like jealousy, demanding the 'red roses' sort of romance

can be appropriate or inappropriate. I recently heard of a married couple who bought each other flowers *every month* on the date of their wedding — their 'monthiversary'. This is so over the top that it devalues itself. The whole point of 'special' gestures is that they should *be* special, not run-of-the-mill. But as Alan Loy McGinnis points out, 'Ritual is one of the universally important ingredients in good relationships'.[3] People need those 'signs of caring', some of which come round regularly and mark the high points in the rhythm of life, and some of which are extra and show the extravagance of emotion. It's all a question of balance.

So far away from me . . .

Ever heard one of those sad old folk songs about the couple on opposite sides of the river with no bridge? Transport may be better these days, but couples who live at a distance still have special problems to face.

Apart from the practical difficulties of getting together, the inevitable on-off-on-again nature of the situation creates its own tensions. You may argue about whether he could manage more time with you if he 'really' wanted. You may feel obliged to be on your best behaviour all weekend because it's the only time you have and it would be a shame to spoil it — so you never say what you feel. You may fight about how to spend that precious time, and whether you can 'waste' it seeing friends. You may save up your resentment all week about some trivial misdemeanour last weekend, till it blows out of all proportion.

All these problems can be overcome if the relationship has a good foundation. That probably means you need a longish time together whenever you can. (This may well be the time when you find there isn't so much there as you thought!)

It's equally important (especially if, as is likely, you met on holiday) to find ways of deliberately linking your relationship with your ordinary everyday life of work, friends, church, family — because this is the bit that won't happen so naturally when you live at a distance.

Whose date is it anyway?

'Can I come in for a cup of your mum's cocoa? I love your mum's cocoa', one of my teenage 'fellers' would say. In this case cocoa wasn't a code word for slap and tickle — he really did like her cocoa. I used to wonder if he liked my mum more than me!

Going out isn't usually just Jack and Jill — sooner or later it'll involve Jill's mum and Jack's dad and Jill's mate Jackie and Jack's football team and the vicar . . . Whether it's Mum saying, 'You're too young', or Dad saying, 'I'm not having my daughter go out with a hairdresser', or the youth group leader saying, 'When are you two getting hitched, then?', everyone wants a look in, welcome or unwelcome.

Should you tell them all: 'Go boil your head, it's my affair'? No. They are involved because they care about you. Your family, friends and church are part of you; your partner's are part of her/him. If you are genuinely interested in your partner's life, that includes the other relationships in their life. After all, if you do end up together for ever, they will be *your* family and friends, for better or worse. And vice versa.

In the meantime, family and friends have real, though not unlimited, claims on you and thus on your relationship. Parents, for instance, who ask their teenage offspring to be home by a certain time, do so because they are genuinely concerned for their daughter's or son's safety. The eager swain who wheedles you into staying out 'just ten minutes more' till you miss the last bus is doing you no favours — if he doesn't care about your relationship with your parents, he doesn't care about you.

If you're lucky, your partner's family may be a positive bonus of your going out. Lizzie found that with each steady boyfriend, his family was a much-valued alternative to her own. I'm sure lots of us have cried more at losing a boyfriend's or girlfriend's mum than at losing the boy- or girlfriend!

One more way in which others can be constructively involved is that, believe it or not, your parents were once young and starry-eyed too. Even if that was thirty years ago, people weren't so very different, and dating already existed. Parents who are willing to talk about their own experiences (rather than just declare their opinions!) can be an enormous encouragement not only to the heartbroken fifteen year old, but to the world-weary thirty or even forty year old.

I said that the claims of others aren't unlimited. Once you're of age (which legally is now eighteen) your family still have a right to express their views about your boyfriends or girlfriends, but not to impose their wishes. Part of being an adult is the freedom to make your own mistakes.

Something similar applies to the rights of other friends. Yes, they are free to say if they feel neglected because you have a new romance. And you are free to disagree with them, although they may be right! But 'the lads' or 'the girls' can't claim as much of your time as they did before you started going out — they must accept that you need time together.

The other side of the tracks

If different interests or views can be a source either of stress or of enrichment, the risks are even greater when you're from different cultures. Even in an increasingly mixed society, Mum and Dad will worry when their offspring turns up with a new love who isn't 'one of us'. It's a problem for Asians, Jews, Afro-Caribbeans and many others. Even different social classes, sadly, can still be a source of trouble.

Parents who worry aren't entirely unreasonable. Cultural differences may not matter in a weekly trip down the disco, but they matter when things 'get serious'. You've probably been brought up with different styles of family life, different ideas of correct male and female behaviour, maybe even different languages. (And this can apply to social class too — if you doubt it, just ask a countess and a cleaner what they call the toilet — or should I say the lavatory, or the loo, or . . .) It's hard enough to relate across the great divide between the sexes, without all this as well!

Celia faced this when she went on an evangelistic mission to India, and met a young man who seemed interested in her. She was wondering whether God was calling her to work there, when the young man's employer offered her a job, and he promptly proposed to her. When she went home to think it over, he arrived to visit her laden with presents. Unknown to her, these, according to his local custom, were engagement presents! Cultural crossed lines like this can take a lot of sorting out. But the clash needn't be this dramatic — it could be as everyday as your views of timekeeping (African views are very different from European!) or what behaviour is considered polite.

I'd be the last one to say people from different cultures shouldn't go out. One of the greatest biblical themes is that Christ breaks down cultural barriers (see Galatians 3:28 for starters). But relationships which cross these barriers will have to deal with the issues that arise. In bringing Jews and Gentiles together, the early church had to face big conflicts. They didn't deny the problems, or go their separate ways; they didn't try to make Jews into Gentiles or vice versa: they searched for God's will together and found a way forward.

Born too late

Age difference is another 'culture gap' that causes concern to anxious Mums and Dads. Obviously it's disturbing if your thirteen-year-old daughter is out on the town with a twenty-year-old escort (or even if your sixteen-year-old son takes his cookery teacher's fancy!). Either there's some exploitation going on, or you're dealing with a rather immature twenty year old, neither of which bodes well.

But even in a romance between bright young twenty-three and slightly jaded thirty-seven, the age gap can't be ignored. It's not just that it's irritating if you're a George Michael fan and your beloved is drooling over Helen Shapiro (who?). Your whole attitude to your lives may be different. You can dance all night; he wants to settle down with a Horlicks and the Scrabble at half-past nine. You fancy a year bumming round India; he's thinking semi-detached and loft extensions. Or maybe you are already dreaming of suburban bliss — well aren't you a bit young to be middle aged? Or maybe he is still into following the hippy trail — shouldn't he have grown out of it by now?

Well, I'm caricaturing, but you see what I mean. People go out with someone a lot older or younger for a lot of reasons, good and bad. Some feel safer, perhaps less 'in competition', than with someone their own age. Some find people of a different age more interesting — Ruth, in her

teenage years, found boys her own age were too shy to have
a proper conversation, but older men 'treated you as a real
person'. Some of us over-thirty women find men in their
mid-twenties are less rigid in their views of women, and
better able to be friends without getting 'heavy' about things.
Sometimes it's just pure chance that two people of widely
different ages get on.

Again, I wouldn't put a ban on younger—older
relationships, either way round (though older women and
younger men face more social disapproval); and the older
you both are, the less the gap matters. But age difference
does have its own stresses, and needs careful thinking about.

Love me, love my God

There is one barrier, though, that might be too big to cross.
I'm referring to that vexed question of the Christian going
out with the non-Christian. Can it ever work?

Clearly, Christians should be friends with others, and seek
to share their faith and experiences. But an intimate
relationship is different. 'I won't get involved' is all very
well but you can't always predict how involved you'll get.

'I'll convert him' is a nice idea. You have to be very
strong-minded, however, to stand your ground in the face
of someone who attacks or ignores your faith or doesn't
mind it so long as you keep it quiet. Unfortunately our
society doesn't encourage strong-mindedness in young
women (and because of the imbalance of the sexes in
churches, it usually *is* young women who have to face this
one).

'Ah,' you say, 'but he really cares for me and respects
my faith.' Fine. But how far can a relationship get when
you have fundamentally different ideas of what life is about?

If Jesus is the centre of your life, he's more than just an 'interest'! As Sally said, 'My faith is such a huge thing — if they don't want to share that, what is there left to share of me?' Either you'll have to stay off the subject; in which case, how honestly are you relating? Or else you'll have to talk about it, and eventually you'll hit a gap that's too great. Maybe one of you will be converted. It may not be him — that's the risk.

The attraction of any relationship rather than none is understandable. Amanda found Christian men often took things so seriously that they wouldn't ask her out at all — so she went out with non-Christians because they were able to be 'just friends' and it 'felt good to be treated like a woman.' But she found differences of viewpoint a problem — especially on sex.

Very occasionally, and usually with an older and well-established Christian, this kind of relationship results in the non-Christian finding a Christian faith. But it's much more common for the Christian to drift away from God. And that's a lot more important than just giving up concerts because your boyfriend isn't musical.

Hands together, eyes closed . . .

One thing Christian/non-Christian couples certainly miss out on is praying together, something many Christian couples value even when they don't find it easy. 'There'd be something wrong if you couldn't pray together', said Rachel. And she and Amanda agreed that prayer could force you to sort out difficulties in the relationship: 'Praying with Simon showed me something about him I wouldn't have known otherwise'.

Many of us feel shy about praying with others, and

whether, when and how often to pray together can itself become a subject for arguments. But it's vital to have some way of explicitly bringing God in on the relationship — if you can't pray alone together, you can at least go to church together.

Prayer should not, however, become a way of papering over cracks, pretending it's all fine because you've prayed about it. You can fool each other, but if you think you can fool God you're only fooling yourself. If you're not in harmony, trying to pray ought to focus this in a dramatic way — possibly because you'll find you can't! The whole point of praying together is that it is a major way of turning conflicts into growing-points.

Translation needed

How else then can we make conflicts into creative, rather than destructive ones? First of all, we need to go back to that question of 'language' that we touched on in the last chapter.

Judson Swihart in *How Do You Say 'I Love You?'*[4] lists eight languages people use to communicate caring.

Meeting material needs — bringing a box of chocolates, or if you define 'need' more strictly, paying for his petrol!

Helping — whether it's washing up or painting the bathroom.

Spending time together — in a restaurant, in the park or just in front of the telly.

Meeting emotional needs — giving appreciation, or even fair criticism (it's not always praise we need).

Saying it with words — not just the same three ones.

Saying it with touch — need I say more?

Being on the same side — standing up for the person.

Bringing out the best in them — learning to affirm and encourage them.

Each of us tends to use one or two of these more than others. Despite being a writer, I find touch often comes quicker than words, and I never really feel wanted by a man until he's reached out to me physically. Others may find touch meaningless without 'sweet somethings' in the ear.

The trouble arises when two people have different languages, and don't realise that they're not getting through. To communicate that we care, we need to find out what language *does* mean something to our partner, and learn it. And I'd add a ninth language — humour (but not sarcasm). It's amazing how a well placed joke defuses a confrontation!

Fair fighting

But sometimes we also need to communicate that we are hurt or confused by the other's behaviour. Giving in may look more Christian; but 'laying down your life' doesn't mean being a yes-man, or yes-woman. If the other person always gets their own way, how will *they* become Christlike?

Rowing, with a bit of grace, can turn into growing — but only if you fight fair. Here are Alan Loy McGinnis' prescriptions for constructive argument, (with my additions in brackets): [5]

*Describe feelings, don't point out faults (not 'You're always pawing me' but 'When you do that I feel a bit attacked').

*Stick to one topic (no 'And another thing . . .').

*Give space for a response (and listen to it!).

*Aim for ventilation of problems, not conquest (rather

than 'I'm right, you're wrong' try 'Something's wrong with us').

*Balance criticism with affection (hold his hand while you're telling him about his breath?).

And of course, love means *often* having to say you're sorry . . .

Jesus the lover

To sum up, I'll look at Jesus as our model. But Jesus never went out with anyone, you cry! True, O wise one, but he also never drove a car, shared a kitchen or played badminton. If we can apply his example of caring and courtesy to any of those situations, I don't see why we can't apply it to courting.

So here are some things I think we can learn from him:

Jesus didn't treat people as Tax Collector, Mental Patient or Religious Leader, but as Matthew, Mary or Nicodemus. There may be many moments when you feel, How like a man, or Trust a woman to do that, or She's getting horribly like my mother, or Why doesn't he act more like someone in love? However in the end you are relating to an individual: Steve or Jane or Susan or John, not Man, Woman, Mother or Lover.

Actually, individuals are a lot more fun in the end — they may not do what you'd planned, but what they do do is sometimes a pleasant surprise! Remember, you're probably not doing what *they* hoped for either. It could be instructive to ask them.

Jesus didn't expect too much of people at once. He chose his disciples because he saw enough potential in them to make them the right people for the job. They let him down continually for three years, but in the end he was proved right, and they lived up to the task of becoming the resurrection church.

Relationships need time to grow, and no one can get everything right at once. If you had good reasons in the first place for starting a relationship with someone, don't give up the first time they dent your image of them.

Jesus loved enough to deal with disagreements. We're told he was specially attached to one disciple, probably John. Yet still, when John was out of order, he told him off pretty sharply (see Luke 9:51—6). It was *because* he cared so much that he bothered. The clash strengthened the relationship.

You've probably started a relationship with a basically selfish goal: to have your needs met emotionally, physically, socially (maybe even financially). The other person probably has much the same hopes. There's nothing wrong with this — who wants to be asked out from charitable motives? But if you believe in Christian love, you need to get beyond this, to a point where you aim, in the words of the prayer of St Francis, 'Not so much to be loved as to love, not so much to be understood as to understand'.

This doesn't mean you should struggle on with a relationship no matter how badly it's going. Loving and understanding a person may mean finishing with them because you realise you can't give each other any more.

Jesus accepted his human limitations. He had appalling doubts in the garden of Gethsemane, just before he went to the cross. No amount of warm feelings could carry him through this. What made him go ahead was the knowledge that this was what his whole life had been leading up to. He had trained for it. He couldn't have done it when he was fifteen or even twenty-five.

I'm grateful to Harry for the remark that 'romantic relationships don't automatically enable you to do things you can't do with friends'. It's true that the 'in love' feeling seems to give us superhuman strength for a while. But it won't be long before the glow wavers, and the batteries need recharging. This is where you discover that going out *is* a friendship, and if you haven't learnt the skills and the boundaries of friendship, no amount of tingling feelings will make up for it. Even Jesus had to learn to love people. Can we expect less?

The crunch

There's one source of conflict I haven't explored. It's going to sound a little odd. I suspect that the biggest problem in male—female relationships is that they are between men and women. This Zundel woman's mad, you exclaim. Bear with me — I'll explain. But I think it needs a chapter to itself.

8

WORLDS APART

*No wonder I'm all confused: one of my parents was
a man, the other was a woman.*

Ashleigh Brilliant
Pot-Shots No. 277
© Brilliant Enterprises 1971

It was easy in the good old days (whenever they were). Men
were men, and women were a mystery to all sane people
(meaning men). Then around 1970 a conspiracy was hatched
among certain dissatisfied women and the result was
feminism, a subversive plot to undermine society and upset
the men. Isn't that how the story goes?

Not quite. For a start, the feminist movement was already
going strong in the 1890s when a disturbing creature called
'new woman' thought she should have the right to vote, and
there was evidence of it in the 1790s when Mary
Wollstonecraft wrote her *Vindication of the Rights of
Woman* and even in the 1690s when the Quakers encouraged
women to preach. Not to mention a couple of thousand
years before, when Paul said, 'There is neither . . . male
nor female, for you are all one in Christ Jesus' (Gal. 3:28),
and Jesus counted women among his closest followers,
talking to them and listening to them in a way no other

religious teacher would. Or a couple of thousand years before that, when Deborah led troops into a battle in which the decisive blow was struck by another woman — and they knew the men wouldn't like it . . .

No one who studies the evidence can blame feminism for the battle between the sexes, or claim that everything in the garden was rosy before the women started complaining. The battle was raging long before Germaine Greer, indeed it started in a certain garden where things were far from rosy ('The woman you put here with me — she gave me some fruit from the tree . . .' [Gen. 3:12]).

Modern woman and 'new man' are just one more variation on the constant attempt to grapple with the fact that the sexes don't cope very well with their differences. But then human beings aren't very good at coping with any differences — just think of all those countries where different racial and cultural groups try to live together (including our own!). If it's hard to live with different neighbours, it's bound to be even harder in the hot-house of an intimate relationship.

One way to cope with differences is to institutionalise them: to settle once for all what a man should be like and what a woman should be like, and never the twain shall meet. Then when difficulties arise, you can just say, 'Oh well, men/women are like that, you can't expect anything different'. This is how it's been done for most of history; and many people, some Christians included, want to bring back this simple formula. Is it the solution? Let's first take a look at the 'traditional' images of men and women and see how they affect relationships.

Me Tarzan — you Jane

'Superman and the Bride' are how one TV programme characterised the media images of men and women. He is the strong silent John Wayne or the playboy James Bond, for whom women are a pleasant but inconvenient distraction from real life. She is the 'feather-brained female' whose chief attraction is her apparent complete helplessness (as Jane Austen ironically put it, 'Imbecility in females is a great enhancement of their personal charms'). Or in a more sophisticated variation, she is the wild seductive creature who will sink into submissiveness at the taming touch of the powerful man who's got what it takes.

In their domestic versions he goes out and conquers the world, 'makes the running' in the relationship, pays the bills, is good at important things like understanding cars and football; she looks, smells and feels good and is generally helpless at everything except trivial things like keeping other people clothed and fed. It's only natural, isn't it?

Even language reinforces our preconceptions. A man with brown hair is a brown-haired man; but a woman with brown hair is a 'brunette', defined totally by her appearance. And how many times have you heard references to 'men and girls' and not batted an eyelid? Yet 'women and boys' suggests 'cradle-snatching'. Why is it our language allows only one sex to grow up?

You Tarzan? You joking!

So how do these stereotypes affect going out?

First of all, they dictate the things we do to attract a partner in the first place. Fashion decrees that it is feminine to have hairless legs, faces and underarms and masculine

to have a hairy chest. So all those women who don't happen
'naturally' to be hairless (i.e. about 100% of us) are
desperately shaving, waxing or creaming their legs etc, while
men gaze mournfully at their two chest hairs and wonder
if rubbing in garden manure would help. (Meanwhile, in
Scandinavia a good growth of female underarm hair is seen
as sexy, and in Britain half the women you ask think hairy
chests are repulsive.)

So there we are: women stuffing their 34A bras with
handkerchiefs while many men prefer (as an acquaintance
of mine put it once) 'sweet and near the bone'; men going
weight-training while loads of women feel nauseous at the
sight of Arnold Schwarzenegger and drool with passion for
Woody Allen. Silly, isn't it?

It's not only our appearance that we feel doesn't measure
up. If men are supposed to be decisive, determined and
daring, pity the poor shy soul who'd rather stay at home
with a book than go on an Outward Bound course. On the
other side, any woman with more than half a brain will have
to hide most of her opinions, or she'll be too threatening
to male omniscience. And the woman who goes on Outward
Bound courses herself had better change into high heels by
the evening, or no one will want her.

Men? Ha! Women? Pah!

When we actually get into a relationship, images of women
and men affect us in all sorts of subtle ways.

Part of the problem is that few of us feel secure in our
masculinity or feminity. Even if we don't believe in the
stereotypes, they are all around us and part of us thinks we
should be that ideal 'man's man' or 'total woman'. But it's
impossible to live up to such distorted aims. So we do the

next best thing: criticise our partner for not living up to them! Why doesn't he push for promotion in his job? Why doesn't she dress how I want her to? Or, if we're more feminist we may criticise our partner for *trying* to live up to them . . . Why won't he share his feelings? Why won't she learn to repair her own car?

But the biggest danger is that the stereotypes give us endless weapons with which to attack, belittle or dismiss our partner's behaviour. He's never there when he's needed? Typical man — you'll just have to learn to put up with it, dear. She uses tears to get her own way? Well, that's women for you. Ignore her.

It's easy to see how all this militates against true communication, because it tells us implicitly that communication between people who are so different just isn't on the cards. Meeting of bodies is possible, certainly; meeting of lives perhaps; but meeting of minds, never. 'A man of sense', wrote Lord Chesterfield, 'only trifles with women, humours and flatters them as he does with a sprightly forward child, but he neither consults them about, nor trusts them with, serious matters, though he often makes them believe he does both.' And while it's more typical of men, such thinking is common among women too — how often have you heard a woman say patronisingly (or should I say matronisingly): 'They're all little boys at heart'?

Pious hopes

It's surprising how many Christians share this dismissive attitude. Christians, indeed, often swallow male and female stereotypes wholesale and give them a spiritual gloss.

Pete, for instance, remarked to Nadia one day, 'When we go on our holiday to the Lake District in September . . .'

'When we do what?!' she exclaimed. Soaked in the idea that the man should take the lead in everything, he had made his plans without even consulting her. Just in case they should end up marrying, he seemed to think he should practise his 'headship' right away. And 'headship', in his view, meant making all the decisions.

I don't happen to think that this is what the Bible means by the husband being head of his wife, but even if it is, they *weren't* married, so Pete was presuming somewhat! Actually I think what was really going on was that Pete was frightened he would be over-ridden by Nadia's strong personality, and so defended himself by making up his mind on things without giving her a look in. His definite ideas about what a relationship 'ought' to be were a convenient shelter to hide behind.

Pete's behaviour illustrates why people retreat into the safety of 'traditional roles'. Psychologists suggest that the less secure people are emotionally the more they tend to emphasise sex differences. We live in a century when women are changing, and asking men to change. Change is threatening, especially when it tells you that what you've striven with all your might to attain isn't worth the effort. Far easier and simpler to go back to the good old days. With enough pretty language about what one writer called 'the beautiful relationship between men and women', you can ignore the fact that those good old days featured as much rape, adultery, sex-inspired murder, male domination and female manipulation as today (look at Judges 14–16, Judges 19, 2 Samuel 11 or 1 Kings 21 for some examples).

In a relationship where both partners have identical views of male and female roles, the traditional formula might work out. But that's increasingly unlikely to be the case. And when people and circumstances change, roles have to change too, or they won't fit any more. What use is 'It's his job to pay for things' if he's unemployed and she's earning well? What happens to a relationship based on his intellectual superiority when he fails his exams and she gets a distinction?

If your view of things amounts to 'Men should always lead and women follow', you'll be lucky to find a woman who'll put up with that for ever, or a man who'll shoulder that burden for ever. And in any case I don't call that a real relationship. It gives men something very close to absolute power, and we all know how power corrupts and absolute power corrupts absolutely.

Why can't a man be more like a woman?

But, you cry, I've already abandoned the traditional images, and so has my boyfriend, and yet we *still* come up against clashes that can only be explained by men and women being different. How do you explain that?

All right, I admit that in practice, the opposite sex can often be incomprehensibly and infuriatingly different from ourselves, who are of course the sensible sex (read this as whichever sex you happen to be). What's up with them?

The most obvious and problematic difference is in the way men and women deal with their emotions. You could almost say men don't on the whole deal with their emotions; they leave it to women to do that. Achieving in the world is seen as men's business, making relationships work as women's business — 'keeping the home fires burning'. As Byron said in *Don Juan*:

> 'Man's love is of man's life a thing apart,
> 'Tis woman's whole existence.'

Byron portrayed what *is*, not what should be; yet I'm amazed how often Christians quote this as though it were gospel teaching!

Here's how Marc Feigen Fasteau describes what he calls the 'male machine': 'It is difficult for him to connect his internal circuits to those of others. In fact, his internal circuitry is something of a mystery to him and is maintained primarily by humans of the opposite sex.'[1]

That ring any bells? It does with me!

It would be unwise to extend this description to all men or all cultures. Maybe it's a peculiarly British phenomenon (Arab men are much more emotional, though that doesn't necessarily mean they understand their emotions or relate to others better!). Maybe it affects men who've had a heavy diet of Wayne and Bond. Fed on examples like these, taught to stand alone, not to cry or show 'weakness', many men have great difficulty even knowing what they are really feeling, let alone communicating it.

I happen to think this is a very sad state of affairs! Ernest Green in his book *Personal Relationships* sums up the Wayne/Bond types as 'handicapped in relating'. These screen idols only know how to be close to a woman physically — when it comes to being close emotionally, they're at a complete loss.

Roger is one victim of this syndrome. He feels his emotions were 'anaesthetised' by the double effect of losing his parents early and being at an all-boys' boarding school, where 'softness' was certainly not encouraged. Maybe this is why he's had a habit of finishing relationships very quickly, before he could be the rejected one.

Campbell's style is to treat everything as a joke. Even if he's telling you his heart's just been broken, he'll do it with a smile on his face and finish the story with some flippant comment. You'd have to know him pretty well before you could detect when he's really hurt.

Joe is more of a 'new man'; he cries easily and unashamedly in public. But crying at work (quite acceptable in a woman, who will just be sent home with the comment that it's probably PMT) is anathema to him. In the competitive male environment he has to be a 'real man', even though he doesn't feel like one.

If you want a really heart-rending account of a man unable to open up emotionally, read Wendy Green's *The Long Road Home*, her account of her husband's death from stomach cancer.[2] Already suffering severe symptoms, Peter felt so strongly that he should be all-capable, that he couldn't let Wendy anywhere near him to find out what was wrong. Even in hospital he refused to admit what was happening. It's one of the saddest stories I know — and the most challenging to the 'macho' image. It probably ought to be on the syllabus for 'social education'.

Your sin, my sin

Lest you think I'm totally anti-men, I do think there's something positive in their training in being 'detached'. Recently — and I've been as surprised by it as anyone — I've come to value the greater calmness men often bring to problems. It can be useful to make your head rule your heart at times. The problem is when it leads to forgetting that you have a heart at all. And if the heart is so little exercised, when men do start using it, it can result in flabby sentimentality, instead of real passion. The equivalent with women is that when we exercise more discipline over our feelings, we can start acting like steamrollers!

It's impossible to tell whether these differences stem from biology or upbringing. We just don't have enough evidence. But in a fascinating article[3], theologian Mary Stewart van Leeuwen traces them back to the Fall, linking them to that mysterious prophecy in Genesis 3:16: 'Your desire will be for your husband, and he will rule over you.'

Men and women, she says, each have their distinctive temptations and sins. The sin of man is to dominate, to think he has the right to rule the world by brute force and keep woman (and all other creatures) in subordination. The sin of woman, on the other hand, is to abdicate from responsibility, to refuse to take her full share in the task of caring for creation, and yet still to seek her own way by manipulation, using 'feminine wiles' and being 'the power behind the throne'.

If you take the traditional image of man as the sturdy oak and woman as the clinging ivy, this means that the oak tries to take up as much space as possible, and stop the ivy growing into anything more than a mere decoration. Meanwhile the ivy refuses to grow sturdy stems of her own, but leans on the oak as much as possible and takes all she can get out of its attention.

Actually, it's more complex than that. According to psychologists Luise Eichenbaum (whose name means 'oak tree'!) and Susie Orbach in their book *What Do Women Want?*[4], men are encouraged to expect praise, attention, a listening ear from women — and they get it, because women are encouraged to give it. So the ivy is in some ways supporting the oak!

Women, however, feel starved of these things from men, who haven't learnt to give them. As a result the ivy may cling too tightly in her effort to get a response, and the oak feels he's being choked to death. If at the same time he's trying to pretend that he doesn't have any emotions and doesn't need the support she is in fact giving him, he'll find her emotional 'demands' even more stifling, because they remind him of his underlying vulnerability.

Devious, isn't it? Is it really like that? Well, this analysis too rings a lot of bells with me, and I wouldn't be surprised if it does with you.

Gosh — you too?

So here are all these women wanting closeness, sharing, love talk, and all these men feeling swamped and threatened by it. Who's right and who's wrong?

All this isn't designed to lay the blame at the door of either sex. We both sin, and we both suffer, because we live in a distorted world. Rather than point the finger it's more useful to think about how to tackle the problem.

Joyce Ames, who with her husband Dave runs marriage-guidance programmes, says that half the problems between couples arise because people don't know the difference between men and women. I know what she means — in dealing with someone who's different it's useful to know where they're coming from. But in the end I'd say exactly the opposite: the problem is that men and women don't know their similarities.

When people truly open up to each other, they'll certainly discover differences, but the most amazing thing is the common ground they find. It's to be expected if they're both made in the image of the one God! Underneath it all women and men are a lot more alike than we're generally encouraged to believe. Both sexes worry about their attractiveness, both get hurt when relationships don't work, both get randy sometimes, both get guilty sometimes, both need friends, both fear loneliness, both are ambitious, both are competitive, both sometimes use their brains and sometimes forget to use them.

As far as I can tell, there's nothing in male chromosomes that makes men particularly good at signing cheques or changing plugs, nothing in female hormones that gives them a natural ability to scrub floors or decorate birthday cakes. Women don't have magical powers of sensing what another person's feeling; it's just that all their training from the word go has taught them to watch other people carefully and to adapt to them. Men aren't automatically programmed by their genes to be competitive and aggressive, to come out top or bear failure with manly dignity — all these things are learnt as much as inborn.

Maybe biology does dictate *some* basic differences. It is true that women have babies and men are (on average) bigger and physically stronger, so one would expect women to have more caring, people-centred skills and men to have more 'survival' skills. When life was short, when few babies survived, and when food had to be hunted, this division of skills was necessary. But we've come a long way since then — must we really take our style of relating from the Flintstones?

It's true too that our bodies aren't just a container for our selves, they *are* ourselves. In biblical, Hebrew thought we are a unity: body, mind and spirit. So our physical selves affect who we are: the fact that we have a particular shape, a menstrual cycle or none, external or internal sexual organs, all these affect the way we feel and think. But Christians should surely not believe that biology, or social history, has to dictate all our actions. We are our bodies, but we are more too. We have choices.

Two-way giving

How then can we exercise our power of choice to achieve more positive relationships?

I want first to look at a much-debated passage of Scripture

on marriage, which I think has something to say to unmarried couples too. It's that famous bit from Ephesians 5: 'Submit to one another out of reverence for Christ. Wives, submit to your husbands as to the Lord . . . Husbands, love your wives, just as Christ loved the church and gave himself up for her'.

Before all the women groan (is she trying to put us back in our box?) let me say that the first sentence, usually separated out by a badly placed sub-heading, is the foundation of the rest. This passage is not about who kow-tows to whom. It's about voluntary, two-way giving. After all, in the relationship between Christ and the church, who sacrifices most? I'd say Christ — and who's asked to be like Christ here? You get my drift.

Now the picture I've painted so far of male—female relationships is one in which women tend to demand as much as they can get, and men tend to give as little as they can get away with. Paul's command is exactly the opposite: men are to give everything, and women are to demand nothing. Who wins in this equation? Both!

Our picture of the oak and the ivy was of an unhealthy, parasitic relationship, in which both were bound by a rigid prescribed pattern. But in a Christian view relationships are not meant to be about one-way dependence or keeping your independence, but about interdependence. I think Paul puts it perfectly in the middle of another much-argued-over passage: 'In the Lord . . . woman is not independent of man, *nor is man independent of woman* (my italics). For as woman came from man, so also man is born of woman' (1 Cor. 11:11—12).

To me this means that adult relationships have got to be relationships of equals, each free to be real, each able to develop and encourage each other to develop, each ready to lead the other in learning the qualities the other lacks.

I'd like to think that men could learn to be tender and affirm others, to show sadness and hurt, and discover that emotion is strength, not weakness. I'd like to think women could learn to speak out firmly, to express the indignation and anger which stands up against injustice (and ironically that might mean they complained less — it's only if you don't feel heard that you go on and on . . .).

The Bible offers us plenty of strong-minded women, from the hammer-swinging Jael to the Virgin Mary, who far from being sweet and docile, came out with a very political prophecy all about how God would depose rulers and impose super tax on the rich (we call it the Magnificat). It also has some very emotional men, from Joseph who wept all over his youngest brother, to Paul who wrote things like 'I have great sorrow and unceasing anguish in my heart' — no stiff upper-lip there! And you know the shortest verse in the Bible: 'Jesus wept'.

Your turn to be It

Does this mean we have to give up all those amusing 'You're a lady, I'm a man' games? I don't think so. Just because I can let my boyfriend cry, doesn't mean I can't also let him carry my suitcase (most men are bigger than me!). I think Martin got it about right when he said of Cindy, 'She's got a demanding career and all day long she has to take responsibility for things and make decisions. In the evening she wants to relax and be taken care of, and have me get the taxi and open the door. So I do'. They had worked out a pattern that suited their situation. As it happened, some of it fitted the traditional roles, but in other ways they were ready to break out of them. Actually, Martin was finding it quite a challenge going out with such an independent person. Maybe 'playing' at her depending on him in some things helped him to feel better about changing in others.

The ideal is that both sexes should sometimes be tough, sometimes soft, sometimes controlling emotions, sometimes letting them out — as occasion demands.

Till we get there, maybe we women have to be patient for a bit longer with our tough and tongue-tied men. But men have got to be as brave as they say they are, and expose their tender hearts for inspection. They'll find they don't get trampled on or laughed at half as much as they expected.

Strong to be weak

Jesus, the model for both men and women, did some very 'unmasculine' things: cooking breakfast, playing with children, washing others' feet. He also did some very forceful things: brandishing a whip at the free-marketeers of the day, calling the religious leaders some extremely rude names. He discouraged men from jostling for leadership, and called them to be self-sacrificing. He discouraged women from being totally absorbed in housework, and encouraged them to discuss theological topics.

Try this question — when was Jesus strongest? When he turned water into wine? When he fed five thousand with five loaves? When he drove the traders out of the temple, or drove demons out of a crazed outcast, or made a blind man see?

I think he was strongest on the cross, where he was utterly passive, helpless, naked, dying and feeling God-forsaken. That's where he conquered evil, with blood, sweat and probably tears. Was he acting in a masculine or feminine way? Or was this where these distinctions are shown for the irrelevance they are? Think on it.

9

YOU DO THINGS TO ME

This book is for everyone who has a sex. And especially for anyone who hasn't got a sex.
James Thurber, *Is Sex Necessary?*[1]

Didn't God make the human body amazing? All that smooth, touchable surface, those super-sensitive spots, those bits that fit so extraordinarily into and around each other (I refer, of course, to shoulders and armpits) . . . But I'm not going to go on about all that. I get annoyed by those Christian books that turn you on in their attempts to turn you off, and gush for five pages about the goodness and joy of sex only to tell you on the sixth why you can't have it.

However, this *is* where I get on to the interesting topic of sex (and I hope you've read the rest of the book first). And I do want first of all to be positive about it — because I think it's a good gift of God, not a distasteful nuisance. So I will get a bit physical — verbally at least. Here goes.

Body talk

When I asked a church youth group at what point a 'friendship' became 'going out', they all agreed that it was the first kiss. When pushed, they admitted it wasn't the kiss alone that signalled a special kind of relationship; there were other codes, such as arranging to see the person again. Kissing might just mean a casual flirtation. But if there was *no* kissing, it was definitely 'just friends'. In other words, you can have kissing without 'going out', but no 'going out' without kissing.

What this tells us is that physical contact is not just a matter of pleasure, whether mutual or one-sided; it is communication. It may communicate a whole range of different meanings, from 'I'm desperately frustrated', or 'I fancy you', through 'I like you and want to get closer to you', or 'I'm committed to you — for now', to 'I belong to you for ever'.

As with all communication, but especially non-verbal, the message the kisser thinks s/he is giving may get through quite differently to the kissee (or co-kisser). It's like the game of Chinese Whispers, or the old story about the front-line SOS, 'Send reinforcements, we're going to advance', which got to HQ as 'Send three-and-fourpence, we're going to a dance' (for those born after 1971 that's about 17p).

I've written in earlier chapters about languages of caring. Body talk is a major one. Now most people learn to speak their native language pretty early. But some, whether by heredity or by circumstances, become particularly good at it, and can use it exceptionally fluently, precisely, and expressively. It probably means they're also good at learning other languages. Some however, find it a massive struggle to say what they mean even in their own language, and need a lot of encouragement to make themselves clear.

I have a feeling it's quite similar when it comes to body talk. Spoken language takes a basic raw material — sound — and then develops many different varieties of it: French, Swahili, Cantonese, Serbo-Croat. It's quite similar with touch: there's the common ground, that people like to touch each other, but lots of different ways in which it can be done, and everyone learns to use and appreciate a slightly different set of gestures.

Some people seem to be born good at doing things that excite or reassure others. Some come from families that cuddle a lot, and having learnt one dialect of the touch language in their home, are probably better able to learn new ones later. Others seem to be born clumsy and fumbling, or have been made by parents or others around them to feel ashamed and awkward about their bodies. Some, sadly, have been physically or sexually abused, and have to unlearn the bad language they've picked up.

Most of us, during our childhood, will pick up a mixture of good and bad feelings about physical contact, made up of things like being hugged by Mum after bringing her a bunch of dandelions, being smothered with wet kisses by our least favourite auntie, creeping under a clothes-horse tent with our friend from next door and playing doctors, or having to hold hands on the school outing with that fat kid with warts. And later most of us (though by no means all) will also engage in a variety of experiments, enjoyable or not, in our teenage years.

How, given this haphazard collection of feelings and knowledge that we're lumbered with, do we then learn to express ourselves clearly, appropriately and rewardingly through touch? How do we acquire the grammar, the vocabulary, the prose and the poetry of body talk?

French lessons?

I vividly remember that first kiss with Percy on a park bench. It was a big disappointment. 'What's the matter?' he asked.

'Don't you like it?' I was lost for words, wondering how I could surreptitiously wipe my mouth.

Though Percy boasted of his experience with girls, I rather think he was fantasising. But is experience, on the part of one or both partners, the answer? In the old days, Percy's father (if rich enough) might have sent him to get an 'education' in the hands of a mature Parisian woman. Educating your inexperienced daughter was not of course considered necessary in the days of double standards — it was enough if the man knew what to do. Nowadays, it's considered desirable for both sexes to get some practice in the 'arts of love'.

I won't go into a Christian moral viewpoint on this yet. But in practical terms I hardly think either the old-fashioned or the modern view is a very satisfactory solution. For a start, I've been kissed equally ineptly by men who were very 'experienced'. Well, maybe their other kissing partners liked it that way — or maybe they never dared to say. Besides, I'd hate to think anyone was snuggling up to *me* simply to gain new skills for future use with someone else! And in any case, what 'works' with one person isn't necessarily right for another — first because tastes differ, and secondly because every relationship and every person is unique.

More seriously, if touch is about communication, what does this thing labelled 'experience' really amount to? Perhaps it'll help you pick up a certain amount of technique, a few tricks to get someone aroused and make their body feel good. But it isn't teaching you to care, to share, to express loyalty and commitment through physical gestures. In fact it's probably doing quite the opposite. Learning, in effect, to tell lies physically with several partners, can hardly equip you to tell the truth with another when you've got some truth to tell.

The Bible's sex manual . . .

Maybe instead we can take a lesson or two from the couple
in that famous biblical love poem, the Song of Songs (or,
as I often find myself calling it, the 'Snog of Snogs'!). The
plot of this verse drama is complicated, and scholars disagree
about who the speakers are. But it's probably a wedding
song, sung during the festivities to help break down the bride
and groom's shyness in the days when they might not even
have met before. Yet in our very different situation, it still
gives us an ideal to which all couples, including those just
'going out', can aspire.

The biblical lovers start out with a potent mixture of kisses
and compliments. She praises his perfume (1:3) — probably
something he put on his beard, but read 'aftershave' for
today. He notices how her matching earring and necklace
set emphasises the curve of her cheeks and neck (1:10). She
admires his energetic running (2:9); he revels in her lovely
face and her sexy voice (2:14).

Later it all gets more physical, as each catalogues the
beauties of the other's body. He enjoys her flowing hair,
even teeth, red lips, rounded temples, beautifully formed
breasts (4:1—5) and later still he starts from her elegant feet
and works upwards via some even more private bits (7:1—5).
She meanwhile explores his tanned cheeks, his melting eyes,
his oh-so-kissable lips, his well-shaped arms and legs, and
even the colour and texture of his skin and the veins showing
faintly through it (5:10—16).

But I promised not to get carried away; read it yourself
if you want to indulge in imagination. What are the lessons
of all this?

First, the lovers respond to and discover each other's
whole bodies — they don't just make a grab for the most
exciting parts. Ever fully appreciated your girlfriend's

temples, or your boyfriend's complexion? Probably not. Most of us are too busy making for the erogenous zones to realise that this person comes to us whole and not in 'more interesting and less interesting bits'. Men — this lesson is especially for you: most of us women respond far more to being tenderly caressed in 'non-sexual' areas than assaulted in the standard places.

Second, all the senses are there: taste (she's equally glad to lick his delicious lips or be fed with raisins by him), sight (they spend lots of time gazing at each other, and both like dressing to please the other), hearing (the whole poem is really a succession of 'sweet somethings' not so much whispered as proclaimed from the housetops), smell (even her clothes retain a wonderful whiff of myrrh) and of course touch — though interestingly, that's only implied, not described in detail. Maybe we get it wrong when we put touch at the top of the list! It's also interesting how much time they spend out of doors, in a pine forest, out on the hills with the sheep, in the vineyard, in the fruit orchard. The fresh air, the scents, sights and sounds of the countryside in spring, all serve to enhance their enjoyment of each other's closeness.

Third, getting closer is initiated in this Bible book by *both* partners. One 1960s definition of petting goes: 'anything a man does that is directly sexually stimulating to a female'. [2] But the Bible has no room for this one-sided view. If anything, more of the running is made by the woman, who is the main speaker for most of the poem, and who takes the initiative when anything threatens the relationship (3:1–4, 5:1–8).

Fourth, these two have no inhibitions about telling each other what they like. As a result, they're building a foundation for coping when something happens that they *don't* like — as in chapter five, when an ill-timed midnight visit leaves him offended at her cool response, and her frustrated after he's gone. If they hadn't already reinforced each other's confidence by all that affirmation, this might break their relationship. But because there is basic trust, they in fact make it up.

Fifth, their physical relationship is connected to the other elements of their lives. They mention his wanderings as a shepherd, her pasturing of goats, her vine-growing, and all these activities become places where they can relate, and word pictures for describing their feelings. Their friends comment on their relationship, and she longs to bring him to her old home (3:4) and to go to his (8:5). So work, friends, family are all part of their loving, not excluded from it.

Last, the lovers exercise suitable restraint. This may surprise you — you've probably been taught that this poem is a 'no-holds-barred' celebration of marital sex. But in fact it's more of an account of courtship, with the physical exploration building up gradually, as the relationship develops. Particularly worth noting is the man's image of the woman as 'a garden locked up . . . a spring enclosed, a sealed fountain' (4:12). That implies that he respects her 'personal space' and won't invade it thoughtlessly; and it's reinforced by the repeated warning, 'Do not arouse or awaken love until it so desires' (2:7, 3:5, 8:4). The overwhelming impression, if you read the poem in one go, is not of unbridled desire, but of tenderness, care and respect — even an air of 'brother-and-sisterliness'.

The personal touch

What all this suggests is that good body talk can be learnt not so much by having a succession of partners, but by giving your full attention and commitment to one. And that does *not* mean, discover what gives the other person a sexual thrill. It does mean: learn to express your feelings to your partner on all levels — the affectionate hug as well as the passionate kiss, the cosy leaning together in front of the fire as well as the rumbustious fight on the hearth-rug.

This is an area where I think women definitely have something to teach men. Researchers have found that in conversation, the amount of friendly touch is greatest between two women, less between a woman and a man, and least of all between two men.[3] Too often for men, touch automatically equals sex. I think it's high time men, particularly reserved Anglo-Saxons, learnt the place of touch in friendship.

So the answer to, How do I learn the language of touch? is not, Touch as many people as possible as much as possible. It is, Think carefully, and talk together as necessary, about what the way you touch is doing and saying and where it is leading. This might well mean less, but more meaningful, touch.

Above all, it means treating your partner as a real feeling person with beliefs and morals as well as likes and dislikes — not just a living doll, whether Barbie or Action Man, designed for your gratification.

Bill and Cathy's story provides a good illustration of how this works. 'With Bill', said Cathy, 'I was more than just an attractive face or body . . . for the first time I knew what it was to be appreciated as a person. With the exception of a soft good-night kiss, the first time Bill reached spontaneously to touch me was after I had made an observation about the role of the USA in foreign policy that he agreed with. That really made my heart skip a couple of beats.'[4]

It's all rather different from the situation described by an Irish girl: 'It's awful when a boy won't talk the whole night and then gets absolutely passionate at the end of the night — this only means that he couldn't care less who she is once she is a girl'.[5] It's also a long way from the attitude of Sir Isaac Newton, who's said to have plugged his pipe absentmindedly with his lady-love's finger while holding hands!

That obscure object of desire

Before we look deeper into the question of beliefs and morals, there are two other questions that need dealing with. The first is met by anyone who relates more than superficially: how important is sexual attraction in a relationship?

Christians often stress that in searching for a partner you should look for integrity, spiritual maturity and a common vision, rather than just going for a dazzling smile and a gorgeous pair of legs. And of course they're right: personality *is* central, if you want to relate to a person and not just a body. Especially if you're thinking along marriage lines, you'd better concentrate on the things that would make for harmonious everyday living, because that's the person you're going to live with for the rest of your life!

But let's face it: if you do marry, that's also the person you'll sleep with for the rest of your life. And if you don't feel much tempted to do so now, you're unlikely to be more tempted later, when they've got thicker around the middle, thinner on top and saggy in vital places. So isn't it rather important that you should fancy them at least a little?

This raises that vexed question of what the magazines call 'physical compatibility'. What is it, how can you be sure of it, and how much does it matter? It's not easy to answer, since no one has all the evidence. But I'll try to make some sense of this from my own limited experience.

First of all, I'm not sure attraction and compatibility are the same thing. The older I get the more I discover that attraction takes many different forms, and it's not always a reliable guide to how you'll actually get on physically. Attraction can happen at a lot of levels. It can travel via the eyes, the ears, the skin, the imagination. It often has a lot more to do with what's between the ears, than with what's between the legs. You may feel drawn to one person at a mainly intellectual level, another at a mainly physical one. You may find one person compelling to look at, yet feel no desire to touch them; another may leave you cold as far as their decorativeness goes, but something extraordinary happens as soon as they touch you. Attraction, in other words, is something that goes on inside yourself. Compatibility is how you relate to someone else. They're connected, but they're not the same thing.

Second, we tend to talk about sexual desire as though it were either there or not, like an electric light being connected to the power supply or disconnected from it. In fact it's a lot more like a living fire, dependent for survival on the conditions around it, how well it's built up, how you feed it and how well it's aired. Desire varies with your mood, the circumstances, the state of your relationship. In a time of intense frustration, you may find yourself lusting after someone you wouldn't look at twice on another day (even, dare I say it, someone of the same sex?). When work's going badly, you may be totally cold towards the person whose body you couldn't get enough of yesterday.

Third, how you get on in the 'preliminary' stages of physical intimacy is no guarantee of instant bliss in bed. Sexual harmony is a skill that has to be learned, and it's likely to be a trial-and-error process, with quite a few disappointments, whoever it's with. Ask anyone who's been in a long-term sexual relationship.

Last, anyone who's kept a relationship going will also tell you that sexual desire is a good roof but a bad foundation. A marriage without a good sexual relationship is vulnerable to harsh winds of discontent and disharmony. But if the foundation and walls of communication have been well built, it's always possible to climb up and replace the missing roof slates. However if the foundation is built of anything so variable as sex, as soon as it's affected by changing health, stress, ageing or the novelty of fancying someone else, the whole house may fall down. Without good communication, what started as the ardent desire of courtship can disappear completely under the stress of daily life. But conversely, a lukewarm start can hot up amazingly if the overall relationship is growing.

All this indicates that sexual pleasure is not an automatic response, like sneezing if you stick a feather up your nose. It's an emotion which expresses itself physically. This means that if you work on your emotional relationship, worries about your physical relationship will return to their proper proportions – and may even be solved.

The Bible seems to have a good balance on the issue. Peter warns us to look for the beauty of 'the inner self' (1 Pet. 3:3–4), not that which came from the Body Shop. (Incidentally, I think this passage is a lot more liberating for women than is often acknowledged; it focuses on what's in our brains, not what's in our bras . . .) But as we've seen, the Song of Songs emphasises the delight of a woman and a man strongly desiring each other's bodies. Fortunately, the way we're made means that we can feel desire for many different people – so the choice isn't limited to just one.

Different for girls?

Now to that second question. Given the variety of sexual responses, a lot of people have tried to classify the types of attraction by dividing them up between the sexes. It makes it much neater and easier to cope with!

The most common opinion is that men are excited by the visual, women by affection. Often, it's taken that men therefore don't have to be good looking to catch a woman − they just have to be kind and gentle (or tough and cruel, if you follow the 'women like them rough' school).

I suspect this conclusion is a convenient male fantasy to console men who don't feel they're good looking enough! (The first man to read this said, 'But I like being consoled . . .') The fact is, girls and women go for a pair of piercing blue eyes, beautifully shaped hands or long legs just as much as boys and men go for a pair of anything else. I've yet to meet a woman who doesn't thrill to the sight of a perfect little bottom!

It may be true that women are more prepared than men to accept a partner who isn't stunning but whose personality they like. This could be because they haven't had much option! In the last 150 years or so women have been discouraged from taking much notice of their own sexual desires, so it's not surprising that those desires have been misunderstood or ignored.

Women have also been encouraged, and have many resources, to 'make the most' of their appearance, but men have tended to think it was unmasculine to look or smell good. It wasn't always so − in the sixteenth and eighteenth centuries, when women's desires were more acknowledged, men preened, powdered and perfumed themselves like mad. And whatever you think of male make-up or perfume, it's only fair to ask that a man should be clean, wear clothes that are reasonably fashionable and suit him, and keep his weight down. Friendliness, courtesy and caring count for a lot, but 'outward things' are a welcome addition!

Nowadays we are more ready to admit that a woman can feel desire for a man's body, not just for the security of being loved. But is there a radical divide between male and female sexuality? Are the ways in which male and female desire are aroused fundamentally different?

Clearly there are real differences in the way our anatomy and our hormones work. Men tend to get aroused far more quickly and dramatically than women, and generally take less time to come to orgasm. On the flip side, men also seem to be able to 'switch off' far quicker if aroused but not satisfied. We women may take longer to get going, but we can also keep going for longer!

These differences, which make themselves obvious in intercourse, also affect us in the lesser intimacy of 'petting'. But they are generalisations, and it's risky to base sweeping statements on them — like 'men can't survive without sex' or 'women are the ones who ought to set the limits'. I think we've hardly begun to find out the real differences because we have for so long had so many unexamined assumptions. If we look at what we really feel, rather than what we're supposed to feel, some other, quite unexpected differences might emerge.

For instance: the only person I ever met who confessed to being more excited by the emotional than the physical was a man! At the time, I didn't understand what he meant; but later I experienced it for myself, suddenly finding it incredibly sexy just to think of how much someone cared for me. That can't have been a particularly female feeling, since it was a man who first described it to me.

Another phenomenon I've noticed is that for women desire can enter by the ear as much as by the eye — especially on the telephone! But again, I don't think it's only women who get aroused by whispered endearments or naughty suggestions. Men are into provocative talk too . . .

Here again the Bible gives us a balance. Apart from the sexually enthusiastic woman in the Song of Songs (and a few others equally ardent but less laudable, such as Potiphar's wife) look at that intriguing chapter, 1 Corinthians 7. In verses 4—6 you'll find Paul saying that in marriage, *both* partners' sexual wishes have equal priority. If we can adapt this for the 'going out' situation, it means that both should feel happy with their physical relationship, and neither should feel abused, exploited or repelled by what's going on. Either partner has the right to make their feelings about sexual matters known and be heard with respect, and either has the right to change the nature of the relationship, or end it, if they are unhappy about their physical involvement.

Time for bed?

All right, we'll have to face it. There is a limit to how much the Song of Songs, or advice about marriage, can help the couple who are going out. For the Song, as a wedding poem, naturally ends up in bed. Is that where a couple who are just going out will also end up?

I expect you can guess the answer I'm going to give, so I won't beat about the bush. I believe in the 'traditional' Christian view: that for *both* sexes, full sexual intercourse belongs only within marriage. Before you throw the book aside in disgust because you don't happen to agree, please be kind enough to give some time to my reasons — which will need another chapter.

10

HANDLE WITH CARE

Christians think no one has a body until they're married

Mike Fearon

When I started this book I told friends I wanted to write about how people relate, not about 'sex and how to avoid it'. So the last chapter was mainly about 'sex and how to enjoy it'. Am I now going to show my true colours and reveal myself as anti-sex after all? No. This chapter is not on how to avoid it, just on how to keep it in its proper place. I'll start, then, by explaining this strange idea that its proper place is marriage.

You'll be sorry . . .

Various reasons have traditionally been given for not 'going all the way'. They're all good reasons, but I don't think any of them is the final reason. However, let's take a look at them:

Reason one: the risk of pregnancy. Obviously this concerns women most, though any man who cares hardly relishes the idea of an unwanted child. In the bad old days

there was little or no contraception. Last minute withdrawal
was unsatisfactory and unreliable. The condom (which is
a lot older than you think — Casanova used a pig's bladder)
was more reliable, but not very romantic. Other methods,
such as half a lemon as a cap, or cow dung as spermicide,
were neither reliable nor romantic!

If prevention failed, it was a 'shotgun wedding', or a
dangerous backstreet abortion, or social disgrace followed
by the trauma of adoption, or the lifelong struggle of single
motherhood. All very high prices to pay for 'love'.

Things have changed a lot, partly for the better.
Contraception has developed, abortion is legal, single
mothers are more socially acceptable, and 'experienced' men
no longer demand a virgin bride. So is the way clear for a
sexual free-for-all, with no fear of 'consequences'?

Not exactly. First, there is *no* 100% reliable contraceptive,
and all have dangers and drawbacks. Even the pill can fail,
and there are risks in taking it too young or for too long.
Moreover, you have to take it absolutely regularly, and most
young people are not noted for doing anything regularly!

Second, abortion is not like having a tooth out.
Emotionally, almost any woman who has an abortion does
so with deep regret, and many suffer grief later. Abortion
has physical effects too — it can lead to pelvic infection,
and inability to have a child later. Nowadays there are girls
who've had two or three abortions before they're even
twenty-one. What kind of start in life is that? And 'it can't
happen to me' is just stupid — it can. I've watched
'liberated' friends worrying about 'what would happen
if . . .'. It seemed sad to me that pregnancy, which ought
to be a joy, became for them the great threat.

Reason two: disease. Another threat often held over
ardent youth, is what were once called 'social diseases'.
Syphilis ruined thousands of lives in the past — it could

cause madness and death, and be passed on to innocent
partners and children. Did you know his father's syphilis
caused Beethoven's deafness?

In recent years drugs have been developed for syphilis and
gonorrhoea and they have become less serious. Then doctors
discovered that cervical cancer was linked not only with the
number of the woman's partners, but the number of women
the man had before her. Then herpes came along, a lifelong
ailment with no cure; then chlamydia; and now we're in the
age of AIDS. People are taking the disease risks seriously
again.

'But what's this to do with me?' you may ask. 'I'm not
sleeping around, my boyfriend/girlfriend hasn't slept
around, we just want to sleep with each other and we think
we may get married later. There's not much risk of disease
there!'

The trouble is, you know what they say about the road
to hell . . . When I was twenty it seemed James and I might
marry. Suppose we'd slept together, then split up. Of course
I'd have slept with the next boyfriend − I'd be used to sex
by then, and miss it. But that one didn't work out either.
Then I had various casual flings. If I'd already been sexually
active, I'd have been more ready to jump into bed with any
of them. And some of them had slept with other women,
who had slept with other men . . .

The risks hardly need spelling out. Yet I'm sure I wouldn't
have thought of all this at twenty with that first steady
boyfriend. I'm glad I just believed that sex before marriage
was out.

Reason three: 'sex is dirty'. Another reason that isn't used
much now is the idea that sex is so nasty and sinful that even
married couples shouldn't do it except for reproductive
purposes. I think I've already shown that this isn't a
Christian view (although many Christians, sadly, have held

it). Genesis 2 tells us clearly that God made sex and was pleased with it.

A particular danger of 'sex is bad' is that when people start to explore it, of course they discover that it's not at all nasty, but very nice. 'How can it be wrong if it feels so good?' they ask. And if you've led them to think it would *feel* wrong, you haven't got much of an answer.

Reason four: 'nice girls don't'. Linked to reason three, this is another disappearing one, but still leaves traces. 'It's something men do — you won't like it', says a mother sadly to her daughter in one novel. And many mothers, friends and counsellors have said, 'He won't respect you if you say "Yes".'

This, frankly, is an awful reason for not sleeping together. It is based on a lie about female sexuality. It locks sexual relations into a battle of wills in which 'If you loved me, you would' tries to out-blackmail 'If you loved me, you wouldn't ask'. Sex becomes a bargaining counter, a 'favour' doled out to the man who's passed the endurance test and paid the 'bride price' of mortgage, ring and Pronuptia dress.

Anyway, if nice girls don't but boys can, then who do the boys try it out wi n? Bad girls, and once a bad girl, you'll have to be one for ever, because nice girls don't, and you have.

Reason five: security. Again, this is linked to distorted views of women. The argument is that (a) women find it harder to achieve satisfaction and (b) a woman will be more relaxed and better able to respond, if she feels secure in the relationship — i.e. if they are married.

This isn't altogether untrue. Many women do need security to function sexually. However, thousands of *un*married couples get past the initial adjustment to each other and enjoy sex — so this argument doesn't stand up to reality.

What's it all about?

Some of the reasons above have a certain validity. But the
trouble with 'think of the consequences' is that consequences
can always be dealt with. When the perfect contraceptive
is invented, or a cure or vaccine is found for AIDS, what's
the next bogy the moral police will use to threaten
lawbreakers?

Besides, what value is there in a morality which relies on
threats to keep people in line? Christian life is not meant
to be based on fear: 'There is no fear in love . . .' says John
(1 Jn 4:18), 'The one who fears is not made perfect in love.'

So in the end, I come to my own sexual morality from
a different angle. The foundation for me — and I think for
the writers of the Bible — is in the *meaning* of sex.

Throughout the Old Testament sex belongs with lifelong
commitment. A man who seduced a woman was expected
to marry her (Ex. 22:16). Women had to be virgins on
marriage — and since ideally all women married that would
go for the men too!

The New Testament re-affirms this view of sex. Paul
writes in 1 Corinthians: '. . . since there is so much
immorality, each man should have his own wife, and each
woman her own husband' (1 Cor. 7:2). He was writing to
Corinth, a city where *Who's Had Who* would have filled
several volumes. People have argued about what
'immorality' meant — was it just prostitution? But to his
original readers it would be obvious what he meant: sex
outside marriage, full stop. Otherwise, why would he
recommend marriage as a cure, instead of saying, 'Stick to
one partner at a time' or 'Only sleep with someone you
love'?

But the Bible's view of sex isn't all about rules and
prohibitions. It tells us what sex is *for*. 'A man shall be

united to his wife, and they will become one flesh' says Genesis 2:24; and Jesus repeats it in Matthew 19:4—5. Sex is about the union, on every level, of two people. That must inevitably imply permanence: 'I love you and want to relate to you on every level but only temporarily' doesn't make a whole lot of sense.

If sex means 'I am one with you, for good', then sex without that commitment is a lie. And relationships, as I've said again and again, must be based on truth.

Experience does count

Arguments based on consequences can be backed up and may be proved by statistics. They can also be *dis*proved! What I've said about the meaning of sex can't be proved — or disproved. It's a matter of faith. I believe it because of my commitment to Jesus and what he stands for, and my view of the Bible.

Faith can, however, be tested by experience. My own experience, and that of others, makes me more sure of my view. I'll be honest — trying to limit physical involvement is a painful struggle. But when I look at the evidence of friends' lives, I see that one sexual relationship after another can hurt just as much. No longer is sex a total self-giving, a way of communicating that you belong. It's just something pleasurable to do, with little connection with how your relationship is actually growing. And when the relationship doesn't grow, sex only makes the disappointment worse.

Kieran, who had the classic 'committed relationship', put it this way, 'Moira and I were serious, so it seemed natural to sleep together. But after a while we realised that when there were problems in the relationship, we'd just say, "Let's

go to bed", and not deal with the problems. Sex can be a
great escape.'

In other words sex wasn't bringing them closer at all —
it was driving them apart.

It's true that even for married couples sex can be a way
of pretending all's well when it isn't. But in marriage there
are more chances to deal with problems — and it's less
threatening to air them, because the commitment's already
made. In the fragility of 'going out', however, all sorts of
barriers and insecurities arise: If I don't want sex tonight,
will he ditch me tomorrow? If I tell her how difficult I'm
finding her, will my supply of sex be taken away? Sex is
so powerful that once it occupies centre stage, we're
reluctant to let it step aside for anything else, even the health
of the relationship.

Take it to the limit?

If you're with me so far, it'll be obvious what the next
question is. It's the perennial youth club talk on
'Relationships' question: then how far *can* we go?

Many Christian books and talks set up a 'scale' of physical
activities, starting with holding hands and going all the way
through 'French kissing' and 'feeling', to mutual
masturbation. Depending on how liberal they are, they then
draw the line somewhere on the scale, always stopping short
of intercourse. I can remember my minister in about 1970,
saying that he thought there should be no touching or
fondling of breasts or genitals (presumably no looking at
them either!). Ten years earlier, a minister might have said
'no passionate kissing' and twenty years earlier perhaps 'no
holding hands'.

What has always happened in practice is that couples have

drawn their own line three or four stages beyond where
the minister drew it. The result for many has been what
one friend calls 'evangelical sex', or 'everything but'. She
adds, and though I don't agree, I can see her point, that
it might be more honest just to 'get into bed and get on with
it'.

Other Christian writers and teachers, reacting against the
'as much as we dare' approach, have reverted to the 'don't
do any of it' ruling. John White in *Eros Defiled*[1] despairs
of determining tricky questions like whether fondling with
some clothing removed is more or less sinful than having
an orgasm fully dressed. Eventually he concludes that
therefore 'the whole bag of tricks is wrong' and you should
refrain from anything that produces arousal. As he points
out that even a caress on the cheek can be arousing that
doesn't leave much!

It seems to me that this 'all or nothing' philosophy is
severely wrong on at least five counts. First if arousal is the
touchstone, then logically it must be OK to go as far as there
is to go as long as you don't enjoy it!

Second and more seriously it focuses unhealthily on *what
you feel physically* as the way of making moral decisions.
This could set up an enormous pattern of guilt and fear
about getting excited or exciting the other person, which
doesn't help people to develop a positive view of their God-
given sexuality!

Third, it implies that sexual desire is wild, raging and
uncontrollable and once it's aroused there's no going back.
This common view is often linked to the idea that men
particularly are unable to stop. (In fact, in my experience,
it is often the man who is much better at calling a halt!) What
this in effect says is that some forms of temptation are
impossible to resist. That's a profoundly un-Christian idea.
I believe there is *no* warrant for thinking that as soon as

we are sexually aroused we cease to be morally aware, decision-making people. We are who we are, even in the back of a car. 'It just happened', is always more accurately translated, 'We just did it'. If we have made up our minds clearly where the limits are, we *are* (though often with difficulty!) capable of sticking to that decision.

Fourth, in John White's view the reason for banning all forms of kissing and cuddling is that God created these as a preliminary to intercourse, and in any other context they are inappropriate. If this is the case, you'd better stop stroking your little niece's hair, kissing your big brother or sister and even caressing your husband except when you can get into bed soon after! God made us beautifully able to express ourselves through touch, and the line between what is sexual and what is not, is a hazy one. I believe many forms of touch have value in themselves, and it's very sad to see them all as just a stage on the way to sex — or to see everything 'sexual' as a threat.

Last and perhaps most important, if the limits on intimacy are so severe as to make the relationship virtually Platonic, it seems to me there's no point going out at all. Don't get me wrong — I don't mean slap and tickle is all one goes out for! What I do mean is that if going out is preparing for a more committed relationship, then you should be learning and progressing in intimacy on all levels: social, intellectual, emotional, spiritual and physical. It's artificial to say, 'You may grow on all the other levels but not on this one'.

Till it is ready . . .

If neither 'all' nor 'nothing' is sensible, then somehow you'll have to decide 'what'. And I mean *you* will have to decide

— I can't decide for you. All I can do is suggest how you might go about it. Let me give you some pointers.

The decision depends on the type of relationship. The basic decision, whether or not full intercourse before marriage is OK, is one you'll have to make alone. But the rest is different in each context. In one relationship even holding hands may be a lie; in another, much more may be perfectly truthful. If you've made all your rules beforehand, you'll be so intent on keeping to them, you'll have no energy left for relating.

The decision should be mutual. Unilateral decisions on anything, not just petting, are bad for relationships. There's a very telling story by Muriel Spark in which the self-righteous, repressed narrator 'lets' her fiancé fondle her breasts, because he's her fiancé, even though she thinks it's really 'not nice'. She doesn't 'let' him go any further than that. Her view of relationships is horrifying. Intimacy is not about what you'll allow the other person — or yourself — to get away with.

But what if you can't agree? In that case, it's only fair to go by the wishes of the one who wants *less* physical intimacy. No one should be pressurised into doing things they don't feel happy about. In many (though not all) cases the casting vote will be that of the woman, who may want to play it safer. Ardent men take note — and take No for an answer.

The decision must be practical. We all discover, sometimes through painful experience, what we can cope with. It's only common sense not to go beyond it after you've discovered your limit. This shouldn't be the sole basis of decisions — it's perilously close to 'what we can get away with'. But it's a factor to consider.

The decision must take account of emotions. If 'everything but' only leaves me and the other person more

frustrated than before, as well as anxious, guilty and feeling
that one or both of us has been exploited, then the whole
thing is hardly loving.

The decision should be both strong and flexible. Strong,
because 'we've decided this but we can always change our
minds' will break in five minutes. If you're always going
beyond what you decided, either your decision wasn't
realistic, or you're not creating the conditions in which to
keep it. (Do you really need to share a bed when he stays
overnight?) Flexible, because as the relationship changes the
decision may need to change. Which brings me to point six,
the most important:

The decision must reflect the whole relationship. The
trouble with most systems of working out how far to go is
that they concentrate on asking, What's allowed? The New
Testament isn't much into that sort of question. Christ sets
us free, and in one sense everything's allowed. But we must
ask, What's appropriate? As Paul puts it in 1 Corinthians
6:12, talking about this very question of sexual morality:
'Everything is permissible for me — but not everything is
beneficial'.

Physical closeness is one (not the only) expression of a
close relationship. A good relationship grows, from distance
to intimacy, and the expression of it should grow with it.
The danger is — and it usually happens! — that physical
intimacy is so compelling and alluring, that it races ahead
of the rest of the relationship. The art is to stop and think:
is this particular action expressing something that's real
about our growing closeness? Or is it just because I feel like
it?

'What's appropriate' also allows for the changing status
of the relationship. A couple out for one evening are just
beginning, and their physical actions should reflect that. An
engaged couple are almost married, and it may be

appropriate to 'almost have sex'. At stations between, adjust accordingly!

Applying these criteria may have some unexpected results. Dave and Ginny, for instance, found as they approached their wedding that 'We felt we couldn't do anything without doing everything', so they gave up even kissing! They found it a great relief of the tensions involved in petting, but it only worked because they had a deadline — it wouldn't have worked for a relationship that was just developing.

It all takes us back to the Song of Songs: 'Do not awaken love . . . until it is ready'. This assumes that there's a time when it *is* ready — and I see no reason why that shouldn't arrive gradually, in sensible stages.

In name only?

One objection I must tackle is the 'hypocrisy' argument. According to this, the engaged or pretty serious couple who have petted intimately, perhaps to orgasm, are hypocritical because they are only technically avoiding intercourse.

I sympathise with this idea, but I don't go along with it. It seems to imply that the point of not sleeping together is to preserve virginity until marriage. Since petting to orgasm only technically preserves virginity, it's only technically chaste.

But staying a virgin is a pretty negative angle from which to view things. From the positive angle of being honest, then if full intercourse means 'We're committed for ever', heavy petting can mean 'We're nearly committed for ever'. And it may well be honest to say that. If not, I can only say there are a lot of hypocritical Christians about.

Though I'm told some people have made it work, I wouldn't dare marry a man I hadn't got quite physically intimate with. I *don't* believe you need to sleep together to find out if you're compatible. But I do think you need to begin finding out how you relate physically — not so you can give up if it isn't perfect, but so you get an idea of what you need to work on.

Take Alan in chapter one. When he was engaged to Christine, he was a bit concerned about her lack of physical response to him. But he put it down to her strong principles. Later he knew better. Had he had more confidence, he might have brought up the question before marriage, and they could have either begun to tackle it together, or called the whole thing off. A 'no touch' rule would only have postponed the tragedy their marriage turned out to be.

Help, I'm human

'But', I hear you complain, 'all this balancing on a knife edge is impossible. When Paul wrote, men and women were kept separate, kids married in their early teens, even kissing was banned. I'm in the twentieth century, when everyone around me is getting it, when people don't marry till their twenties or thirties, when I have loads of freedom to be alone with my partner. I can't cope!'

Congratulations: you're human. So am I. It *is* tough to keep things within limits in our society. We make mistakes. Some of them are such fun that we decide to make them again before learning from them. Some of them are pretty serious. Maybe you've already done more than you planned to, and are finding it hard to stop. Maybe you're divorced or widowed, and after an active sex life you find it easy to accept substitutes.

There *are* practical ways of taking the pressure off, but I'm sure you can work them out for yourself. Things like only meeting in public places for a while, going out in a group, staying away from hot-house situations like sitting late at night in your car ('Being in a car with a girl', observes one writer, 'seems to turn a boy's mind to sex the way nothing else can'[2]). Though I said in the last chapter that the great outdoors can enhance a physical relationship, it can also be a good way of 'cooling it': first because it can make things less intense, and little things like kissing more satisfying in their own right, and second because it's hard to misbehave when the park keeper may arrive at any moment!

One note of caution: praying together about your physical relationship is not necessarily a solution — 'good prayer leads to good sex,' says Charlie Shedd.[3] For some of us the spiritual and the sexual are very close, and if you're one, you'll know what he means. It all comes down to knowing what our own 'danger points' are.

Most of us, whatever limits we set, will go beyond them sometimes. We may wish we hadn't; or we may realise they were unrealistic. That's for us to sort out with ourselves, our partners and God. I'm glad to say God understands that we're only human, and is a lot more compassionate than most Christian guides to sexual behaviour are.

I've said it before: *no mistake — no, let's be frank and say 'no sin' — is unforgivable.* Just because you 'lost' your virginity (perhaps through no fault of your own), doesn't mean you have to sleep with anyone who asks, for ever. It also doesn't mean you're 'married in God's eyes'. That Old Testament law about marrying if you'd slept together was written to protect women in an ancient society. It still speaks powerfully about responsibility and the significance of sex — but we have to apply those principles differently today. And we're under the grace of Christ now — not under the law of 'every sin must be paid for' (he's already paid).

Damaged lives can change, with new understanding, help
from others, prayer and common sense. If that isn't true,
the Gospel isn't good news.

Therapy for free

If the last bit was all about the struggles, let's be positive.
What sex therapists generally do is to set couples a task. They
have to spend time, undisturbed and in pleasant
surroundings, exploring each other's bodies and reactions
but without stimulating the genitals or having intercourse.
Thus they can rediscover, through gentle and restrained
contact, the joys of affection and tenderness, and how to
build up slowly.

   Unmarried couples who've decided not to sleep together
have a terrific opportunity to do just this, and without even
paying the therapist's fee. Yes, it can be a strain, but all
the time they are building up skills and knowledge, learning
to consider the other person and to take time, instead of
short-circuiting it all by getting straight into bed. I think
that's something to celebrate.

11

IS THIS IT?

If we were wise
In love we'd rise,
Still we fall in love . . .

Lesley Duncan[1]

'Thank you for a very useful weekend,' wrote the fifteen-year-old boy on a questionnaire after a youth training event; 'I met my future wife.' The girl in question was fourteen.

If that boy's reading this in 2000 or 2010, I hope he'll write and tell me whether he married her or someone else, or no one. I doubt very much if things worked out as neatly as he hoped — in fact probably by the time he was sixteen he had met some other future wife, and the next year another . . .

But before you laugh at his folly, how rational are you about finding a marriage partner? You've probably never gone up to a virtual stranger and declared, 'The Lord has told me to marry you', but maybe you've rushed home from a dance, a service or a lecture thinking, This is it — the perfect person I was looking for! and rung up all your friends to tell them, only to be greeted with, 'And what happened to the last perfect person?'

Or maybe you've found yourself in the midst of that

all-absorbing romance you'd always hoped for. You can't
understand why he or she suddenly announced they were
having doubts and thought you should give it a break. Was
it all an illusion?

Or perhaps you've got a relationship that seems to be
developing OK, and after the last ten chapters you're
congratulating yourself on how many pitfalls you've
managed to avoid and how maturely you're relating. The
problem is, you're not sure where to go from here. Yes, you
do get on well, but can you spend your life together? Would
you want to have children with them (terrifying thought!)?
On the other hand, if you don't think it's permanent, how
long can it go on as it is?

I've already stressed that going out has value in itself, and
that it can be counter-productive to see every relationship
as the first step to the altar. But most of us are looking for
a permanent partner, and particularly as you get older, the
awkward but fascinating subject of marriage can't be
avoided. As Nick said ruefully, 'At my age I don't want to
waste time . . .'

How do you answer that impossible question of whether
this is 'it'? Maybe we should look first at what we mean
by 'it'.

This thing called 'lerv'

'Some enchanted evening', the song goes, 'you will see a
stranger across a crowded room and somehow you'll know
. . .' Well, most people over fifteen aren't quite so starry-
eyed as to believe in 'love at first sight'. But many times
I've heard Christians make comments like this: 'You'll just
know when it's the right one; if you have doubts the answer
should be No'. I've also seen plenty of people agonising

because they didn't 'just know' (particularly if the other person was keener than they were)!

What people usually expect is an indescribable (but still much described) feeling of 'being in love'. 'We're in love' is the excuse for all sorts of silliness, and 'Do you love him/her?' is the standard question to those suffering from doubt.

The trouble is, 'being in love' can be the most deceptive and ill-founded feeling known to humankind. Men who at forty 'just can't help loving' their secretary seem to forget that at twenty they 'just couldn't help loving' their wife!

But the mythology of love in Western society has a very strong grip, and we're none of us free of it. Originally this chapter was going to be on, How can I tell if this is real love and not just infatuation? But I've since realised that this is a question soaked in the 'being in love' culture. You couldn't ask it unless you believed that 'real love' and 'infatuation' were very similar to the naked eye and hard to tell apart.

In this view both conditions absorb most of our attention and energy and make us inconsiderate to people other than the beloved; they both produce disturbing but pleasant flutterings of excitement in the stomach and other bits; they both make us exaggeratedly aware of the other person's best qualities and conveniently blind to their faults. In fact the only reliable way of telling them apart is to wait long enough — if it lasts longer than a couple of months it's probably real love, and you can close your eyes even tighter and stumble up the aisle.

It doesn't take much thought to see the shortcomings of this approach. After all, even if you do feel thrilled about every single aspect of the person and the relationship, the feeling is far too exhausting and stressful to be sustained for more than a year! As a medieval writer said, 'Love is a species of agony caused by excessive meditation on a member of the opposite sex.' You can't live in agony for long. And what's going to take the place of the agony when it wears off?

Earlier generations had a very different perspective. Marriage was too serious a business to be entrusted to the strength of an elusive and unpredictable emotion. I like this passage from the great Christian preacher George Whitefield, writing to the parents of his prospective bride:

'This letter comes like Abraham's servant to Rebekah's relations, to know whether your daughter Miss Elizabeth is a proper person to engage in such an undertaking; and if so be whether you will be pleased to give me leave to propose marriage to her. You need not be afraid of sending me a refusal; for I bless God if I know anything of my own heart I am free from that foolish passion the world calls love.'[2]

I don't suppose Miss Elizabeth was much pleased by this self-confessed indifference! However, one does have to admire George's practical-minded concern as to whether Elizabeth was 'a proper person to engage in such an undertaking'.

Should we return to a similarly pragmatic approach today? Should we abandon all thought of looking for 'this thing called lerv'? Or is it just our definition of love that's wrong?

The way we see it

In the hope of getting things clearer, let's listen to a few real people's ideas of what they're looking for in a partner.

Rachel was that fifteen year old who climbed out of the back window to avoid an unwelcome suitor. Now in her

early 30s and still single, she's matured a lot since then . . .
'I can't predict what kind of person is right for me — there
are so many different kinds of people I can get on with.
What makes a good relationship is mutual respect, and not
asking the wrong things from each other. In my last
relationship, he was leaning on me too much for emotional
support, and he was jealous of my job, because he was
insecure about his own career . . . I'm a strong person, and
I'd like someone to know how to handle me.'

Simon feels the same about weakness and strength: 'If
I feel secure enough to dominate someone, it's probably
someone I'm going to get bored with very quickly. I used
to choose women who were less intellectual than me because
I didn't have enough confidence — but then we were
intellectually incompatible . . . It's important to be with
someone who compensates for what you lack — for instance
I can't handle money, and I need a woman who can!'

Kate takes a practical view too: 'Every man I've gone out
with has represented a particular lifestyle, and I've made
my decisions on the basis of whether I wanted that lifestyle.'

And a similar question comes up for Malcolm: 'With my
last girlfriend I began to discover we had different goals for
our future — she felt called to go overseas as a missionary,
which wasn't right for me at all, and I felt I was holding
her back.' However Malcolm, being an artist, also looks for
a high degree of emotional input: 'Every relationship seems
to get to a stage where you know the basics of each other,
and you start to wonder, are we stimulating each other
enough, do we fit? Can I imagine waking up next to this
woman every day, coming home from work and telling each
other what we've been doing, and would we be committed
enough and involved enough to make it a stimulating
relationship? In each case we were, but not enough.'

For Amanda the key factor is respect: 'For his spirituality,

for how he relates to others, how stimulating I find him as
a person, how physically acceptable . . . I want to marry
a man who can be my best friend, and the physical side can
grow out of love and respect — when the physical thrill goes
off, if friendship isn't there, there's nothing.'

How are we doing?

So far Amanda is the only one who's mentioned 'love' at
all, and even she links it with respect, rather than a woozy
feeling in the stomach. Maybe it's because Amanda & co
are all old enough to have gone through a few 'great loves'
which may have been enthralling at the time, but in the end
didn't amount to much. They're also old enough to know
the value of lasting friendship, and it's friendship above all
that they want from marriage.

It seems people are getting more practical about marriage
these days, partly because a lot of people are marrying later,
after quite a few serious relationships, and partly because
marriage is seen much more as a partnership. These are the
sort of issues a practical approach leads us to look at:

Our lifestyles. What are my aims and goals in life, what
are the other person's, and how do they fit together?

This is about 'big' things like work (what sort? what
priority does it take?), children (do we want them? how
many? what if we can't have them or have more than we
planned?), money (how important is it to us? how much
have we got or might we acquire, what do we think about
managing it/spending it/giving it away?) and, biggest of all,
faith (how committed are we both as Christians? how would
we react to a particularly demanding or unusual call from
God to one or both of us?). It's also about smaller, but just
as important things: leisure/social life (how much

socialising/exercise/hobbies do we expect to do?), domestic set-up (are we both town or country people? are we into getting a mortgage on the perfect new suburban development or doing up a derelict mini stately home in the wilds, or will we feel at home in an inner-city tower block?).

If aims and plans are very different, that doesn't make the relationship a write-off. But you then need to ask: am I flexible enough to let go of/alter my plans to fit in? (And is the relationship worth doing that?) You can't just hope the other person will let go of theirs! And a word from the over thirties: the older you get, the harder it is to be flexible . . .

Our relationship. Do we trust each other? I don't mean just do we trust each other not to go off with someone else, but can we talk about our real feelings and ideas without fearing rejection or lack of understanding? Can I let the other person be themselves, do things in which I'm not involved or interested, have different views from me and argue them through together — or does it threaten our whole relationship? Can *I* be myself with them? Can I give in to them on matters of personal taste, and stand up to them on matters of principle? Do we have real equality, or does one of us dominate the other unhealthily?

Development is a key issue. Have we known each other long enough to build good foundations? (This of course varies with your own age and maturity.) Is our relationship continually growing, or has it got stuck? Has it reached its full potential and started to stagnate? If the latter, that doesn't mean it was a mistake — it might just be a good 'temporary friendship' (or a permanent one?) and need to be acknowledged as such.

Teamwork is important too. Can we organise, make and revise plans, and carry them out, together? Can we make joint choices? Or does one person always have to abdicate and let the other do it all?

Our other commitments. How does this person get on with my family? My close friends? My church? My colleagues? How do I get on with theirs? It's true that first and foremost you marry an individual, not a clan or a community. But that individual is part of a clan and a wider community, and you'll become part of it too. I used to want to marry an orphan, so I wouldn't have to cope with in-laws. But even if I'd found that lone ranger, he'd still have to relate to my mum and dad.

Our peace of mind. I'm not necessarily talking about that indefinable 'spiritual peace' here. 'God didn't give me peace about it' can be a cover-up for avoiding the commitment or the uncomfortable emotional issues that a relationship confronts us with! I'm talking more about a basic question: does being with this person make me happy or unhappy? Do I prefer the idea of them, when we're apart, to the reality when we're together?

And finally, *the strength of our attachment.* And note, I mean strength, not present intensity. Realistically, how long would it hurt for if we broke up now? And why would it hurt — because it was inconvenient to be alone again? Because I'd miss the kisses? Because my romantic fantasy bubble would be burst? Because I'm desperate to get married, no matter to whom? Or because this person is really important in my life? As Jason pointed out, 'It's easy to say "I love you" just because you want that to happen.'

Love with its eyes open

But that brings us inevitably back to that tricky four-letter word. Is there any room left for love in a Christian approach to choosing a marriage partner? If so, how does a Christian view of love differ from the 'woozy feelings' one?

Popular wisdom tells us 'love is blind'. My mother gave me a more sophisticated version of this when she said, 'The important thing is that his faults shouldn't irritate you'. But this doesn't tell us what to do when you stop being blind to their faults, or with constant repetition they do get irritating!

If we look at Jesus' love for people, we get a different picture. '. . . he knew what was in people', John tells us (Jn 2:25, my version). Yet knowing people through and through, he could still love them and take on the terrifying commitment of dying for them. Look at his encounter with that superficially self-confident young man who comes asking how to get to heaven, in Mark 10:17—22. Jesus reminds him of the Ten Commandments, and the young man blithely replies, '. . . all these I have kept since I was a boy.' Jesus, Mark tells us, 'looked at him and loved him'. I don't suppose for a moment he was taken in by the man's naive belief in his own virtue. But he loved him for his good intentions.

In the Gospels, we see the human Jesus feeling different kinds of love for different people. 'Jesus loved Martha and her sister and Lazarus', says John (11:5). And John himself was probably 'the disciple whom Jesus loved' (13:23, 21:20). Yet not everyone for whom he felt a special love was called to be part of his band of twelve disciples. John was; Lazarus and his sisters and the rich young man weren't. So his feelings of love were one thing; selecting people for a special task was another.

God's love is universal — he loves everyone. 'For God so loved *the world*', says that famous verse, 'that he gave his one and only Son' (Jn 3:16). But that love is not indiscriminating. It isn't greater or less for different people, but it expresses itself differently.

This is what I'd call 'love with its eyes open'. We love someone when we can carry on caring for them, not in spite of their faults, not because of them, but *with* them. That, after all, is the way we love ourselves; and it includes wanting to get rid of the faults, without expecting to do so instantly.

As Jesus' example shows us, love with its eyes open means being realistic about how that love is most suitably expressed. I may truly love someone, yet they're still not necessarily right for me to spend my life with. Love may mean saying, 'Because I love you this must end'.

Dying for love?

But what about 'laying down your life'? Didn't Jesus say that no one could have greater love than to lay down their life for their friends? Didn't Paul say 'love bears all things'? Doesn't that confirm the idea that with God's help we could love anyone at all? (Provided they're of the right sex!)

Erich Fromm, the great psychologist, claims: 'In essence all human beings are identical. We are all part of One; we are One. This being so, it should not make any difference whom we love.'[3] I have a lot of sympathy with Nathaniel Branden, who replies:

'If we were to ask our lover why he or she cared for us, consider what our reaction would be if told "Why shouldn't I love you? All human beings are identical, therefore it doesn't make any difference whom I love, so it might as well be you".'[4]

Quite! Apart from his heretical idea that we are all mystically part of God, I think Fromm confuses two different forms of love. Yes, we are called to love in the same self-giving way Jesus has loved us: 'A new command I give you: Love one another. As I have loved you, so you must love one another' (Jn 13:34). This love applies to everyone — the colleague who really annoys you, the woman at the bus-stop, the tramp who asks for money on the street. It also applies in marriage, where plenty of 'laying down your life' is called for!

But in marriage this self-sacrificing love finds a special expression, more intimate, more binding, and sometimes more demanding than any other. And for this particular way of loving we need both a natural motivation to love a particular person, and a determination to keep loving them. One without the other just doesn't work. If it's all based on natural inclinations, there's not enough to sustain it when things get difficult. If it's all 'grit your teeth and get on with loving', our human frailty will make it impossible even to get started.

I like the way Henry Stack Sullivan gets the balance between 'natural' feeling and Christlike self-giving: 'When the satisfaction, security and development of another person becomes as significant to you as your own satisfaction, security and development, love exists'.[5]

I have to add that it may take many years of life together before we learn even to love one person like this! Identifying that this person *can* be as important to us as ourselves, and resolving that they *will* be, is only the beginning.

A little of what you fancy . . .

There's something I haven't mentioned yet. I expect you've noticed. It's that good old question, Do you fancy them?

I've left it till last, because people will ask it without any prompting from me. But it should probably be last anyway.

I'm still uncertain about this myself, but I think I'd say this: in an ideal world everyone would find a partner with whom they could communicate well, who had similar goals, who was a good friend and who also drove them wild with desire. But this is not an ideal world. Given the choice between someone you can live with, and someone who just drives you wild with desire, I'd advise anyone to choose the first, and work on the desire bit. After all, making love is not the only thing you do together.

Maxine highlighted the issue when she described her feelings for Julian and Pete: 'I couldn't let Julian out of my sight, but we were totally incompatible — we'd have hated each other if we'd lived together. But Pete I felt I could live with.'

As Ernest Green says, 'Sex is passionate interest in another's body; love is passionate interest in another's life'. A person's body is part of their life, of course — but only part.[6]

Free trial offer?

But isn't all this guesswork rather risky? If we're going to be practical about finding a partner, wouldn't it be most practical of all to live together and find out as much as you can?

Christians who believe in reserving sex for marriage, obviously don't generally support living together. But I think there are other arguments against it too.

In the first place, knowing that you're being 'tried on' like a new outfit isn't likely to make for great security and openness, even if the 'trying on' is mutual. Sharing the whole of your daily life is a big commitment, and it becomes a lot harder to make it work if there's a constant 'let-out clause'.

Second, statistics seem to suggest that marriages where

the couple have lived together before, are *more* likely to break up than those where they haven't. Not only that, but one survey discovered that the most frequently quoted factor in studies of successful marriages was *lack* of pre-marital sex![7]

No one knows quite why this is so, but I rather suspect that many couples manage all right while they still feel it's temporary, but feel trapped when it becomes permanent. Perhaps, too, living together feels pleasantly like a naughty game; but once they've 'made it legal', they slip into acting out stereotyped 'husband and wife' roles based on their ideas of 'proper' marriage. There may also be many couples who blindly hope that getting married will solve their difficulties!

Actually, logically there's no such thing as a 'trial marriage', any more than there's 'trial death'. If marriage equals permanence, you can't try it out, since you can't have 'temporary permanence'. In its very foundation, a conditional commitment is dramatically different from a total one.

Pins in the Bible

If a 'trial run' is not a real option, then clearly even when you've rationally weighed up all the arguments for and against, you'll still want that extra factor to help you in your decision: God's guidance. Does this mean voices from heaven, or sticking a pin in a Bible till you find a suitable verse that hopefully confirms the decision you'd half made anyway?

Certainly some people *have* had dramatic confirmations of their decision — such as coming out with the classic, 'The Lord's told me — has he told you?' and getting the answer 'Yes'! But people have also been very misled, like Vanessa

who got engaged, disastrously, to Greg because of a verse
in their daily Bible reading (fortunately they later got
dis-engaged).

For most people, though, the process of deciding is more
like Dave and Ginny's: 'We couldn't see any prospect of
splitting up, and we couldn't carry on the intensity of the
relationship without marrying . . . We felt God had
provided us for each other to ease our loneliness.'

God, despite many people's ideas, is a pretty intelligent
sort of person, and doesn't usually lead us into things that
don't make sense. So yes, we should pray for guidance, and
we should pray for it together, but we should expect it to
go hand in hand with using our own common sense.

Confessions of a married woman

It's time to come clean. When I wrote chapter one I was
footloose, if not fancy free. During the writing of the first
nine chapters I started to go out with someone. It wasn't
exactly 'eyes meeting across a crowded room'. Although his
first words to me were, 'I think you're fascinating,' my
mental reaction was, Oh, what a nuisance!

My first impression of Ed was that we were so different
that there was no chance at all of a serious relationship. I
went on thinking this for most of the next two years, even
when we *were* having a serious relationship! However, two-
and-a-half years after meeting, we got married. This is one
explanation for how long it's taken to write this book!

In that time I made a difficult journey from extreme
reluctance to 'taking the plunge'. And I'm sure there'll be
many more times when I wonder if I wouldn't have been
better off with someone else, and he may well think similarly
— until we get the next problem sorted out, and we realise

once again what it was that made us take this risky step of
commitment . . .

A reasonable call

What was it, then, that decided me?

I realised at once that he was someone I could trust, who
would greatly help my self-confidence, which had just taken
a nasty dent from another man. (Anyone who calls you
fascinating will boost your confidence, but in his case I felt
he meant it!) When life got rough, he was the one I ran to
for reassurance.

On our first meeting I also had one of those strange
'prophetic' feelings, which I'm not often given to, that this
was someone who would be very important to me. I think
I needed that to sustain me through the struggles that
followed!

As we spent more time together, our relationship grew
and became more equal. We discovered our ideas weren't
so different, though our experience and abilities were. The
idea of sharing life seemed not so unreasonable. As Mrs
Thatcher said of Mr Gorbachev, I felt I could do business
with him! I wasn't 'in love' — all those feelings had been
lavished too recently on someone who would probably have
done me no good at all. But I knew Ed genuinely loved me,
and I cared about him. We could laugh, cry, work, play,
fall out and make up together. Whenever I'd decided to
finish it, something kept me going back.

Two things convinced me in the end. One, it seemed on
the whole a reasonable idea. Two, I felt that God was asking
me to say 'Yes', and I'd always regret it if I didn't.

Marriage is a departure, not an arrival, as I'm discovering.
And the point of 'going out' is not to find that other half

of yourself, the only one in the world for you, with whom everything will then be plain sailing. It is to learn to relate to real people, with all their cussedness and their pleasant surprises, so that if and when you meet someone you can realistically spend your life with, you and they will be on the way to being mature enough to do so. And if you don't meet them, you'll still have learnt a lot about being friends with those peculiar but lovable creatures, the other sex.

12

OVER AND OUT

When I was a child, I talked like a child, I thought like a child, I reasoned like a child. When I became an adult, I put childish ways behind me . . . Now I know in part; then I shall know fully, even as I am fully known.

1 Cor. 13:11,12b
(my version)

The last chapter, like the rest, wasn't designed to make your decision for you, but to help you make it yourself. OK, so you've made it — what next?

Maybe you've decided that yes, you're onto a winner — this one *is* strong enough to last a lifetime. In that case, my good wishes and prayers go with you, and you can find lots of advice on the wedding and the lifetime after, in other books.

But suppose that your decision is, No, I/we really don't think we are meant to stay together. Perhaps you've got a list of reasons; perhaps you just sense that this isn't God's call to you both. Probably it's a combination of the two. Or maybe you yourself are sure this is the one for you — but the other person doesn't agree, and nothing you say will change their mind. How will you get through the break-up and the time after?

A good goodbye

Obviously all that I said in chapter five about dealing with
unrequited love applies here too — the importance of saying
'No' firmly but kindly if you're the one having to say it;
the need to keep things in proportion and to get support
from other people in that lonely time when there's only one
of you again. But ending a relationship is more painful than
just not starting one, so I'll expand on those points a bit
more.

First, *say goodbye, don't act it out*. Mike ended his
relationship with Jenny by suddenly not communicating with
her at all, even though they lived in the same college. What's
more, Jenny got the false impression that he was now going
out with Patsy, whom Jenny didn't like at all! Ending a
relationship like this is cruel, confusing and indeed plain
rude. It made Jenny feel she couldn't learn the lessons of
the relationship, since she was never able to find out *why*
he'd finished with her.

However hard it is to come out with it, do *tell* your partner
how you feel and what you want to do. Have an open talk
in which you can both have your say, and try not to let it
degenerate into a row — even if you have to have a third
party there to see fair play.

Second, *make a clear break*. Dragging on, not sure if
you've really finished or not, is usually agony for one and
a burden for the other. 'We'll just have another go and see
how we get on' is creating false hope — if you didn't get
on before you won't now, unless one or both of you are
prepared to change radically.

On the same basis, *don't try to be 'just friends' too soon*.
It may be that you can salvage a good friendship from the
ruins of a romance, and sometimes this is the best kind of
friendship there is. But dates 'for old times' sake' ought to

be put off until the old times really *are* old!

Most importantly, *don't rush into a new relationship*. It's tempting when you're used to having someone, and a new admirer can help your self-image, but 'rebounds' can rebound upon you! While you're grieving for one relationship, you can't come to a new one with a clear mind. I have to confess that much of my getting to know Ed was haunted by my hanging on to unfulfilled longings for another man, and though I was grateful for Ed's support in the hurt, I don't think it did our growth as a couple any good.

As with any time of grieving, it can really help to *pray*. Pray together when you part, if you can manage it. Pray for each other in the weeks following the break. And pray for yourself to learn and grow through what has happened. Don't let your sense of failure, anger or disappointment keep you away from God — talk to God honestly about it.

And finally, *reflect*. If 'going out' is a learning process, it includes what the management experts call 'de-briefing' (no rude jokes please . . .!). You need to think over in a detached way what you have learnt from the relationship, good and bad. Or else you might have to repeat the lesson with the next one . . . 'Nothing is a waste of time', says Harry, 'unless you haven't learned from it.' (He may not have got it all together yet himself, but he's full of these profound remarks!)

What — not settled yet?

Well, there's another one gone. Was it worth it?

Growing up, finding our true identity, learning how to relate deeply to others — none of these things are easy. Sex has always been much more readily available than love. And it sometimes seems the more we focus on finding that longed-for rewarding relationship, the more it eludes us.

Maybe you've just about given up. Ten years, even twenty years of relationships, few or many, actual or hoped for, serious or less so, and where has it got you? Can you face ever trying again, should you get the chance?

In the Apocryphal book of 1 Maccabees, written between the Old and New Testaments (you'll find it in a Catholic Bible), there's one of my favourite Bible stories: that of King Antiochus, who, after a military defeat, 'fell into a lethargy from acute disappointment, because things had not turned out for him as he had planned'.

I know the feeling. Things rarely turn out for us as we had planned, especially in the area of man/woman relationships. But maybe thinking that we can get it all sewn up is one of those childish things that we have to leave behind us.

Too often we spend ourselves in a desperate search for a lifelong partner, because we're taken in by a series of wrong assumptions — that marriage is the only way of deep loving and belonging, that a husband or wife will automatically meet all our needs, and that the goal of every man/woman relationship is to find a marriage partner. It's not surprising that we swallow all this: social life is very much structured around couples, and sometimes any partner seems better than none. Our dear and loving families can be less than helpful too: 'My mum asks me on average three times a week when I'm going to get married,' complains one unfortunate young man.

I think the only answer is to shift the focus — to concentrate, not on finding the solution in someone else, but on being whole in yourself. I don't think this is something you can learn on paper. Many other people have written about the pains and pleasures of singleness, and how to lead a satisfying life as a single person; but books can only go so far in helping, especially the sort that are full of homely advice on how to fill your time productively. Anyone who's been single and lonely knows that it's love that's needed, not advice.

It's easy to say, 'Give love and you'll get love'. But it's impossible to give love unless you have first received love; 'We love because [God] first loved us' (1 Jn 4:19). Learning to feel loved and to give love is never simple. It can take a lot of help to get us beyond dissatisfaction and self-pity. But it can be done, if we believe it's worth attempting.

Single vision

Even if you're not that happy about it, being without a partner has plenty of compensations. At least being alone is better than being locked into a love-hate scenario. If you've ever had a really destructive relationship, you'll remember the great relief (however mixed with regret) of shaking the burden off!

And, of course, being without a romance doesn't mean you're without relationships. Jan, after some serious teenage romances, didn't go out with any men for the whole of her 20s. She felt it was an immensely freeing time, allowing her to relate in depth to a whole range of people, not just spend all her time with one. She could be an individual, not X's girlfriend, and be emotionally intimate with friends without getting entangled in the tensions of physical intimacy. In fact she actively avoided a 'going out' relationship, feeling it would be too binding! In this she echoes many Christians throughout the ages who have found as great a depth of love, for God and others, in singleness as anyone could find in marriage.

Jan's view, however, highlights one danger. Especially as
the years relentlessly march on without your having 'tied
the knot', it's only too easy to get so independent that you
refuse to open up to anyone. The whole point of the
Christian tradition of celibate singleness is that it should free
you to love more people in a self-giving way — not that it
should allow you to become self-centred! As D. S. Bailey
reminds us, 'A man or woman is free to adopt the celibate
life, but not to evade the duty of partnership'.[1]

Paradoxically, becoming a more whole, contented and
open single person, rather than running after a partner like
a headless chicken, makes you a more attractive person, and
more likely to find a partner. It's not a matter of 'pretend
you don't want a partner and you'll get one,' like some kind
of divine ' "I want" doesn't get'. It's just that the more you
radiate warmth and responsiveness rather than discontent
and frustration, the more other people will respond warmly
to you. On the other hand, if you give off vibes of being
uptight and desperate, you may still get a response — but
most likely from another uptight and desperate person.

Image vs reality

This is where we come to a radical divide between the
generally accepted view of the dating game, and a Christian
view. In his book *A History of Courting*, E. S. Turner lists
the following ways in which animals make efforts to attract
one another: 'The display of bright colours or adornments
. . . special tactile contacts; dances or other antics; pursuit;
music, vocal or instrumental; the discharge of scents . . .
and the presentation of prey or of inedible but otherwise
stimulating objects.'[2]

Sound like anything you've seen at parties? The purpose

of such behaviour in the animal kingdom, Turner says, 'is to cloak the association of male and female with such enrichment and mystery that they shall be attracted to each other for . . . long enough to produce and rear a family.'

Humans, Turner implies, are not so different. Mystery, enticement, intrigue — that's what it's all about. And many would agree with him. 'How could you love a girl whom you have always seen?' asked a Berber tribesman.

The view I have tried to present in this book is the exact opposite. Yes, when we are teenagers our main object will be to convince a member of the opposite sex that we are a figure of romance and hidden depths. But our goal should be not to perfect this image until it's good enough to ensnare a really good catch (and never mind the disillusionment afterwards). It should be to grow out of such pretences, into someone who has the capacity to know and be known, in all our human frailty.

Erich Fromm observes that 'most people see the problem of love primarily as that of *being loved*, rather than that of *loving*. Hence the problem to them is how to be loved, how to be lovable'.[3]

But Christ calls us, not so much to be lovable, as to love — to love God and to love our neighbours as ourselves (which of course means learning to love ourselves, too!).

This is a call which good friends can help us answer: by challenging us when we fail to act lovingly, by encouraging us when we feel inadequate to the task, by communicating to us the love of Christ which we can then pass on to others.

If we approach 'going out' in this spirit of neighbour love, it will become just one way of relating as a person to people, of growing in the knowledge of God and of his wonderfully varied creatures. It's a goal none of us will attain perfectly. 'Now we know in part' . . . But aiming for it could have surprisingly good effects on our relationships.

Past imperfect

My own 'going out' days are finished — and not too soon.
They were lots of fun, and they caused me lots of pain. I
don't regret anything about them, except that I probably
hung onto my teenage romanticism far too long, and as a
result hurt myself and other people more than necessary.
I'm glad I stayed single long enough to begin to learn how
to be single constructively. I think I was just getting the
knack when I got married and had to start a whole new
learning process!

Writing this book has been part of growing up for me.
I haven't finished doing it yet, and I suspect it will be going
on for the rest of my life. So this book isn't the final word
on how to date without tears. It's just a word from someone
who's still learning to relate, to others who are also still
learning. I've offered some of my own experience, some of
others' experiences, and some reflections on them. It's over
to you for the rest.

Notes

In the Beginning

1 D. S. Bailey, *The Man-Woman Relation in Christian Thought*, Longmans 1959
2 Tim Stafford, *A Love Story*, Zondervan 1977 (UK edition Lakeland 1978)
3 Quoted in E. S. Turner, *A History of Courting*, Michael Joseph 1954, Pan 1958

Take Your Partners

1 David Klimek, *Beneath Mate Selection and Marriage: Unconscious Motives in Human Pairing*, Van Nostrand Reinhold 1979
2 Robin Skynner & John Cleese, *Families and How to Survive Them*, Methuen 1983
3 Mark Cook & Glenn Wilson, *Love and Attraction*, Pergamon 1979

Getting Somewhere

1 David Klimek, *Beneath Mate Selection*
2 Jack Dominian, *The Growth of Love and Sex*, Darton, Longman & Todd 1982

Love and War

1 Alan Loy McGinnis, *The Friendship Factor*, Hodder & Stoughton 1979

2 Patricia McNally, *What Boys Don't Seem to Know*, Irish Messenger Office 1968
3 Alan Loy McGinnis, *The Friendship Factor*
4 Judson Swihart, *How Do You Say 'I Love You?'*, IVP 1977 (UK edition Kingsway 1978)
5 Alan Loy McGinnis, *The Friendship Factor*

Worlds Apart

1 Quoted in Ernest Green, *Personal Relationships*, McGraw-Hill 1978
2 Wendy Green, *The Long Road Home*, Lion 1985
3 Mary Stewart van Leeuwen, 'The Christian Mind and the Challenge of Gender Relations', *The Reformed Journal*, Vol. 37, issue 9, September 1987
4 Luise Eichenbaum & Susie Orbach, *What Do Women Want?* Joseph 1983, Fontana 1984

You Do Things to Me

1 James Thurber & E. B. White, *Is Sex Necessary?*, Penguin 1976
2 Evelyn Millis Duvall, *The Art of Dating*, Association Press, New York 1967
3 Mark Cook & Glenn Wilson, *Love and Attraction*
4 Ernest Green, *Personal Relationships*
5 Patricia McNally, *What Boys Don't Seem to Know*

Handle With Care

1 John White, *Eros Defiled*, IVP 1977
2 Art Unger, *Datebook's Complete Guide to Dating*, Datebook 1967
3 Quoted in Josh McDowell, *Givers, Takers and Other Kinds Of Lovers*, Tyndale 1980 (UK edition Kingsway 1981)

Is This It?

1 'Watch the tears', Lesley Duncan/Jimmy Horowitz, Sunlight Music/G H Music
2 Quoted in E. S. Turner, *A History of Courting*
3 Erich Fromm, *The Art of Loving*, George Allen & Unwin 1957
4 Nathaniel Branden, *The Psychology of Romantic Love*, Tarcher, Los Angeles 1980
5 Quoted in Ernest Green, *Personal Relationships*
6 Ernest Green, *Personal Relationships*
7 David Knox, *Marriage: Who? When? Why?*, Prentice-Hall 1975

Over and Out

1 D. S. Bailey, *The Man-Woman Relation in Christian Thought*
2 E. S. Turner, *A History of Courting*
3 Erich Fromm, *The Art of Loving*

The Salvation Army

WORDS OF LIFE

Words of Life is a helpful day-by-day study of the Bible, systematically covering nearly every part of the Bible over a four-year period in a thought-provoking and informed way.

Its attractive design includes a full page for each day's study, prayer and points to ponder, and margins for your personal notes.

Words of Life is written by Major David Dalziel, who taught biblical studies and church history at the Salvation Army Training College in London.

John Woolmer

THE SILENT VOICE

Very few Christians 'hear' God's voice audibly, guiding them. For most, God's is a 'silent voice', speaking to them through other people and things.

This illuminating book on guidance examines five basic methods God uses to communicate with His people today: reading the Scriptures, prayer, worship, observing nature and discerning circumstances. The place of words of knowledge and prophecy is discussed and illustrated, as is 'the mystery of guidance' — when God appears not to guide.

'He illumines this important theme with penetrating shafts of light. His distinctive but careful biblical approach is immensely helpful and refreshing.' — *David Prior*

JOHN WOOLMER is Rector of Shepton Mallet and Doulting in Somerset. After his ordination in 1971 he remained on the staff of Winchester College before moving in 1975 to St Aldate's, Oxford, first as a curate and then as priest-in-charge of St Matthew's, Oxford.

Tom Davies

THE MAN OF LAWLESSNESS: VIOLENCE, THE MEDIA AND PROPHECY

'There was no set date as such, but one day in the recent past, almost all of us began to feel unsafe when we left our houses. And more than a few of us felt unsafe actually inside our homes.'

Davies sets out to discover the villain behind this rising tide of violence and crime. In pursuit of his quarry, he visits Norman Mailer in New York, a lonely Outsider down in Cornwall and examines the link between a famous novel and the death of John Lennon. The investigation continues with a look at the intellectual womb which gave birth to Rambo and with a visit to Hungerford, where, after the biggest peace-time massacre in Britain, the author finds a charred video recorder.

Marching up the Falls Road, Davies wonders at the never-ending drama of terror and interviews a beguiling mouthpiece for the IRA. As the hunt closes, he goes to America for a round-up of the evangelists who belong to an electronic church with no name, and learns that the media has substituted the photo opportunity for true political debate.

Davies documents the gathering of an enormously evil power and uses the title 'The Man of Lawlessness' as a metaphor for the object of his investigation. This threat to society was prophesied long ago by St Paul; Davies speculates that in the growth of the mind of the modern media, we are witnessing its fulfilment.

TOM DAVIES is a journalist and author of *Merlyn the Magician and the Pacific Coast Highway*, *Stained Glass Hours* and many novels.

William Griffin

THE FLEETWOOD CORRESPONDENCE

An accomplished young demon, Fleetwood is taking a break from his high-powered position in the American mass-temptation industry to answer his uncle's challenge to tempt successfully just one individual, a young woman recently moved to Manhattan to launch herself on a career in advertising. The demonic minion tries every technique at his disposal to win the soul of the beautiful young temptand — from whispering philosophical arguments in her ear to introducing her to unprincipled young businessmen. But Fleetwood has to contend with a bevy of intelligent, if angelic, bouncers! Will Fleetwood win, or might the road to Heaven be paved with diabolic intentions?

THE FLEETWOOD CORRESPONDENCE is in the tradition of C. S. Lewis's much-loved and widely-read *Screwtape Letters*. In this hilarious yet thoughtful satire, Griffin depicts the reality of a personal devil and tackles such timeless issues as church division, fornication, materialism, religious apathy and flippancy.

'A delightful story . . . A faithful mirth that laughs out loud . . . though the issues here are serious indeed.'

Walter Wangerin

WILLIAM GRIFFIN, playright and highly-regarded biographer of C. S. Lewis, is a regular contributor to *Publishers Weekly*.